THE MIND OF THE QUR'ĀN

by the same author

THE EVENT OF THE QUR'ĀN

THE MIND OF THE QUR'ĀN

Chapters in Reflection

Kenneth Cragg

London · George Allen & Unwin Ltd
Ruskin House   Museum Street

First published in 1973

ISBN 0 04 297030 X

Printed in Great Britain
in 11 point Fournier type
by Unwin Brothers Limited
Woking and London

Preface

The Qur'ān has several names for itself—book, guidance, reminder, criterion. All of them suppose community and intelligence. The command to "read in the name of the Lord" was the genesis of Muḥammad's mission. Hence reading and book-relatedness have always been the central factor in Islam and calligraphy the familiar feature, and puzzle, of the mosque.

All literature is the art of transaction with other minds. The more sacred the text then the more crucial the readership. The meaning *of* a book is always meaning *for* a people. The truth of the one stands in the awareness of the other. The title *The Mind of the Qur'ān* intends this reciprocal situation—the book related to readers and readers relating to the book. Only in such relation does a scripture wield its authority. Once the book exists, and what is written is written, and the meaning thus entrusted to words, its writ and its content are with the minds and wills that read.

This fascinating quality of all literature, in the unique shape of the Qur'ān, is the theme of these pages. Their aim is to reflect on the characteristic thoughts of the Islamic Scripture in the receiving of Muslim thinking, and to do so by the clue of its dominant terms of vocabulary. This is not, however, merely a semantic study. It is, rather, a sequence of essays in religious thinking, responsive to the impact of Quranic style and emphasis. It is meant as a companion book to *The Event of the Qur'ān* and pre-supposes the understanding, there outlined, of the Qur'ān in its actual genesis, as a historic phenomenon in religious experience. From those dimensions of origin, this study traces the implications of the Qur'ān in the related fields of man and history, evil and forgiveness, unity and worship, wonder and the hallowing of the world. It does so—as in duty bound— with a respectful, if also critical, eye for the classical commentators, three of whom are translated here in their exegesis of three important Surahs. Traditional commentary, though in part an incubus, is also a vital index to the Quranic mind, its qualities and instincts, as these are set by the practice of memorizing and challenged by the bolder liberties of the mystics.

But the underlying concern of these chapters is with inter-religious converse and responsibility in the contemporary world. There is, however, no explicit contrasting or comparing of doctrines. The Judaist Christian controversies in and with the Qur'ān find no echo here. There may be hope to take up in another place what may be seen to belong with *The Christ of the Qur'ān*. Meanwhile, as in the earlier study, we stay with the main thrust of Muḥammad's mission against Arabian polytheism and paganism in his own time. That mission, wrought into the fabric of an ultimate Scripture for a large segment of mankind, means a continuing liability for human direction in the world today. This in turn deserves and requires a community of attention wider than its inner people—an attention, burdened by the common human bewilderments and shaped by the differing vision of redemption. If that vision must finally take the human tragedy in terms deeper and more radical than those of the Qur'ān, it remains partner with it in the sense of the human significance.

Gonville and Caius College, Kenneth Cragg.
Cambridge.
September, 1972

Contents

George Appleton
Najib A. Qubain
Hasan B. Dehqani-Tafti

consecratores
dilecti

1970

Chapter I
A READER'S INTRODUCTION

To venture by a series of reflections into the mind of the Qur'ān is an enterprise liable to arouse a complex of reactions. The ardent Muslim will take it to imply an independence of judgement which will be highly suspect to his traditional devotion and probably alien to his sense of Quranic authority. The casual believer within Islam may well find it a puzzling notion to come from outside his community. For he himself may seldom think consciously with his Scripture in the easy complacence of his Muslim identity. The impatient stranger will think it a scarcely relevant proposal. For him the Qur'ān is an ancient document, remote and uncongenial, suited only to shaikhs and specialists. Even the sympathetic reader, who is external to its people, will perhaps be dubious. It could be that he has already found his interest baffled and frustrated for lack of the necessary clues and so lost hope of the interest he had registered without them.

The chapters that follow have a care for all these points of view, while refusing the discouragements within them. The intention is to concentrate on a few deep areas of thought and meaning in the Quranic world as these bear upon the modern scene. It is to reflect on mankind today under the tuition of the central religious text of an important segment of it, and to do so as an exercise in religious relationship. Devoted rigorism, or supercilious possession, or intellectual aloofness, or vague sentiment, or, indeed, any other attitude to the Qur'ān, are best answered, for present purposes, in terms of one question, namely: what might it mean to be Quranically minded in the contemporary world?

It is the beginning of wisdom in such an intention to recognize how exacting it is. The Qur'ān, for Muslims, is the ultimate literature. Having it means a human literacy reading a divine writing. There is first the literacy[1] of Muḥammad in the vocation of prophetic word and

[1] 'Literacy' is meant here in the communicative, or revelatory, sense of awareness of

action 'in the name of God': then the Scripture in the active possession of the Prophet's hearers, reading and rehearsing his words as the directive of their being and the bond of their community. 'Everything in the world', wrote a French poet, 'exists to come to climax in a book.'[1] In a very different idiom, that is what Muslims find in their Qur'ān, 'the one great book' which is the utmost in language and meaning, the crux of truth in literary form—not a book *about* something more ultimate than itself but itself the sum and centre.

This climactic quality the Qur'ān claims as the gift of the divine will, by an act of revelation final in history. Utterance and import, form and content, are so fused in this final communication of truth as to constitute a single reality, an entire inherence of revelation and record. By virtue of it Muslims are incorporated as the book-centred community. Islam is thus the world's most striking expression of what might be called documentary faith. Response to the book's meaning creates the *Ummah*, or household of belief, the society of the Scripture and the scriptured, in their mutuality, the one definitive and the other derivative. There is the text from God and its communal custody, the documentation of truth given and acknowledged. Committing the words to heart in memory and recitation, the Muslim believer participates in the mystery of the divine concern with man. The Qur'ān is, literally, 'the Reading', and Muslims are 'the readers'. They are not merely perusers, but confessors, of the book, whose status as the final revelation is, in turn, the clue to their own identity as its possessors.

In view of a bond so strong between the Islamic Scripture and the Muslim peoples, is there either hope or wisdom in the outsider's venture? 'Let none touch it save the purified', says Surah 56: 79. However we take them, the words seem to hint at a powerful dissuasion.[2] It is clear that many Muslims instinctively question, if not suspect, an alien interest in their book. Though the scholarly resources may be impeccable by western standards, they can still look dubious to

the divine will. It does not here involve the further question of 'ability with letters' on the part of Muḥammad and how this relates to his role in the Qur'ān. A historical account of the phenomenon on the Qur'ān, which Islamic dogma formulates in the terms here summarized, was attempted in the author's *The Event of the Qur'ān*, London, 1971, to which the present volume is closely linked.

[1] Stephane Mallarmé, 'Tout au monde existe pour aboutir à un livre'. See Jacques Scherer, *Le Livre de Mallarmé*, Paris, 1957.

[2] 'The purified' may simply exclude those with unwashen hands. But other interpretations indicate some form of authentic membership within the faith or of ritual fitness.

the insiders. These feel that they have suffered, and may yet suffer, at the hands of strangers. They prefer that all study of their Scripture stay within believing purview. The outsider, it seems to them, must have his prejudice or, at least, something prejudicial. The external reader lacks the vital quality of Muslim surrender. The Qur'ān, like other Scriptures, is a document of faith to faith and speaks rightly only to participants. To seek, or concede, an exterior comprehension would then involve a sort of contradiction and disquiet. The conclusion might be drawn that we may not rightly think with the Qur'ān unless we think as Muslims and with them.

Our initial task, then, is with the recognition of this problem. The situation cannot be surmounted unless it is acknowledged. Some of the more technical aspects, relating to chronology, language, background and arrangement, which obviously bewilder the new reader, will be considered below. The larger and more immediate question is with the permeability of faiths to one another and of their documents to general readers. If we were to conclude them inherently impenetrable to the careful, open-minded student, would it not mean that they were incapable even of believers' comprehension? A Qur'ān that was immune from all but Muslims would be closed to Muslims also. The credentials of faith have to be, in some measure, an open book. Else how are they credentials? The Qur'ān repeatedly describes itself as 'a mercy to the worlds'. The worlds—certainly the present—are wider, larger, greater than Islam alone, as they are wider, larger, greater than any single faith.

Islam, further, claims to be culminatory, to finalize all previous revelation, to correct and complete all that went before. If this claim is to be heard, that correction and completion must be feasible of measure and of comprehension. The implications must be taken into the whole context of humanity. If the ultimate is reserved from access how can its ultimacy be known? There cannot be any discernible development if there is a climax of immunity.

Nor can there be anything but irony in religious self-seclusion. For the will to isolation is itself untrue. All about us in contemporary history are urgent factors demanding an active pursuit of human unity. Problems of peace and population, of hunger and resources, of world economy and development, of technology and the meaning of man, confront the several cultures of men with a common urgency. What tests and threatens cultures in their deepest reaches of decision and of will also brings to reckoning the religions that inform and shape them. The single crisis of humanity in its bearing on the traditional faiths requires these in turn to face each other in mutual awareness and an open honesty. The world, it has been pointedly said, began in the twentieth century. Only now, in its long terrestrial existence, has it become effectively a single habitat with a critical proximity of all to each. Thus the religions have more compulsion to common concern than in any earlier generation. They have also more opportunity, despite—and even in measure because of—the political and psychological factors which in the post-imperial day dispose them to antipathy. To respond to current history is surely to allow each other's seriousness and this, equally clearly, begins with their most sacred themes and forces.

But if, so moved and prompted, outsiders take up the Qur'ān in the endeavour to think with it, can they ever surmount the difficulties that await them? Will not an apologetic instinct in some cases assert itself, or some controversial stance? If they be secular humanists will they not be tempted to depreciate, if Jews or Christians to contend, if Hindus or Buddhists to detect intolerance and lose heart? Will they not find themselves in the toils of competition of thought, or ill at ease in a daunting, different world?

There is no doubt they will. But the resources to surmount the inward and outward barriers are not far to seek, given the will they should be found. Truly there are legacies of many centuries which need time and patience to outlive. But the Qur'ān has interrogatives that reach beyond the boundaries of institutional Islam and these are lively enough to create a community at least of study, if not of spirit, or evoke an interest that means neither condescension nor compromise.

> 'No law controls
> Our traffic free for heaven',

wrote Richard Crashaw, a seventeenth-century poet, about Teresa of Spain, and he continued:

> '. . . we may maintaine
> Peace sure with piety, though it dwell in Spain.
> What soul so'er in any language can
> Speak heaven like hers is my soul's countryman.
> O 'tis not Spanish. . . .'

Himself a recent convert to the Roman Catholic Church in a time of acute national and religious enmity, he knew how fiery were the passions embroiling hostile worlds of faith and closing off their frontiers. If there is something in the parallel too ardent and poetic for our calmer purpose, it avails to point a way. Across traditional estrangements the Qur'ān can be greeted from without and known in a kinship of thought that is not only Muslim. Controversies that certainly remain can then be seen in better perspective and worthier dimensions. The Qur'ān deserves better than the forbidding possessiveness with which Muslims have often deterred others from its study and more than the disinterest so liable to neglect it from outside.

'O 'tis not Spanish', however, is a phrase to give us pause. The Qur'ān, on all counts, is most forbidding Arabic. Teresa and Crashaw at any rate had their common Latin liturgy. The non-Arab has to have the Qur'ān in translation and may not know enough at the outset to realize his deprivation. The Islamic Scripture involves a very special relation of language to meaning. Arabic eloquence, understood as characterizing 'an illiterate prophet', (Surah 7: 157 and 158) lay at the heart of its credentials as the miracle of *waḥy*, or inspiration. It gave rise to the *I'jāz*, or incomparability, of the book, understood as a literary matchlessness which attested its divine source and authority. So its being Arabic was, and is, inseparable from its being Qur'ān. It is not merely, as with all great literature, that translation is impoverishment even when successful with the sense. It is, further, that its quality is essentially bound up with its whole significance so that each is necessary to the other.

Its Arabic form, furthermore, was certainly part of an Arab experience. In several crucial passages the book insists on its Arabic state (12: 2; 20: 112; 39: 28; 41: 3; 42: 7; and 43: 3, etc.). The emphasis can be taken as sustaining, if not indeed requiring, the conclusion that the 'illiterate prophet' of 7: 157 and 158 means in fact the 'unlettered prophet', in the sense of a 'prophet for those as yet without Scriptures'. In the event, the Qur'ān made a 'people of the book'—of this book—as cohesive and as confident as those earlier Scriptured people, the Jews and Christians, whose books, and book-centred identities, had so deeply attracted Muḥammad and yet finally inspired him to a countering independence. In this sense, 'the Arabic Qur'ān' coincided with a powerful people-consciousness which, from those beginnings, still lives with its impact and its story.

The task of the non-Arab, Muslim or otherwise, is therefore exacting and there is no easy answer for the foreign reader who must refuse to be deterred. World Islam itself is predominantly non-Arab by every quantitative measure and all those multitudes possess the faith of the Qur'ān without native Arabic and, for the most part, without Arabic at all. This fact alone is proof sufficient of the range of Islam beyond the reach of Arabic and its capacity to give authentic religious existence with a translated or, in the literary sense, an alien, Scripture.

As with most difficulties, there is opportunity in its very texture. Several dependable translations exist in English and the careful student can compare them.[1] The theological and spiritual themes we have to study do not turn on inaccessible enigmas of speech. On the contrary, the effort to elucidate the intention or the development of crucial terms and phrases which translation requires is often itself the first ingredient of an intellectual reckoning. The external student is free to imagine the fascination of the poetry for the Arab-born, without the temptation to stay with the fascination alone. His very externality may turn into an asset, provided he is alert and humble enough to subject it always to the authority, and the decision, of those who are, or were, to 'the manner born'. In such an expectation the common denominators of our present situation must be presumed to be our allies. What languages and literatures are today in the love of their own has to be aligned with the whole around them and with all men in it.

The literary wonder of the Qur'ān had its deepest relevance in the immediate context of the time and place. For modern generations of Arabic-speaking Muslims it is axiomatic. The centuries exchanged a doctrine of excellence for the first fine rapture the Prophet's contemporaries knew. While the emotion of the music of Quranic chant can never be the same outside the language community, time has done much to put the insider and the outsider on more equal ground.

Chronology, within that first generation, is another of the initial perplexities for the unfamiliar reader. The non-chronological arrangement of the Surahs of the Qur'ān and the composite character of many of them leave him bewildered about the sequence of events and the

[1] Notably that by A. J. Arberry. Translated verses here are those of the author throughout, not for any wilful independence of recognized versions, but for the reason that translating is integral to intelligent discussion. But reference to published texts in English is everywhere assumed.

bearings of the contents. The readiest answer, perhaps, is to invite him to work from the last page back to the first, since he will, in a rough fashion, be closer to chronology that way. The earliest deliverances are mostly in the last fifth of the 114 Chapters, while the long, extended, legal and social provisions of the late years occupy (and lengthen) the ample paragraphs of Surahs 2–6. Thus the pattern of arrangement according to length, from longest to shortest Chapters, runs broadly counter to the development of style and theme, from the ecstatic to the discursive, from the poetic to the prosaic.[1]

Growing familiarity—and this very hurdle can well serve to it—soon yields a sense of the main lines of interior progression, in style, form, material and event. The resourceful and determined reader may even in the end appreciate a book which confronted him with obstacles so germane to its understanding. To discover how Muḥammad moved steadily and critically through the early hesitancies and mysteries of vocation, into the long bitter controversies, the citation of the patriarchs and the warnings to a bemused, scornful, angry, violent Mecca, through the crucial emigration and into the state-building, the community-establishing, the victory-completing at Medina, is to follow the sequence of the Qur'ān's chronology by dint of its own clues. It is to know the whole more validly by not being told it *in extenso*. The effort to trace makes for an active reading. Non-chronology may not have been meant this way. It is, in fact, something of a mystery. But if it has this consequence for the careful reader it might, by a sort of paradox, be regarded as appropriate.

But it needs a careful reader. There is, of course, the single dating of every Surah, as either Meccan or Medinan. But this only ranges them on one side or other of the central watershed of the *Hijrah*. The distinction may not always hold for the entire contents of a Surah. For the rest, vocabulary, theme, style and content suffice as guides, with the events that, for the most part, can be readily identified. Taken broadly, the whole situation tallies with the truth that the Qur'ān is not a Scripture about a personality, or a history, to which, as a narrative or a source, it is itself secondary. Rather, it constitutes in itself the revelatory reality. As such it engages with incidents and impinges

[1] There are, of course, re-arrangements according to chronology, such as those attempted by Nöldeke, and the versions of Rodwell, Bell and Dawood. But these require 'keys' to locate, are sometimes lacking in justification, and are distracting or tedious to use.

upon a history. It accumulates through the episodes that happen in its incidence and this 'accumulation' is a fundamental element in its nature.[1] But, so doing, it is the revelation *per se* in its literal shape as a document. Hence it does not need to be biographical, presenting any central personage vital to its significance (except as instrument to its availability to men as document). Still less could it ever approximate to autobiography, as do certain of the psalms or Paul's epistles. Its contents in themselves, not *about* something beyond themselves, are what signifies eternally. Occasions of course they are bound to have, else they could not be in history. But, in orthodox understanding, the occasions are not otherwise significant. Both in practice and in theory the chronology question leads us back to this ultimate idea.

The non-Muslim reader—and many Muslims too—will not be taking the Qur'ān in terms of this account of how meaning and event relate together, of how revelation and history inter-act. But it is vital to appreciate it. We thus come to another introductory matter, namely the right mental attitude of the outsider to the orthodoxy whose most sensitive territory, in the Qur'ān, he is proposing to enter.

It might perhaps best be described as a sincere partnership of courtesy and realism, a lively awareness of the status and authority of the book as these are in the conviction of Islam. Too much western scholarship, in its pursuit of academic liberties, has been insufficiently alive to the susceptibilities of Muslims and to the damage magisterial and unfeeling attitudes may do to the very ideals of untrammelled knowledge which presumably inspire them. It is right to handle the Qur'ān at all times with a sense of the near presence of multitudes whose beliefs it determines and whose reverence it commands. The point has been well made by Charles Adams.

> 'The Islamicist now finds himself drawn into personal relations with the modern representatives of the tradition he is endeavoring to study. But (by) the responses that his work inevitably evokes, if he is at all sensitive, he is made vividly aware that he is speaking of historical events, develop-

[1] See, for example, Surah 20: 114: 'Be not impatient for the Qur'ān before its revelation is completed for you.' Surah 6: 7 points out that a book 'sent down' *in toto* would have been plain sorcery. Its meaning and integrity could only belong in the tide of related events and issues.

ments, documents, personalities . . . that have a profound and immediate religious meaning in the lives of some millions of his contemporaries . . . If he is alive to human feelings he does not deal lightly and indifferently with things that represent the most precious insights and values of others.'[1]

The readiness to be in such relationship, rather than in an abstraction of academic opinions irresponsibly indulged, is the first condition both of fruitful thought and constructive scholarship.

It is with this hope that, in the three succeeding chapters, attention is given to the tradition of Quranic memorizing and to the basic principle of exegesis laid down, if somewhat enigmatically, in Surah 3: 7, with some notice, too, of classical commentary and the temper of its spirit. This is a proper prelude to a concern for the kind of questions that arise in the context of the modern scene and in the conscious neighbourhood of faiths. It would be too vast and diversionary a task here to attempt any adequate review of Islamic exegesis in the sequence of the centuries. But it is important to measure and to acknowledge the massive prestige which it enjoys. Some expositions of Islam see the famous exegetes wielding an authority derived from a divine inspiration. Thus, for example, Frithjof Schuon:

'The (orthodox) commentaries spring from the oral tradition which accompanied the revelation itself, or else they spring through inspiration from the same supernatural source. . . . The commentaries are providentially part of the tradition, as it were, the sap of its continuity.'[2]

There can be no question, therefore, that such commentary merits sustained deference as both the home of the traditional soul of Islam and an institutionalizing of the mind of the Qur'ān.

Such courtesies, however, must live with a proper realism. The fact of long credence does not close all questions. Sensitivity to the prolonged dominion of the great commentaries can yet explore an intelligent independence of them. To do so is the better to discover the resilience of the Qur'ān itself, its capacity to transcend its own devotees, and so to disconcert a merely pedestrian loyalty. This may be no

[1] See the essay: 'The History of Religions and the Study of Islam', in *The History of Religions: Essays on the Problem of Understanding*, edited by J. M. Kitagawa, Chicago and London, 1967, pp. 188–9.

[2] *Understanding Islam*, translated from the French by D. M. Matheson, London, 1963, p. 46.

less a path to awareness of 'what is repugnant to the Qur'ān' than a bare recourse to venerable margins around the text. That very concept of 'repugnancy,' so frequent in twentieth-century constitutional and social debate,[1] is potential of wider range, and open to greater enterprise, than many of its exponents realize. Its converse in a true congruity with Quranic themes and meanings is a criterion well able to disqualify the unimaginative and kindle the perceptive, as may appear below.

To diverge from established interpreters is, no doubt, to risk disallowing whole stretches of Muslim thinking down the centuries. The outsider can never do this without patient converse with its present heirs. Many of these, however, such dialogue aside, are actively given to some renewed possession of their heritage. The debate continues. Every reader, in his integrity, becomes a part of it.

But there has to be realism in another sense also. The book of Islam, like other Scriptures, suffers a conspicuous neglect in many quarters. For many, even within Islam, reciting is a forgotten piety and the art of *ḥifẓ* a relic of the past. Belief in revelation comes oddly to the modern temper with its secular pre-occupations and its sceptical bent. So the Qur'ān has lapsed into a symbol from the ages, the core of a culture, to be championed if it is externally attacked and otherwise honoured in an inattentive esteem. The study of it competes unequally with the clamorous demands of education for a scientific age and the assumptions of people dominated by technology. There has long been a painful dualism in Muslim education. Theological and exegetical learning, with all its erudition and minutiae, is seriously remote, both in temper and in content, from the areas of life and study proper to engineers, technicians, physicists and men of affairs, struggling to overtake the pace of change. They find little leisure for what their criteria regard as the irrelevancies of shaikhs and mullahs. The latter, in turn, retreat from the real issues into bastions of dogmatism, or rely on harmonies of religion and science which do justice to neither. So there is disquiet on the one side and impatience on the other. The full Quranic meaning goes by default even where it is professionally served and finds no hearing where it has most need of being heeded. It would be sanguine to suppose that this situation could be easily resolved.

[1] As, for example in Pakistan in the successive efforts for constitutional definition since 1947.

Aside from the attitudes of the secular mind and the decline in the public influence of religious personnel, there are aspects of the Quranic world within itself which expose it, in perhaps a unique way, to the counteraction of contemporary thought. The point at issue here is difficult to state. Moreover, it needs to be carefully balanced by compensating considerations that are deeply present and tend to the opposite conclusion.

The point in mind is that Quranic theism, with its dominant transcendental emphasis, discourages what we may call here the interrogation of God and of the idea of God. There is so instinctive a fundamentalism at its heart that it has little ready accommodation for the modern mood of agnosticism and revolt. There is much in that mood which leads insistently away from theism, proved or claimed, so to speak, from above. But there is much in it also, and by the same token, which can lead back to theism, as it were, from below, from the experience of man in the mystery and anguish of his being. Many today move Godward, if at all, only from man, his grandeur and misery, his stature both of mastery and tragedy. The atmosphere around us is more liable to psychology than metaphysics, more given to the inward, than to the celestial, direction of inquiry, finding the reality of God more readily in the human meaning than in the revelatory assertion, more in 'the wound of absence' than in the word of command.

In this climate, the Quranic sense of God, being strongly monarchical and authoritarian, would seem to incur the sharpest tensions, to be more at issue than any other with the current technological sense of the exclusive competence of the human. For it does not ride readily with Promethean views of humanity. Its accent is on man the subject, man the creature, man the subordinate. It is forthright, almost political, in its requirement of obedience. In its characteristic emphases it has little room for the more relational and immanentist criteria of the divine which, elsewhere in our generation, have come to the aid of faith and of a renewed integrity in worship.

These reflections are in no sense complete. They return in more adequate discussion in Chapter 8, 'No God but Thou', following an earlier appreciation of the Quranic picture of man to which they must be carefully related. Their immediate and introductory purpose is to keep a reading of the Qur'ān as close as possible to the demands of contemporary relevance and, so doing, to take it in its own seriousness.

Its most urgent concern is undoubtedly the rule of God—the theme which might be described as the urgent unconcern of secular man. We are less than honest with either if we do not hold them resolutely and imaginatively together.

Islam is now in the final decade of its fourteenth century. It has often expected renewal when the centuries turn. This one is like none before it. The consequent disquiet of the traditional mind is everywhere apparent. It coincides with an instinctive distaste, in conservative circles, for surmise and mental exploration. There is a posture of thought which wants only the reverent perpetuity of the familiar, and so questions questioning itself.

> 'I answered a question in theology, went home and my heart was empty of the grace of God which He gives to Muslims. I arose, bathed said a prayer, humbled myself, repented, and wept until it returned to me.'[1]

For such the sense of grace lies in the closed circle of truth. For others it must come in the open world of uncertainty, where the proven is only so in the encounter with experience.

Among Muslims of whatever mood and instinct these issues necessarily centre in the Qur'ān, in the meaning and possession of the conclusive Scripture, in the understanding of the mind of the book in the mind of its community of faith. The student can hardly have the one without the other. The sacred volume is the mentor[2] of believers and belief is the minding of the given word. The hope of the ensuing chapters is to explore that reciprocal situation, its habits of thought and centres of conviction, and to do so from the impulse of a common humanity and a religious concern.

The alert reader will probably register omissions he may want to question or emphases he would dispute. In a sphere so wide, so cumbered with erudition, so prone to pretentious zeal, it is well-nigh impossible to avoid criticism and displeasure, wide and erudite and zealous. To study, anyway, is to select and selection is itself already a judgement of significance. But the silences, it is hoped, are neither culpable nor distorting. The purpose in hand does not turn, decep-

[1] Quoted by A. S. Tritton in 'Discords and Differences in Islam', in *Essays in Honour of G. W. Thatcher*, edited by E. C. B. McLaurin, Sydney, Australia, 1967, p. 93.

[2] The word is well chosen. For the Qur'ān calls itself *Al-Dhikr* (the Reminder), *Al-Furqān* (the Criterion) and *Al-Hudā* (the Guidance).

tively, upon them. On the contrary, it lives through and by the positive areas which, in the Qur'ān, have sustained and kindled it. We are pre-supposing the historical inquiries considered in *The Event of the Qur'ān*, and proceeding upon the understanding of it there suggested. The aim now is to attain a sense of its intellectual and spiritual possession of and by its people. For is it not in such active possession that wells of God irradiate and irrigate the souls and societies of men? As Ibn Khaldūn observed:

> 'Even the flow of springs and rivers stops in waste areas. Springs flow only if they are dug out and the water drawn. . . .'[1]

[1] In *Al-Muqaddimah*. See *The Muqaddimah: An Introduction to History*, translated by Franz Rosenthal, New York, 1958, vol. 2, p. 314.

Chapter 2
HAVING THE TEXT BY HEART

That to have is to have by heart has been from the earliest days the instinctive Islamic conviction about its Scripture. The way to receive the Qur'ān is to become its *ḥāfiẓ*, committing it entirely to memory so that its phrases and themes are constantly present for quotation and its meaning and music treasured in the heart. This *ḥifẓ* of the Qur'ān is its continuity through the generations of the faithful. It is also the traditional prerequisite of all further education. The Islamic scholar is required to have a Quranic memory. Only as a *ḥāfiẓ* can he aspire to do justice to the academic and religious expression of his allegiance.[1]

This phenomenon of Quranic recital means that the text has traversed the centuries in an unbroken living sequence of devotion. It cannot, therefore, be handled as an antiquarian thing, nor as a historical document out of a distant past. The fact of *ḥifẓ* has made the Qur'ān a present possession through all the lapse of Muslim time and given it a human currency in every generation, never allowing its relegation to a bare authority of reference alone. It has also conditioned the mentality of those generations and their patterns of emotion. *Ḥifẓ* has effectively Quranized the instincts of mind in Islam to a degree which could not have been the case if the Scripture had been only a written court of appeal.

Further, the habit of recital in strict sequence fixed the juxtaposition of Quranic incidents and phrases, endowed them with a sort of sacred logic. Adjacence became significant of meaning and sense was linked strongly with proximity. To have a literature thus scrupulously by heart is to think instinctively in its idiom and its content. It is

[1] The root verb Ḥ F Ẓ means 'to keep, or preserve' and so, in turn, 'to have by heart'. The idea of *ḥifẓ* does not readily go into a single English word, unless 'memoriter' ('by memory') could be noun as well as adverb. 'Recital' is too stylized: 'memorizing' has no necessary vocal element: 'rote' is too thoughtless and pedestrian: 'to have on heart and tongue' is a phrase.

to imbue all other thinking with that pervasive association of themes and ideas. In this manner, the Qur'ān has held mental sway over the attitudes of Islam. Its status as an external reality was corroborated by its cherished presence as an interior shape of mind. Muslims were guided by *ḥifẓ* to think Quranically, not simply as acknowledging their oracle of truth but as possessing in it the mould of their imagination. Having the Qur'ān readily and *verbatim* in their minds and on their lips, reciters, we may say, were participating in the deepest sacrament. For they were engaging their powers of memory and speech in a literal appropriation of the divine words. Such memorizing might be well defined as ideology by *anamnesis*.

Before considering some of its larger consequences for religious life and mentality, it will be wise briefly to note the more technical aspects of *ḥifẓ al-Qur'ān*. The art of recitation is a matter of much expertness for the initiate and certainly of fascination for the observer and the auditor. It is technically known as *'Ilm al-Tajwīd*,[1] the science, literally, of 'doing well' by the Qur'ān, of reaching the proper excellence or skill by which the splendour and eloquence of the book may be evident, unmarred by clumsiness, ignorance or error.

Qur'ān itself means, of course, reciting and is so used, for example, in 75: 18, which speaks of 'its (i.e. the Qur'ān's) *qur'ān*, or recital'. From this active sense, the word passed to being the name of the book itself. From the beginning within Muḥammad's experience, the utterance was encompassed with dangers and temptations, from which immunity had to be sought by invocation of God. This sense of preciousness and so of precariousness in a holy trust is present in a different way in all reciting of the Scripture and gives to the practice of it an aura of special sanctity and duty. The act of recital solemnizes the tongue and heart and calls for the disciplined skills that have come to belong with it.

Qur'ān, or reciting in this active sense, is known as *tilāwah*, or reading aloud. The book is divided into thirty *ajẓā'* (sing. *juẓ'*) or sections, each of which has two *ḥiẓbs*, or portions. These sixty *aḥẓāb* (pl.) may each be sub-divided again into four quarters, making two hundred and forty short divisions. The whole Qur'ān may be recited, of course, with varying frequency, the most onerous being that by thirds, making ten *ajẓā'* at a time, comprising Surahs 1–9, 10–30, and 31–114. The Caliph 'Uthmān, it is recorded, recited the Qur'ān every

[1] From the verb *jawwada*, 'to do well'. See Edward Sell, *'Ilm al-Tajwīd*, Madras, 1915.

seven days, beginning on a Friday and concluding on a Thursday. The divisions in such a sequence are Surahs 1–4, 5–9, 10–16, 17–25, 26–36, 37–49, and 50–114. The initial letter of the seven Surahs that begin each of these sections, namely *fā*, *mīm*, *yā*, *ba*, *shīn*, *waw* and *qaf*, make up the sentence *famī bi shauq*, meaning 'my mouth (is) in longing', which affords the name for this pattern of rotation. If the thirty *ajzā'* are followed, as in the thirty nights of Ramaḍān, the month of fast, then we have a monthly period.

The numerous points of meticulous scruple in *'Ilm al-Tajwīd* do not call for notice here, save as indicating the overriding sense of veneration which the Qur'ān commands. The schools differ over them with a Talmudic inventiveness and insistence. There is, however, general recognition of seven classical readers and their norms, respecting pronunciation, emphasis, intonation and punctuation. There are certain points at which *takbīrs* may occur (i.e. saying: 'God is most great') and after certain rhetorical questions in the Qur'ān it is proper for the reader to make a response. Thus, for example, 77: 50 ends with the question: 'What saying after this will you believe?' to which reply is given: 'We believe in God, the Lord of the worlds.' After 95: 8: 'Is not God the most just of judges?' one may say: 'Yea! I bear witness of Thee.' Verses which refer to *sujūd*, or the act of prostration, are said to require a *sajdah*, or prostrating, either there and then, or at the end of the reading.[1]

There are also points in reciting where one may halt and ask for pardon (*waqf al-ghufrān*) where themes of particular urgency or injunction are involved, and the whole is to be prefaced by prayer for protection and sincerity. 'Accept my recital as an act of worship: let me read it thoughtfully. Truly Thou art merciful and gracious' runs one such devotion. Or: 'O God, increase my yearning for it and make it the illuminator of my sight, the healer of my heart and the dispeller of my pain and grief.'

With these and other points in the art of recital, is the fact that it constitutes the sole engagement of the vocal capacities of man in the immediate religious expression of Islam. There is, of course, the voice of the preacher in the mosque *khuṭbah*, or sermon. But congregational music does not exist, nor instrumental music. There are no choirs, chorales, anthems or hymns in Muslim worship. Nor, further, is there

[1] 7: 206, 13: 15, 16: 50, 17: 107, 19: 58, 22: 18, 25: 60, 27: 26, 32: 15, 38: 24, 41: 38, 53: 62, 84: 21, and 96: 19.

congregational audition of the Qur'ān in the manner of the reading of the law in the synagogue or the lectionary in the church. The mosque sermon quotes frequently from the Qur'ān as also from Tradition. But the Qur'ān, as a text, does not need such public reading for the attention of its community since it is already possessed in memory by the faithful Muslim.

Thus the whole vocal articulation of Islam is in the individual recital of the Qur'ān and in the phrases of the liturgical *Ṣalāt*, or prayer, where the *Fātiḥah* regularly occurs, and most other clauses have Quranic origin. The believer speaks the sacred text for himself, both in the phrases of the prayer and in his *ḥifẓ* of the book. Just as the legitimate artistry of Islam keeps its energies and cares for calligraphy, so the musical arts are focused on Quranic chant. The *tajwīd* engages the art of sound with the same devout monopoly as the inscriptions of the mosque employ the arts of line and colour.

'We have made the Qur'ān easy for remembrance' says Surah 54: 17 and 32, though the 'ease', as it goes on to hint, comes only for the attentive. Certainly in the power of rhyme and rhythm lies the secret of Quranic recital. 'I shall preserve my affection for you as the rhyming syllable is preserved from alteration of vowel or consonant', wrote the blind poet, Abū-l-'Alā al-Ma'arī[1], and this sense of the surely coming rhyme both serves and enthuses the recital. Arabic lends itself superlatively to these arts. The Qur'ān's literary and poetic eloquence calls out for the sort of vivid enunciation that *tajwīd* brings. The ear rejoices over the resounding long syllables of the regular plurals. It savours the assonance given by the structure of *ṣarf*, or word derivation, repeating particular consonants and syllables by regular patterns through a diversity of roots. It registers the insistent *shaddah*, or consonantal doubling, and rides with the *waṣlah*, or linking *waw* by which the flowing sequence of merging words gives vocal counterpart to the cursive flow of the Arabic script. With these is the limpid quality of the 'l's (the *lāms*) of the definite article, standing in their own value where the initial letter in the word that follows is 'lunar', or demanding the ever welcome *shaddah* where the letter is 'solar'. Either way, the quality invites the ready energies of the speaker, in a zeal which less vigorous languages do not understand and less lively diction cannot esteem. Arabic, broadly, does not take to the

[1] From Letter 30, in *Letters of Abū-l-'Alā al-Ma'arī*, translated by D. S. Margoliouth, Oxford, 1898, p. 137.

complex, dependent, subordinate clauses so characteristic of Latin, Greek, and Indo-European speech. Even to the point of abruptness, 'it proceeds,' as N. Bammate notes, 'through a juxtaposition of principal sentences, simply drawn in line through conjunctions'.[1] The resulting forthrightness is notably vigorous in Quranic Arabic.[2]

These practiced inflections and emphases, these long accented vowels and reverberating consonants are further enlivened by deliberate nuances in the recital, conforming to the sense of the glad and the grim, the light and the dark, in the meaning. This must not be overdone, however, since the sanctity of the Qur'ān forbids histrionics or theatrical ways. Its own range or sound and content, of eloquence and power, need no extraneous treatment. It is the innate excellencies that the fidelity of the reciter aims both to cherish and to utter. No sympathetic listener can doubt the awe of the professional chanter as he feels and breathes them.

So it is that, with these qualities of the Qur'ān and its *qur'ān*, of the Reading in the reading, the book becomes a sort of accompaniment to life, in the musical sense of the word—the theme by which the believer is articulate, like the singer in the song. The sequences of the Qur'ān are apprehended as the setting that runs parallel to daily life. They are a sort of 'key' in which the emotions and aspirations find a vicarious context in the patriarchs or in the Prophet, in the events and phrases of the Quranic scene. The human situation is 'set to words'—to *these* words, which warn, or chasten, or exhort, or encourage it, in a sort of engagement of these with those, of now with then, in the fabric of the text. *Ḥifẓ* means its prompt availability for guidance or for the imagination, not as something to be tediously recalled out of near oblivion, but as a familiar framework of imagery and theme.

Ḥifẓ, means further the participation of the believer in the divine speech. For it is the point at which the earthly, mortal apparatus of mind and tongue has, in an immediate activity of recollection and of utterance, the words which in their sequence are understood to belong to God. The phrase 'to mouth' has come to have a derogatory sense in English. But if it could be rescued from this, for a properly dignified and literal meaning, then it could be said that by the art of recital the

[1] In 'The Status of Science and Technique in Islamic Civilization', in *Philosophy and Culture, East and West*, edited by Charles A. Moore, Honolulu, 1962, p. 182.

[2] For the Greeks this was *parataxis* and it is interesting to note that where it occurs it has sometimes availed to detect an author using Greek with Aramaic as his mother tongue. Cf. J. B. Lightfoot, *Biblical Essays*, London, 1893, p. 135.

Muslim is 'mouthing' that which is of God and from God. Islam has not used for this the language of sacrament though it might well have done so. For at this point the divine *tanzīl* and the human experience come into closest relation. To repeat the words of the Qur'ān is, therefore, by Islamic faith a sacramental participation. What God has vouchsafed to men constitutes in recitation an exercise in the consecration of lip and thought whereby these become its human vehicle.

This fact is symbolized in the term *dhikr* which has very wide significance in both Quranic and devotional usage. It is at once a title of the Qur'ān and a vital element in Muslim religious practice. The word means 'mention', or 'recollection', or 'reminder', and occurs frequently as an imperative. 'Remember your Lord in your soul with humility and reverence and without ostentation: remember Him morning and evening and do not be negligent.' (7: 205.) But, reciprocally to man's remembrance of God in His Names, is the divine reminder to men, the book itself, called 'the *Dhikr*', or 'the Remembrance', in frequent passages.[1] It may not be necessary or obligatory in all these passages to see the reference as being to the whole Qur'ān. But they certainly relate to the revelatory status of the warning and exhortation which, as in many instances here, the scoffers and detractors refused or despised. The word has the sense of bringing to mind the retribution awaiting evil-doers, as well as the intimations of the divine will and mercy. Indeed, the contents of the Qur'ān may be said to be that to which all human cognizance of God, in penitence and worship or in refusal, is reciprocal. The human awareness of God is schooled and educated by that which holds the divine summons to men. The mutuality in the divine address to humanity and the human response to God is unmistakable. It is this which the single term *dhikr* expresses and which Quranic memorization achieves.

Clearly there is no way so complete as memorizing for having the revelation in mind. God is to be addressed 'in His Names', and it is these (7: 180) which knowledge of the book teaches. In rehearsing, the believer is recalling them. Such *dhikr* belongs with the practice of liturgical prayer (4: 103) and it is explicitly related also to the rites of pilgrimage (22: 34 f.). 'We brought to them their reminder', says Surah 23: 71, 'Yet from their reminder they turned away.' But the

[1] 15: 6 and 9; 16: 44; 36: 11; 38: 8; 41: 41; and 68: 51 and 52. The Qur'ān, in 38: 1, is described as *dhī al-dhikr*, 'the possessor, or the ground, or the reminder', so that it may be right not to think of the term *dhikr* as wholly synonymous with the term *qur'ān*.

faithful exclude such a negation, by the contrast of their intense and solicitous absorption into active memory of every word, in order that they may 'refer to' the divine by the very language received as the divine 'reference' to them.[1] The double sense of *dhikr*, as including both directions of this relationship, is the surest clue to what Islam understands by the duty and vocation of *ḥifẓ al-Qur'ān.*

Dhikr, it is true, has wider and more technical connotations than these, particularly in the Ṣūfi Orders, where it signalizes the art of concentration, through various devices, on the divine Name and Unity—an art which congenially very often dispenses with the more literal and pedestrian skill of the memorizers. *Dhikr* then develops a quality of self-transcendence and mystical ecstacy far removed from the deliberate mental disciplines of the sober reciter. These aspects are not here our concern. The mystic, for his part, is liable to hold lightly to the recognized patterns of orthodox discipline which *ḥifẓ* involves.

It follows from this will to fill the memory with the words of the divine that devout Muslim reactions to life-situations fit characteristically into Quranic precedents and parallels. These, conversely, determine and permeate the understanding of situations. Where the Qur'ān is not known by heart, the professional reciter is recruited to solemnize or celebrate the occasion in view. Where it is so known, he brings the charm, and the merit, of his more skilful powers to its enhancement. The book is thus the shaper of emotion and the *vade mecum* of Islamic experience. It sets them in its own framework of perspective and interpretation and its vocabulary serves for the fears and hopes which life generates. Where the Qur'ān, in memory, and Tradition suggest no clue to events, they surely reinforce or illustrate positions independently reached. Examples are legion from every field of public affairs and of personal existence.

Such suggestibility in the Islamic mind in line with the memorized Qur'ān is reinforced by the many repetitions within the book itself. These were natural to the situation of education and controversy in Muḥammad's mission. The Scripture would be much reduced in volume if its contents were distilled into a form that excluded all

[1] It is perhaps feasible to borrow for parallel of this 'set' of the spirit, John Donne's poem, *Riding Westward*, in its different idiom. He was physically facing *away* from the place of Christian event, but knew himself 'toward' it in heart:

'. . . these things, as I ride, are from mine eye.
They're present yet unto my memory,
For that looks toward them.'

reiteration. But then it would lack its existential quality and its cumulative force. It was precisely in its refrains and recurrences that steadfastness was proved and the revelatory ends achieved. Memory now combines with these, echoes their frequency, rejoices in their quality, and so doing makes itself their ready servant.

The Qur'ān in the currency of corporate Muslim memory is far too vast a theme to exemplify in particular references. But it may be useful here to reflect briefly on its part in the *magnum opus* of later medieval Islam, the famous *Al-Muqaddimah* of Ibn Khaldūn.[1] This classic example of Islamic historiography is a work of profound range and deep perception, an attempt to analyse and explore the wealth and welfare of nations within the totality of human circumstance as conditioned by race, climate, territory and culture. It stands deservedly as one of the finest monuments of Muslim thinking and has a relevance far beyond the local and immediate setting from which it sprang within the author's travels in Tunis, Spain, Cairo and Damascus. Its perceptive scholarship is everywhere tempered by careful piety and chastened by strenuous experiences suffered amid the vagaries of politics and fortune in the disturbed conditions of the fourteenth century.

Ibn Khaldūn quotes the Qur'ān repeatedly. His combination of far-reaching themes and steady devotion make his pages a revealing setting in which to study what *ḥifẓ* of the Qur'ān may do for authorship. Genius, in this, is not atypical. The quoting instinct is representative. It could scarcely have more varied scope than in the wide perspectives and scholarly ambition of *Al-Muqaddimah*.

An unsympathetic reader might soon conclude that the author's recital of Quranic phrases is merely pious decoration. He is far into the first volume before he encounters a citation which significantly bears upon the argument.[1] It has to do with the caliphate or dominion of man by which, according to Surah 2: 30, the creature is set in authority over the material world. From this fact Ibn Khaldūn argues the necessity for social organization grounded in the divine will to settle the world under responsible tenancy. The point is an integral element in the author's case and provides a theology for his analysis of human ways. He relies on the Quranic theme of signs and measures to elucidate the data he observes about the zones of time, the effects of latitude and longitude on climate, and the patterns and instincts of

[1] Ibn Khaldūn, op. cit. See p. 24 above. [1] Ibid., vol. 1, p. 91.

animal and human behaviour.[1] His theological orthodoxy and distrust of metaphysical speculation are sustained for him as faithfulness to the mind of the Qur'ān. He borrows such passages as 17: 85: 'You were given but a little knowledge', and 'God is beyond them, encompassing', to clinch his intellectual reserve.[2]

At other times, however, the connection between the precise concern of the exposition and the import of a quoted verse can be seen only in the most approximate terms. Familiar Quranic language is used to despatch a conclusion in pious or merely decorative guise. 'God give me more knowledge', from 20: 114, ends a survey of the revenues of dynasties.[3] 'God has power to execute his commands', cited from 12: 21 and closely echoed in 13: 41, figures in an omnibus comment on the vicissitudes of thrones and politics.[4] That 'God has no need of the worlds', as 3: 97 and 29: 6 aver, closes a discussion of petty wars in Spain,[5] and a passage on the flux of poverty and wealth.[6] 'This is God's way with his servants', taken from 40: 85, serves to summarize the matter, in line with: 'You will find there is no changing the way of God', which is applied *inter alia* to the varieties of climate, race, physiology and character.[7] The fact that 'God gives his kingdom to whomsoever He wills', in 2: 247, argues the claim that luxury is an obstacle on the way to royal authority,[8] while Surah 13: 11: 'If God has willed evil for a people nothing can avert it', supports Ibn Khaldūn's central thesis of the 'vitality' or '*aṣabiyyah* which is the ethnic secret of the flourishing of cultures, the loss of which in any people reveals itself in lack of leadership and general disintegration.[9]

Here, as elsewhere, the theory of the historian readily fits the potential of the Scripture and is re-inforced by the association with it. But the text does not require, and need not be supposed to intend, the theory. The coincidence of meaning is thus a work of devotion, rather than a necessity either of the authorship or of the authority. Yet there can be no doubt that the piety is alive in the scholarship and the scholarship informed by the piety. The partnership is deep and

[1] The theme of the *Āyāt* or 'signs' of the Qur'ān is the major concern of Chapter 9 below.

[2] Ibn Khaldūn, op. cit., vol. 3, pp. 36 and 38.

[3] Ibid., vol. 1, p. 371.

[4] Ibid., vol. 2, pp. 130, 238, 286, 291; vol. 3, p. 34.

[5] Ibid., vol. 1, p. 336.

[6] Ibid., vol. 2, p. 276

[7] Ibn Khaldūn, op. cit., vol. 1, pp. 57 and 173; vol. 2, p. 99. The verse is Surah 33: 62, Surah 35: 43 and Surah 48: 23.

[8] Ibid., vol. 1, pp. 287 and 378.

[9] Ibid., vol. 1, p. 295. Compare vol. 2, p. 122.

authentic, even if at times it is tempted to triteness and foreclosure of inquiry. Thus the truth of Surah 2: 29 that 'God knows all' explains why Maghribī rulers use mercenaries,[1] while 16: 8: 'He creates what you do not know', serves to buttress the claim that outside the temperate, or Mediterannean zone, the inhabitants, i.e. negroes and Slavs, are 'like dumb animals', whose religious conditions are wretched, since they are ignorant of prophecy and of religious laws.[2] Ibn Khaldūn significantly exempts Ethiopians and some Slavs and 'Turks' from this diagnosis, on the ground of their being Christians. Otherwise he writes off the intemperate zones in the north and in the south as totally lacking in scholarship and religiously deprived.[3] Such prejudicial use of the Quranic text is in no way required by its content. The author's own attitude, in the double sense of the word, betrays his use of it.

The same temptation is present in the oft-repeated formula about the paucity of human knowledge in contrast with divine omniscience. A citation terminates further commentary, whether it be on the curiosity of theologians or the complexities of politics.[4] It is general in *Al-Muqaddimah* to find Quranic quotation at the end of the paragraphs, rounding off the immediate business and consigning all problems, conjectures and opinions to the divine guidance or the divine inscrutability. Its case is clearly comforted by this Quranic reliance and is commended to the reader thereby as loyal and reverent.

This reciprocity of the book and the pen is discernible through all the pages and topics of Islam's great masterpiece of historiography. The modern reader, impressed by the range and perception of the author's mind in fields of sociology usually considered as only a recent territory of science, is aware at the same time of a strangely docile atmosphere of religious duty. There is a persistent mutuality of lively theorizing and willing veneration. The spirit of the man is imbued with his Scripture and the Scripture dwells in the instinct of the man. Independence of mind there is, and certainly a freedom of imagination. The text is flexibly associated with the purposes and hypotheses of a widely ranging intelligence and a fertile historical judgement, ready to analyse and to assess. Yet all is suffused with the temper that returns steadily to the themes of its great sustaining source, as a needle to its pole, for satisfaction and finality.

[1] Ibn Khaldūn, op. cit., vol. 2, p. 81. [2] Ibid., vol. 1, p. 169.
[3] Loc. cit. [4] Ibid., for example, vol. 1, p. 79 and vol. 3, p. 36.

In his long and erudite treatise on the lore of the Qur'ān, Jalāl al-Dīn al-Suyūṭī, the great fifteenth-century compiler, quotes a poem composed by a certain Shaikh 'Alam al-Dīn on the difficulty of *Tajwīd al-Qur'ān*—a difficulty that yields only to steady practice and ripe excellence of diction.

> 'Have no exaggerated measures of *tajwīd*
> Stressing where you have no warrant of the word.
> Do not weigh too heavily
> On the *hamzah* that follows the long vowel.
> Do not chew your letter like a drunkard
> Or mouth your *hamzah* like one about to vomit,
> Scaring the listener to flee from the mess!
> Each word has its weight: do not crush it
> Like a tyrant, violating its due worth.
> When you open a syllable, use all gently,
> Without histrionics:
> Open or closed, give them their due.
> Thus to excel with the text
> Is to have its excellence.'[1]

Perhaps there is a parable, from diction and recital, to possession and interpretation. Mastery, either way, pre-supposes a cherishing care and a patient art. In his quoting of the pivotal verse in Surah 3: 7, which is the theme of the next chapter, Ibn Khaldūn observes that 'only those possessed of minds remember'. May we not assume that the intelligence which deals rightly with the text for the hearing is no less vital in dealing rightly with it for the understanding? 'Only those with minds' might be read as a warning that *ḥifẓ* itself may be barren unless it serves a responsible, even an enterprising, fidelity. Having the Qur'ān in mind would then imply, not merely a devout recital of words, but a discerning recollection of meaning—a recollection no less alert to the present context of existence than to the text received to guide it. Knowing by heart obviously presumes a prospective relevance, as well as satisfying a retrospect of piety. To commit to memory

[1] *Al-Itqān fī 'Ulūm al-Qur'ān*, Cairo edition, 1941, vol. 1, p. 175. The translation is necessarily somewhat free, especially in the final line, and no effort after rhyme is made. 'Use all gently', *ji' bihi mutalaṭṭifan*, is uncannily close to Shakespeare's advice to the players in *Hamlet*. The *Itqān* (or Setting in Perfect Order) is a compendium of Quranic sciences, not an original work.

is to provide for a future as well as to venerate a past. It is to carry the document of faith into the commentary of every new present.

That being so, everything turns on the 'minds that remember'—minds that can inherit the traditional without bondage and the communal without servitude. The classic art of memory has served a long pattern of scriptural nurture in familiar terms. In subsequent chapters, after a review of other technical matters, we will explore some contemporary aspects of an ongoing Quranic loyalty, actual or potential. At a time when, statistically, there is much less caring for the Qur'ān than in earlier Muslim generations, there may yet be, for that very reason, a finer care of it.

Chapter 3
THE EXPLICIT AND THE IMPLICIT

'The Qur'ān is God's word truly enough', wrote Muḥammad 'Alī in his autobiography, 'but it is, and must be, in man's ill coin.'[1] The likeness seems a harsh one, in a writer of undoubted piety of mind. 'Coin' is a metaphor from the commonplace of currency and 'ill' a sharp word in this context. But the writer has a large matter in view. He is thinking of human language as the medium of revelation and sees that what coins are to value, words are to truth. Without vocabulary, meaning has no circulation. Terms are the counters of its worth. The very purposes of revelation require its place in earthiness. Its enterprise is eternal: it must therefore participate in time. Unless it is exposed to misunderstanding it cannot be understood. It fulfils itself only where it stakes itself. Its values turn on human sounds and images. The more total the authority within it, the more critical the risk around it. It is perpetually conditioned by the usages of its recipients. In having them it suffers them.

Coinage and currency, then, are apt, if also lowly, parables for the giving and receiving of scripture, for truth in expression and truth in reception, for the word and the words of revelation. Muhammad 'Alī had in mind, it would seem, not simply the disservice unworthy commentary and obtuse custody may do to the text. His concern, rather, was with the central problem even of worthy and imaginative exegesis, the problem of human language itself in its own time and place bearing the themes of eternity, of human

[1] *Muḥammad 'Alī: My Life, a Fragment,* Lahore, 1942, p. 276. The work is in fact a sizable book. The 'fragment' in the title refers to the (unfulfilled) intention to write a full scale exposition of Islam, to which the autobiography would be the preface. The author was a noted leader of Indian Islam in the period during and after the First World War in the Khilāfatist Movement. His reflections on the Qur'ān derived from long study during political imprisonment under the British. He was buried in 1931 within the Temple Area in Jerusalem in tribute to his leadership in world Islam.

metaphor carrying the stamp of transcendent meaning. He spoke of Muslim theology, 'setting itself right with itself', and added:

> 'It is the very recognition of my ignorance that makes me careful not to attribute to the mind of the Divine Author of the Qur'ān that which belongs only to the mind of so human and fallible a reader as myself.'[1]

We are concerned here for this carefulness not in respect of this or that particular exegesis, but in its total bearing on the idea of revelation. The need for it belongs with Scripture *per se*. 'The mind of the Divine Author' and the mind of the fallible reader are meeting, by the very hypothesis of revelation, in the same verbal territory. The one is necessarily using the categories of speech and literal symbol which are the realm of the fallibilities, and of all the right apprehensions, of the other. 'The Qur'ān', Muḥammad 'Alī insists, 'is not a riddle, except to those who make it so, in the interests of their own variety and subtlety.'[2] But, in that it is not a riddle, it is certainly a responsibility requiring and pre-supposing, as all scriptures must, a readership that actively co-operates with its character. Revelation might well be defined as the divinely given material of such co-operation. Belief in it is the will to receive it in those terms—terms that are *ex hypothesi* both man's and God's, both received and given.

This 'getting right with itself' of all theology derived from a scripture, and of all spiritual existence so sustained, brings us to the pivotal passage in the Qur'ān about its own exposition—a passage in which all the issues of metaphor and meaning, of word and sense, of letter and spirit, may be said to have their criterion. But it is a clue which itself becomes the focus of all the questions. The verse is Surah 3:7.

> 'He it is who has sent down to thee the Book, wherein are verses that are explicit. These constitute the matter of the Book. There are also other verses which are implicit.'

The crucial words here are *muḥkamāt* and *mutashābihāt* (plurals, fem.) variously translated as:

[1] *Muḥammad 'Alī: My Life, a Fragment*, Lahore, 1942, pp. 217 and 220.
[2] Ibid., p. 276.

categorical	allegorical
clear	conjectural
definitive	figurative
precise	metaphorical
perspicuous	allusive
literal	analogical
decisive	susceptible of different interpretations.

The first, we might roughly say, are those that need, or seem to need, no translation in the mind that reads them. They mean what they say and they say what they mean. The second must needs be translated. For, if taken directly as they stand, they would tend to obscurity, contradiction, or even absurdity.[1]

Our purpose in this chapter is to study this basic distinction and attempt a reckoning with its implications for the contemporary reader. The necessity of discrimination which it enjoins has been operative, in a variety of ways, from the beginning of exegesis. But, in so far as there is no decisive clue to the identification of either category, the implementation of the meaning of the distinction involves judgements which cannot be inclusive, nor always objective in themselves.

For this reason 'ambiguous', though current,[2] is hardly a sound translation of *mutashābihāt*. It is true, of course, that metaphors often have double meanings and that language lives by the sensitivities it kindles as well as by the statements it makes. But such imaginative potential of the Qur'ān's allusive and figurative elements is better expressed by a term that does not imply mere doubtfulness of sense.[3] Poetry and picture must be seen as an instrument, not an impediment, to truth.

The two types of verses might be distinguished in a preliminary way, as 'literal' and 'literary'. For these are the associations of the roots from which they derive, and of the form of the derivative. The *muḥkam* (sing. masc.) is that which is decreed or determined from authority, whether of rule or of wisdom. It denotes the legal and

[1] 'Translation' here, whether required or not required, refers to language *per se*, to transposition by the proper clue, not transition to another speech—though the latter no doubt searches and alerts the former.

[2] For example, A. J. Arberry in *The Koran Interpreted.*

[3] Compare Martin Buber's perceptive remark: 'It is not the unambiguity of a word, but its ambiguity, that constitutes living language.' *The Knowledge of God*, translated by M. Friedmann and R. Gregor Smith, London, 1965, p. 114.

the authoritarian, the 'thus-it-is' quality of a sovereign will or of a competent tribunal. *Mutashābih*, however, has artistry and allusion in its nature. It relies on an image or a figure from one realm for the illumination and expression of another.

The two might be broadly characterized as the factual and the figurative. The Qur'ān makes statements that are entirely explicit and belong with simple fact. 'Muḥammad is not the father of any man among you' (33: 40). 'Eat of their fruits at fruiting time and bring the due thereof on harvest day' (6: 141), relating to produce, to olives, pomegranates and the rest. 'Fight them until sedition is no more' (8: 39). 'Messengers sent before you were the butt of ridicule' (6: 10). Such verses are precise, concrete and direct, either in assertion or command. But at other times the Qur'ān is highly metaphorical. To assume a literal sense would then betray the meaning. 'Their deeds are like a mirage in the desert' (24: 40). Or God 'seated Himself upon the throne' (7: 54, 10: 3, 13: 2, 20: 5, 25: 59, 32: 4, and 57: 4). Or 'Your women are a tillage for you. So come to your tillage as you will and bring about your progeny in the fear of God' (2: 223).

On the one other occasion besides 3: 7 where *muḥkamah* (sing. fem.) is used, namely 47: 22, it relates to 'a decisive surah', giving clear directive about warfare. *Mutashābih* occurs in passages of simple comparison, for example various kinds of similar fruits, resembling each other (2: 25, 6: 99, and 6: 141).

But, given this specific sense of the two words, there is need to see the distinction as something that is always qualified and never absolute. Hence the preference for 'explicit' and 'implicit' as translations. One cannot exclude factuality from the intention of the implicit type of statement: nor can one escape subtlety in what would be accounted explicit. The case is such in all literature. If, for example, we say with Thomas More in Robert Bolt's *A Man for All Seasons*: 'You have yourself like water in your hands', we have used a *mutashābih* sentence, a similitude. Yet it stands, surely, as an eloquent, explicit and authentic judgement of fact. Conversely, George Fox wrote in his *Journal:*

> 'As I was walking with several friends, I lifted up my head and saw three steeple-house spires, and they struck at my life. I asked them what that place was and they said: Lichfield.'

Here we seem to be dealing with bare facts, until the sudden turn with the words: '. . . they struck at my life . . .' which seem to tell of something more than a walking with friends, seeing a three-towered cathedral and asking a name.

Quranic usages have a comparable quality. That Muḥammad had no son, in the context of 33: 40, is a factual matter, simple enough—and tragic. But is the statement not also to be understood as implying a search for an heir, and relevant, therefore, to questions of marriage and perhaps also of strictly human status? Or does it intend the sense that his sole significance lay in prophethood and not in the founding of a dynasty? The explicit has an implicit quality, even if it cannot be immediately interpreted. Likewise in the metaphor linking husbands and husbandry, sexuality and agriculture. The capacity of either of these to be images of the other is a profound illumination of each.[1] But what the explicit directive teaches in its implicit context is open to a wide interpretation.

It seems right, then, to take the two categories of 3: 7 as concerned, not finally with exclusive lists of verses ('some . . .' 'others . . .' in that sense), but rather with a double quality of Quranic expression belonging, in varying degrees, to the verses as a whole, or to very many of them. The importance of this view will be evident in all that follows. It might seem, however, at first sight, to be excluded by the words of 3: 7 to the effect that the *muḥkamāt* are *umm al-kitāb*, translated as 'the mother . . .' or 'the matter . . .' or even 'the basis . . .' of the book. The phrase is widely understood to denote the Qur'ān in its eternal essence or pre-existence, preserved on 'the inviolate tablet' (85: 22), the original whence, by *tanzīl* or descent, the revelation came into time, in Arabic, on the lips of the Prophet. But it would appear necessary not to take this as excluding the *mutashābihāt* passages. For all the contents of the Qur'ān have the same source and status. *Waḥy*, or prophetic experience, is a unity with a common authority and an equal origin. There is nowhere any indication that the two 'qualities' of the Qur'ān imply or involve any divergence within the phenomenon of inspiration on which Islamic reception of

[1] In Biblical imagery also man springs from the ground and makes it productive and, despite the danger of an allusion derived from fertility rites, the prophets were ready to think and speak of a 'marriage' of soil and soul, of territory and people. Buber suggests a link between the name 'Adam' and *adama*, or 'fertile earth'. *Israel and Palestine: the History of an Idea*, translated by S. Godman, 1952, p. 10. Sophocles has the imagery of the plough and marriage and in Egypt Ptah Hotep gave this advice to husbands: 'Treat your wife with goodly devotion: she is a fertile field for the Lord.'

the Qur'ān relies. The explicit/implicit question belongs with the discernment necessary in understanding and exegesis. In the context of 3:7, therefore, *umm al-kitāb* may be taken to mean the gist of the 'explicitness', the firm directives of the book.[1] These the imagery and the literature sustain and make vivid, as music the words of a song.

Support for this conclusion may be claimed from a single use of the word *mutashābih* in 39:23, with reference to the whole Qur'ān, there described as *kitāban mutashābihan mathānī.*[2] This clause, which must be read consistently with 3:7, has probably to do with the integrity of the Qur'ān as 'symphonic' through all its contrasts of style and content. What is definitive in it and what is allusive are in mutual and complementary relationship. The metaphorical brings lively emphasis and kindling emotion to the service of the plain directives which, in their turn, control and recruit the allegorical to their purpose. Through all the sequences there is a continuity of theme, served, and not obscured, by the changes of mood and pace and character.

Surah 3:7, however, still leaves us with one further issue for debate. It clearly implies that the *mutashābihāt* are the special temptation and pitfall of the mischievous and the immature.

[1] The concept of the *I'jāz* of the Qur'ān is relevant here, the doctrine, that is, of the 'matchlessness' of the Quranic eloquence and style. Impressiveness in a literary sense would seem to belong much more with metaphor and imagery than with legislation and precept. Inasmuch as this literary dimension is the crucial 'sign' and demonstration of Quranic origin and authenticity, it can hardly be relegated to a subordinate status.

[2] The phrase is variously translated. Part of the problem is in the third word, with its suggestion of 'pairs' or 'repetition'. Some have taken this to refer to the contrasted 'refrains' of promise and of threat, of blessing and curse. Others understand it in relation to the rhymes, couplets or metrical measures of the Qur'ān. The translations read: '. . . A book, consimilar in its oft repeated' (Arberry); 'a scripture, consistent, paired' (Pickthall); 'a book in unison with itself and teaching by iteration' (Rodwell); 'a book uniform in style, repeating (promises and threats understood)' (Dawood); 'whose different verses are consistent with each other, some repeating themselves' ('Abdul Laṭīf); 'a book consistent with itself, repeating (its teaching in various aspects)' (Yūsuf 'Alī); 'a book conformable in its various parts' (Muḥammad 'Alī). The word *mathānī* recurs in 15:87 which reads (lit.): 'We have brought to thee seven of the oft-repeated and the mighty Qur'ān.' This verse is generally taken to refer to the seven verses of the *Fātiḥah*, or to variant recitings of the book. Since the phrase in question is preceded by a clause in apposition, referring to the Qur'ān as 'the fairest discourse', or 'the most beautiful converse', it may be best to take the meaning to be literary. The book, it seems to say, employs metaphor repeatedly and does so consistently, i.e. congenially to its purposes. In this sense the whole Qur'ān may be said to be *mutashābih.* If so then the *muḥkamāt*, as 'the mother of the book', must be understood to be such, not by isolation within the whole, but by summation in the whole.

> 'Those in whose hearts is aberration are the ones who go for the figurative parts, with a view to dissension, desiring to make the interpretation of it their own. Only God knows its interpretation and those who are steadfast in knowledge say: "We have put our trust in it: all is from our Lord." '

The reason for the charge in the immediate context of Muḥammad's mission can be readily recognized. History offers many examples of the kind of perversity which takes occasion from allegory, such as plain prose might have precluded. Anthropomorphisms can be distorted by literalists and so plague the labours of theology and the sensibilities of religion. But this should not blind us to the opposite problem, no less chronic in the things of belief, when the categorical becomes the excuse the authoritarian temper takes to 'make the interpretation its own'. Punditry that way can well be a worse menace than a free-ranging fancy. Those in whose hearts there is a feel for tyranny find the *muḥkamāt* as congenial an invitation to self-will, as the conjecturers do the *mutashābihāt*. The potential of the allegorical for quixotic minds is not, of necessity, a greater danger to the religious temper than the arbitrariness to which dogmatic souls are liable in possession of explicit claims. Interpretation needs to be freed both for and through the imaginative mind.

It should be remembered further that the categorical, even when received in full sincerity and with a right integrity, may still enshrine far-reaching questions of exegesis. Then, the more categorical the form, the more crucial the meaning. Thus, for example, Surah 4: 64 declares: 'We have sent no prophet except that he should be obeyed (*li yuṭāʿa*) by the divine permission.' Does this 'obedience' mean the heeding of the message, or the establishing of a polity, or the acknowledgement of a mystery? 'The obeyed one', as understood by many Muslim theologians, goes beyond all merely political or moral allegiance, and is linked with the very *amr*, or *fiat*, of God, by which the worlds were made. Obedience in such terms to the Prophet of Islam, joined repeatedly in the Qur'ān with obedience to God, becomes a duty of almost metaphysical force. The verse has clearly a potential range of political, spiritual and perhaps cosmic meaning, of which, at first glance, its simple directness gives no hint.

Or there are frequently both immediate and potential aspects of 'clear' verses, where the question arises as to what their contextually explicit meaning may be understood to have, as it were, in reserve implicitly for the future. Thus, for example, in *The Struggle for Pakistan*,[1] Ishtiaq Husain Qureishi, sets on the fly-leaf the words of Surah 7: 133.

> 'We have made a people who were looked [down] upon as weak the inheritors of the eastern and the western parts of a land that We have blessed.'

He may well be sound in his borrowing. But is it the simple parallel arguable between east and west Pakistan now and east and west Jordan in the Old Testament narrative of the entry into the land? The latter is the immediate context of Surah 7. Or is there, beyond that chance tally, the larger issue of statehood and territorial independence as the answer to minority status? How far was the making of Pakistan analogous to the entry into Canaan? What precisely is here explicit and what implicit? How should the verse be characterized by the clue of Surah 3: 7 ? Examples of this kind are legion.

We may, in awe of these complexities, fall back altogether on the diffident docility of the concluding sentences of 3: 7, and put our trust in God all-knowing. Representative of this stance are the words of Abū-l-Kalām Āzād, himself no mean commentator on the Qur'ān. Explaining that the *mutashābihāt* belong to aspects of life beyond the reach of human intelligence, such as the being of God and life after death, he continues:

> 'Reference to subjects such as these is made more or less in a figurative language, not totally incomprehensible for man. He who ventures upon any disquisition in these subjects very often involves himself in varying misapprehensions. So men of right understanding regard the *muḥkamāt*...

[1] London, 1965. The author was formerly Minister of Education in Pakistan and is a leading scholar. Examples of implicit meaning, much more fortuitous than this, were present in the anticipations of science briefly noted in Chapter 5 below. In quite different vein there have also been many playful ventures in exegetical ingenuity. Witness the story in Ibn Ḥazm's *The Ring of the Dove*, translated by A. J. Arberry, London, 1953, pp. 239–40. Here a young man, madly in love, is found sitting with his beloved by a passing friend, who invites him to share his house. The youth promises to come very soon, but never appears. Hearing the story, a third friend volunteers a complete exoneration of the lover: 'I will discover a perfectly valid excuse for him from the Book of God, where it is written: "We did not break our engagement with thee of our own willing, but we were charged with heavy burdens—the ornament of the people" (20: 90).' The context has to do with the excuse of the people when chided by Moses over the golden calf.

> as what primarily matter in the field of thought and action and do not run after the *mutashābihāt*... since no probe into them will bear fruit.... These . . . are certainly not repugnant to the intellect of man, but they decidedly are beyond its grasp. Man can believe in them: but he cannot catch their reality. So people of right understanding say: "We believe in all that the Book of God contains", and go no further. On the other hand, those who are perverse entangle themselves in the *mutashābihāt* and thwart the development of faith in them.'[1]

Yet, intelligible as this posture is, it can hardly be denied that the development of faith also requires and engages the liveliness of soul which allegory suits and to which metaphor ministers. These are inseparable from the nature of revelation itself. In so far as a scripture is a cypher, it fails to disclose. To say: 'We believe and go no further' is to qualify belief itself. The very authority of omniscience to which faith defers needs minds for its ally. Its very use of language means that it supposes those minds to be active. No text can have adequate readers, however reverent, if they are not also partners with it in an active apprehension.

We may, of course, set this co-operating awareness vis-à-vis the text one stage further back and see it as happening within a closed circle of *charisma* or *gnosis*, to which alone truth is intimated and from which it may be mediated to those outside the circle. This has been the characteristic pattern in Shī'ah Islam from the early centuries, whether through the *Imāms* or, from the time of the 'hidden' *Imām*, through the *mujtahids*. *Tafsīr*, or commentary, on this reckoning, is excluded. Careful scholarship and popular devotion alike fall short of the necessary illumination only the élite can receive. The simple believer is wholly dependent on the mediation of meaning by those in its mysterious possession. The literal sense, in effect, ceases to exist. *Ta'wīl*, or esoteric elucidation, emerges as the perquisite of a hierarchy of insight and so becomes an infinitely subtle thing where allegory is total and the categorical quality is virtually transferred from the text to the oracle.

[1] *The Tarjuman al-Qur'ān*, edited and translated by Syed 'Abdul-Laṭif, vol. 2, London, 1967, pp. 139–40. Maulānā Abū-l-Kalām Azād (1888–1958) was a leading thinker and statesman in Indian Islam, a protagonist of Hindu-Muslim political unity, whose Quranic Commentary and Memoirs (*Tadhkīrāt*) are among the most significant documents of Indian Muslim religious experience in the crucial years before and after Independence and Partition.

Islam in its Sunnī form, however, has vigorously rejected this solution. It is one which collides sharply with the sense of the community as the sure repository of Islamic faithfulness and of *Ijmā'*, or consensus, and of that communal mind as being the place where the possession of the Qur'ān properly belongs. It runs counter also to the deep significance of personal *ḥifẓ*. There can hardly be point or relevance in Quranic recital if the text has no intelligent business with the ordinary man and with the day-to-day world. The Muslim, after all, is not invited to acquaint himself with an enigma. Even the *mutashābihāt* must somehow be covered by the Qur'ān's own formula for itself as 'a Book wherein is no dubiety' (*Kitāb lā raiba fīhi*, 2: 2, 10: 37, 32: 2).

Yet, in medieval Sunnī ways, if we substitute the expert and the scholar for the Shī'ah *Imām* and *mujtahid*, there was a comparable tendency to withdraw the book into an exclusive purview of interpretation—the purview, that is, of the pundit who was suitably equipped with the minutiae of his task, and fortified with the privilege of his special skills, grammatical, traditional and erudite. Commentary could almost then be thought of as having, as it were, a private ear for revelation, becoming, at remove, a sort of special confidant of scripture.

But the explicitness of Surah 3: 7 might well be taken as scarcely compatible with such exclusive powers of comprehension. Can the categorical, it might be asked, really be in need of a professional expertise for its understanding? And though the implicit may still leave occasion for the learned and his learning, there is a logic in the contemporary situation returning the text to the ordinary folk, with whom it first began. The secularization of life and the laicization of thought and education tend in this direction. The pundit is in diminishing demand. Explicit and implicit thus emerge, not simply as questions of a text, but as questions of a society. Explicit for whom? Implicit to whom? What the Qur'ān means comes to turn upon where it is heard and how it is taken among its loyal people. Only from them, in the flux of circumstances and in the intentions of faith, can it be known what is rightly enjoined in the *muḥkamāt* and enfolded in the *mutashābihāt*.

Such a confidence, however, in the generality of Muslims as being the surest clues to the Qur'ān has to reckon rightly with a deep contention through the centuries which has critical bearing on all modern commentary. This is the thesis that the Qur'ān, in its metaphors and allusions, intends an audience of the seventh century which, according to this view, was innocent of theological perception and unaccustomed to mental abstraction. The book brought itself within the range of popular comprehension by pictorial language. Where it was not legally explicit, it taught implicitly by the kind of allegory suited to the limitations and the circumstances of its hearers. It deferred to their level of sensuous experience and relied on *argumenta ad homines*. This, it is claimed, is peculiarly the case in its portrayal of the future state. It would, therefore, be wrong, for example, to take its vivid characterization of celestial delights on silken couches in entrancing gardens, or the bitter anguish of the quenchless fires, as literal truth. They are imagery required by the mentality of the time and place. Numerous other themes besides judgement and eschatology are said to be as they are because of what their hearers are.

This notion of the Quranic style turning on a temporal, and temporary, situation can, of course, be used to justify wide exegetical liberties. It is, therefore, severely and rightly suspect. Yet it cannot be totally rejected without absolutizing the moment in the seventh century and thus endangering the whole concept of a scripture given into a history. It is an argument which, at least since Al-Fārābī (AD 875–950) has been invoked to reconcile intellectual speculation with Quranic loyalties and, in effect, to by-pass its contents wherever they were awkward or obstructive to philosophic interests. But treating the Qur'ān as an *ad hoc* volume, beyond a certain degree, is to jeopardize its abiding authority.

The essential question would seem to be how far the argument *about* time can become virtually an argument *against* content. Time and date, it is true, cannot be escaped if revelation is to occur. But, if revelation in them is to endure, they must have a perennial quality in themselves which an honest sense of a new time need not doubt and can dependably perceive. The point of incidence of a scripture must somehow abide *within* the significance of its revelation—a conviction which strongly undergirds all that is attempted in the pages that follow.

The question at issue here is not simply that of chronology, of a book for a setting and at a time. It is, by further implication, that of a distinctive audience at any date. Is there an élite which alone conceptualizes the meaning truly, while the non-élite must lie, as it were, in the shallow end of the pool where symbol and picture allow them to tread water? If so, then much in revelation becomes almost a popular disguise of truth, withheld from the penetration of minds not sophisticated into its clues and idiom. Or, putting the matter the other way round, is it the popular guise of truth, which the really perceptive ones defer to in a concessionary sort of way, for prudential or practical reasons, without genuinely receiving it for themselves? Such intellectualism was not infrequent in the hey-dey of Islamic philosophers. The like phenomenon was by no means unknown in western thought in ages of dogmatic authority.

An illuminating instance of the view that esteems the Scripture for its uses among the 'vulgar', while assuming a philosophic self-sufficiency for the intelligent, may be found in Abū Bakr Ibn Ṭufayl al-Qaisì (*c.* 1110–85), author of the famous philosophical romance, known from its hero as *Ḥayy Ibn Yaqẓān*.[1] This 'Alive, Son of Awake' is a sort of Robinson Crusoe on a desert island who, by gradual but unfailing self-education through sense-perception and acute intelligence, builds his own universe of knowledge and ethics as he grows in years. He finds it all confirmed in the Islamic faith, when the latter is brought to him in his island seclusion by one, Asal. He greets the hitherto unknown religion with instinctive acclaim. But he is perplexed by what he feels to be the crude language of the Qur'ān, especially phrases about God seated on a throne, about heaven and hell and final judgement, pictorially so stark and unrefined. He is also deterred by the minutiae of the Qur'ān and its magisterial tones in regulations about buying and selling, marrying, divorcing and inheriting, and the like, which, 'Alive' thinks, ought to be extraneous to truly religious lives, or at least instinctively sensed without such tedious explicitness and commonplace style.

> 'Why did the messenger of God, in describing most things which relate to the divine world, express them to men by parables and similitudes and did not give a clearer revelation of them? This occasioned men to fall into grave error, namely asserting corporeality to God and attributing to the essence of the One Real things from which it is absolutely free: and so, in like manner, concerning those things which relate to the rewards and punishments of a future state.'[2]

[1] There are innumerable editions of the work. The author lived under the Almohad (*Al-Muwaḥḥidūn*) caliphate in Spain. He was secretary to the Caliph, and a noted scholar and physician. The Almohads were a sharply puritan and rigorist community.

[2] Paragraph 112. It is not entirely clear whether Ḥayy was abandoned on the deserted

The answer he receives from his mentor, and which clearly the author means to commend, is that this pattern of things is necessary to the common throng. The book is how it is because the generality of men are incapable of a finer competence with truth and the eternal world. It is to be noted that Ḥayy's stance does not essentially turn on the distinction between *muḥkam* and *mutashābih*. For he feels a certain scandal in both the detail of legal provision and the atmosphere of the figurative. His views, therefore, do not avail to solve our basic issue within Surah 3: 7 specifically. But they do illustrate the question that issue involves, namely that the clue to the Qur'ān has to be found in its readership.

It is noteworthy, in Ibn Ṭufayl's romance, that Ḥayy's dismay over unphilosophic religion is not lacking in compassion. He is stirred by commiseration for the ordinary world and eager to serve the dissemination of the purest truth. He proposes a mission to inhabited territory, with his colleague teacher. It ends in failure. His lofty sophisticated religion achieves no viability in the rough and tumble world. Chastened by this further awakening, Ḥayy returns to his island to live out in appropriate isolation the pure concordance of reason and faith which he had earlier attained. He confesses the practical wisdom of a vulgar form of religion, such as avails for the brutish life of men enchained by their senses and unable, without sensuous rewards and literal pictures, to seek or apprehend eternal verities. He is content to leave them to the wise rule of Salaman, the practical and 'literal' Muslim, whose engagement with the concretness of the Qur'ān is the only practicable thing outside a private utopia.

The very popularity of this romance is witness to its bearing on a vital problem, extreme as its drawing of the alternatives may be. Numerous questions lurk within this aristocraticism of truth and the assessment of explicit regulation and implicit figurativeness as simply concessionary to human dullness. Symbol and imagery are surely more than necessities to frailty or a crutch for the obtuse. Allegory is surely more than a device to light up the abstract for the slow-witted. Metaphor and allusion belong with the subtle mysteries of

island soon after birth, or whether the reader is meant to understand that he came mysteriously into being by supernatural genesis. The intention of the story either way is to exempt him altogether from parental and educational influence, in order to demonstrate the inherent intelligibility of the world, the innate 'construction-kit' of the human intelligence, and the rationality of Islam which is immediately recognizable despite the forms of its 'popular' shaping for and in the common world.

language and will in their inter-action. They recruit and employ the potentialities of land and territory and *mores* for the illumination of the crisis of hallowing or 'submission' on which those factors turn in the human custody.[1] Metaphor ministers, where logic only states. It deals with the art, within the argument, of truth. To comprehend the imagination within a scripture as a method unnecessary to the wise is liable to debase both word and wisdom. It may well make insoluble the vital problem of rightly relating reading and readership as these two are held together in both the fact and the concept of *Qur'ān.*

Yet still the modern question of sophistication remains. The audience of the book after fourteen centuries of Islam is plainly different from that after fourteen months or fourteen years or fourteen decades. It has itself shaped the reasoning and fed the imagination of generations. Meanwhile human liability in religion has come to embrace and confront things then undreamed of and unknown. What was *ad hoc* then, in the deepest sense, has to become *ad hoc* now, if its impact is to be contemporary and loyalty with it alive. Manifestly 'then' and 'now' are utterly far apart: yet not so far apart that present generations of Muslims in their possession of their Scripture cannot determine the connection. We arrive at the aphorism that what the Qur'ān means *in* itself is what it means *to* its readers. The ultimate implications of *muḥkam* and *mutashābih* will be those of a readership taking them duly. The right qualifications of readership may be in perpetual debate. But can there be any 'right' decision about the explicit and the implicit other than that of readers in the right?

Islamic history contains one other broad stream of Quranic attentiveness, different from both the orthodox and the philosophical, and relating quite critically to the import of Surah 3: 7. It is the *Ṣūfī* or mystical instinct in Islam. This has read the Qur'ān according to its own lights and liberties and taken its own counsels with the *mutashābihāt.* Its main, if not always articulate, sense of things, it may be conjectured, goes back to the phenomenon of the Prophet himself in the actual recipience of the Qur'ān.[2] The book itself seems to invite kindred minds to a yearning after the disciplines—if we may not speak of 'techniques'—which served it. If the very Scripture itself

[1] For a study of landscape and the human scene within Quranic imagery, see *The Event*, Chapters 5 and 6.

[2] Some attempt was made in *The Event*, chapter 1, to explore the nature of prophetic *charisma*, though whether this can well be seen by Muslims as at all a matter for emulation —in its form—must remain controversial.

belongs with mystical apprehension in its actuality to the Prophet, may not an ardour to be like-minded, or like-willed, be the deepest and surest form of recognition and submission—and that, without in any way impugning the uniqueness of the revelation? Numerous passages are to hand as potential or actual texts for this position and the whole, rich canvas of *Ṣūfī* possession of the Qur'ān will concern us in Chapter 10 below.

Taken this way the book becomes no longer simply the manual of the student, the lore of the pundit, the treasure of the reciter, the criterion of the faithful: it becomes, beyond all these, the *rendezvous* of mystic love with mystic truth. Or, in the metaphors of Jalāl al-Dīn Rūmī, prince of *Ṣūfīs:*

> 'You say: "I filled the sheep-skin from the sea, and the sea could not be contained in my sheep-skin." This is absurd. Yet, if you say: "My sheep-skin was lost in the sea", that is excellent: that is the root of the matter.'
>
> 'The Qur'ān is a bride who does not disclose her face to you, for all that you draw aside the veil. . . . The act of drawing aside the veil has itself repulsed and tricked you, so that the bride has shown herself to you as ugly, as if to say: "I am not that beauty. . . . But if you do not draw aside the veil and seek only its good pleasure, watering its sown field and attending to it from afar, toiling upon that which pleases it best, it will show its face to you without your drawing aside the veil." '[1]

Enquiry, intellection, discourse, will seek and not find. For finding means a different search, a submission of heart and a discipline of yearning.

So arguing, however, the mystic is a law unto himself. Neither insight nor argument can finally resolve the sharp tensions of his intuitive world with dogma and tradition. That issue persists into the very criteria needed to adjudge it. Our concern here must leave that controversy in its necessary perpetuity. There is a tradition that 'the Qur'ān has many reciters whom the Qur'ān curses'.[2] It is one which

[1] *Discourses of Rumi*, translated by A. J. Arberry, London, 1961, pp. 122 and 236–7. (Spelling changed from 'Koran'.) Jalāl al-Dīn has another intriguing passage about a gnostic and a grammarian. 'The grammarian said: "A word must be one of three things . . . noun, verb or particle." The gnostic tore his robe and cried: "Alas! twenty years of my life and striving . . . have gone to the winds. For I laboured greatly in the hope that there was another word outside of this. Now you have destroyed my hope." Though the gnostic had in fact attained that word which was his purpose, he spoke thus in order to rouse the grammarian.' Ibid., p. 165.

[2] Quoted in ibid., p. 94.

can obtain in either or any direction, abjuring the scholar in the name of the mystic, or the mystic in the name of the grammarian, or each in the name of the philosopher, or all in the name of the sectarian. What matters, for our immediate conclusions, is the range of the implicit and the test of the explicit which these histories reveal, against the long background of their ventures, their debates and their convictions, disclosing and yet concealing their great original. 'Poetry,' observed Wallace Stevens on one occasion,—'poetry is the subject of a poem.' One might almost be tempted to conclude similarly that the theme of the Scripture is the Scripture.

It is wise to recognize, in sum, that there are meanings hidden except to humility, that truth is always responsive to capacity and that capacity is a quality of heart as well as an activity of mind. For the rest, there is the stimulus of community—community which, in present situations, must be no longer merely familiar and religiously congenial, but as broadly human as are the questions of the time. Through and in all these, there must surely be the will to plead and, as far as may be, pursue, the hint of Surah 39: 23 about the Qur'ān as affirming, almost like refrains in music, certain consistent themes that are its steady care. *Kitāban mutashābihan mathānī*—a book of recurring fidelities to be read in its situations as parabolic and expressive, a book addressing the will and the imagination and declaring truths that demand re-iteration both for their own sake and for the frailty of their human audience.

This, to be sure, is no more than a broad paraphrase of a single, significant clause. It may, nevertheless, be reasonably understood as inviting a contemporary reckoning with the Qur'ān that is loyal to the generations of the past in their reverence and to the present in its crisis. Decisions may well differ as to how these themes may best be set down and pondered. But any such venture requires that we first have clearly in retrospect the mind of traditional commentary.

Chapter 4
THE EXEGETICAL TRADITION

'O you who believe, do not ask about things which, if they were revealed to you, would only trouble you. If you raise your questions about them while the Qur'ān is being given, they will be made clear to you.' So runs a notable passage, in Surah 5: 101. The check to mere curiosity is characteristic. It is, however, qualified, by the pledge that within the period of the Qur'ān answers will be there. The time element here may be taken to mean, either the whole prophetic span of Quranic incidence, or the particular moments of separate revelations within it. Whichever it be, it is clear that the questions and the time belong together. There are occasions, for example in Surah 2, where paragraphs begin with some popular question, usually of a practical kind, which is then elucidated. At many points the Qur'ān was responsive to human interrogatives, though 5: 101 is careful to add that there is pardon for such questioners. Perhaps this means that in any case there was an element of presumption in asking to understand.

But what of questions, and questioners, that arise outside the chronology of the Qur'ān? It might be thought that these can have no answer once the volume ends. Inclusion in the sacred text cannot occur when it is concluded. But, since its relevance is by no means confined to the period of revelation, it must certainly bear on these later, excluded issues, by vital, intelligent interpretation—an interpretation which extends and applies the chronologically located text to the questions of ensuing time. These, of course, multiply in bewildering range and variety—never more so than today. The problem, then, is how to reach and formulate the discernible directives and implications of the once-for-all content, so that the revelatory finality believed of it may have its operative authority in every age.

In the immediate decades after the completion of the Qur'ān—

perhaps even for two centuries—Tradition provided part of the answer. For it illuminated the where and why and how of many passages, by recollection and explanation of attendant circumstance. It thus became a source of guidance, responsive to those issues and questions that could be comprehended within its form of extension of Quranic dicta. But by its biographical nature, however freely enlarged, Tradition could not hope to suffice for the questions of the lapsing centuries. Time took it beyond the feasible range of its significance for the obligations of exegesis, as these grew apace. To such a degree is this the case today that there are those in Islam who feel that there is little point in now addressing modern problems to the scriptural sphere, as being altogether too distant and too different a realm.

To hold this view unproven and unwarranted, as we do, is to be liable the more to honesty with the problems. The first duty of such honesty is surely a mind for traditional commentary—a mind both reverent to its devotion and independent of its dominance. For centuries classical exegesis has enjoyed so massive a prestige as to be almost sacrosanct. Yet there are significant ways in which it rests like an incubus on the Quranic meanings it is supposed to serve. It may help to our double purpose of feeling for what piety cares about and yet pursuing the fuller, freer dimensions of the text, if we preface our own questions with some broad assessment of the characteristics of the traditional exegetes. It soon becomes clear that many of the most famous commentators are pre-occupied, to the point of tedium, with questions we do not now ask, but which strongly impede the ones we do. The margins of the Qur'ān are so copiously filled with interpreters and their erudition that the book itself has been taken into a sort of protective custody and needs saving from the very custodians.

This is not to say that a contemporary reader owes no debt to their pains and cares. The sustained deference of the centuries is part of the history in which the Qur'ān reaches him. Their grammatical finesse and technical skills still have significance. But the tasks that were once necessary in those fields have been thoroughly completed. To be only so equipped today is to be unready for the necessary liabilities that have supervened. It is to say: 'I can say little more than I have studied and that question's out of my part.'[1] Commentary, by its very nature, means that the text is subject to a sort of scrutiny, a catechism of question and answer. What sort of scrutiny is the vital matter.

[1] William Shakespeare, *Twelfth Night,* Act 1, Scene 5, lines 179–80.

Typical of the great masters was Fakhr al-Dīn al-Rāzī, author of the many volumes of *Al-Tafsīr al-Kabīr*, or 'The Big Commentary', also known as *Mafātīḥ al-Ghaib*, or 'Keys to Hidden Things' (AD 1149–1209, AH 543–606). He was a widely travelled, highly reputed figure in his generation, reared in the Ash'arite tradition and gifted with strong resources of mind.[1] His commentary worthily represents the conventions of exegesis and the intricacies of dogmatic theology. It breathes a religious sincerity, deeper than intellectual debate in which, as the author wrote in his will '. . . I found neither the satisfaction nor the peace to equal the satisfaction and the peace which I found in reading the Qur'ān'.[2]

Only quite extended translation fully communicates the balance of discussion, the revealing pre-occupations and the significant silences of this notable work and abridgement is here imperative. But the reader need not fear that it here distorts what he needs to observe, namely the habit of reaching for tradition, the care to tabulate even what is disapproved, the capacity to be unalert to possibilities outside assumed criteria, the quaintness of parable and parallel, the interest in numbers and the ability to say much and conclude little, to leave much with little said. Through all there is the ready retreat into the inexplicable.

The extracts that follow relate to the crucial Surah 97, which runs:

'Truly We revealed it on the night of authority.
Would that you knew what the night of authority means!
Better than a thousand months is the night of authority.
Thereon come the angels and the spirit down
By leave of their Lord, for every behest.
It is a night of peace till the breaking of the day.'

Taking the first verse, Al-Rāzī proceeds:[3]

'There are several points at issue here:

(1) Most of the commentators are agreed in the view that it is the

[1] He is not to be confused with his greater namesake, Abū Bakr Muḥammad al-Rāzī (AD 865–925, AH 251–315), the celebrated physician, who was known to medieval Europe as an enthusiast for Aristotle, and a doughty controversialist. Bar Hebraeus (1226–1286) in the next century compared him with Origen, for the range and quality of his mind.

[2] See his *Controversies, Islamic Culture,* vol. 12, 1938, p. 137.

[3] Extracts are translated by the author from the Cairo edition of *Al-Tafsīr al-Kabīr*, 1962, vol. 32, pp. 27–37.

sending down of the Qur'ān which is meant. But the Most High omitted to say so explicitly and this redounds to the greater glory of the Qur'ān in three senses.

(*a*) He is the sole and exclusive authority for its descent and

(*b*) His use of the pronoun rather than the specific noun signifies the eminence of the Qur'ān in that He dispenses with the use of the name . . .

(*c*) This magnifies the time at which the revealing occurred.

(2) In some places the Most High says: "Truly I . . ." and at other times He uses "We" as in the verse here. . . . Sometimes the purpose of this plural pronoun is to indicate greatness. It cannot possibly be taken as a literal plural. For it is clear on absolute authority that God is one. If indeed there were many gods, they must all be of lesser rank than the divine, for if each were utterly perfect each would be able to dispense with every other. Yet, if any were so dispensed with, he would lose something of his right. So each would be lacking something, whereas on the other hand, if each were not utterly perfect he would likewise be wanting. Thus we know for sure that the plural "We" denotes not plurality but majesty.

(3) The question is raised as to the meaning of its being sent down on the night of power.

(*a*) Al Sha'bi said that the night of power, being in Ramaḍān, was the beginning of its descent.

(*b*) Ibn 'Abbās said that it was sent down *in toto* as far as the heaven of the earth on that night, and then onwards in the piecemeal way. For God said: "Do I not swear by the fallings of the stars?" (Surah 56: 75). The question is in mind, too, in the verse (2: 185): "The month of Ramaḍān in which the Qur'ān was vouchsafed."

But on this basis, why does He not say: "We sent it down to the heaven . . .?" because its coming forth may be understood as its downward revealing to the earth. We say that its descent to the heaven is tantamount to its descent to the earth. For God would not set something in train and fail to see it through. It is comparable to an absent person who comes to the environs of a place and word spreads of his arrival or rumour of the purpose of his coming. So, too, the Qur'ān's descent to the earth's heaven is to kindle in men a longing for its arrival here, just as when there is news of a message come to one's father or mother, and he grows the more eager to read it for himself. As the poet says: "Yearning is intensified when proximity grows."

Heaven is a realm we share with the angels—a common territory.

> It is their dwelling place and our ceiling and splendour (as the Qur'ān says: "We set the heavens for a roof . . ." 21: 32). The sending down of the Qur'ān thus far really means its coming hither to us.
> (*c*) The purport of the phrase is to indicate the blessedness and eminence of the night of power.'

Fakhr al-Dīn then turns to the intricacies of the term *qadr*, or power, withits complex meanings—authority decreeing, disposing, ordaining, revealing, an ordering of all things in nature, in history and in destiny. He takes his cue from 54: 49: 'We have created everything according to its measure.'[1] Aside from the 'measure' of the divine will, he says, it may denote honour and glory, in which case it may be

> '. . . the night of glory, because a glorious book was that night brought down, by the agency of a glorious angel, to a glorious people or *Ummah*, and perhaps this threefoldness of time, means and nation is why God Most High repeated the word *qadr* three times in this Surah.'

Or it may be the night of power for the reason that, to angelic beings, earthly missions are arduous. For this world is a cramping place.

Our commentator next broaches the hard question as to the 'date' of this great night of revelation. It is here perhaps that he vexes a modern patience most sorely.

> 'God Most High has left this night undisclosed for a variety of reasons.
> (1) He has concealed its date, as He has the rest of things. He has not, for example, made specific the pleasure He takes in particular acts of obedience so that men may desire them all, nor His wrath in particular acts of waywardness that men may guard against them all. He has likewise concealed His special "associates" (*wali*) among men that they may magnify all. He hides the answer to prayer-petition so that men may persist in all prayers. He has not let His supreme Name be known so that all the Names may be exalted. He has not identified "the middle prayer" so that every prayer may be earnestly performed.[2]
>
> He has kept secret the aspect of repentance which He accepts so that the penitent may bring an entire repentance. He has hidden, too,

[1] A much cited verse which has been a battleground of 'determinism' and 'liberty', according to whether the 'measure' here is an arbitrary, or a scientific, concept.

[2] *Al-Ṣalāt al-wusṭā* (Surah 2: 238), an enigmatic phrase on which the exegetes differ.

the hour of death that men in their alertness may ever fear. Thus, in like manner, He has left this night unknown so that all the nights of Ramaḍān may be honoured.

(2) It is as if He were to say: "Knowing as I do your presumption and proneness to rebelliousness, if I were to designate the night of power, your ill-disciplined excess might make you insurbordinate that very night and you would fall into evil. Such conscious sin would be much more culpable than if you sinned without knowing the time. So for this good cause I have left it concealed."

It is narrated of the Prophet that he went into the mosque and noticed a man sleeping. So he told 'Ali to arouse him to perform the ablutions. Whereupon 'Ali woke the man up and then said to the Prophet: "O Apostle of God, you are the source and spring of good deeds: why did you not awaken him yourself?" "If he had reacted to you angrily [was the reply] it would not have been a damnable sin. I did it that way to lighten his punishment if he had refused." If such is the considerateness of the Apostle, it will give you some idea of the mercy of the Most High. It is as if the Most High were to say: "Had you known when the night of power is, and had observed it with meticulous obedience, you would have gained the reward of a thousand months, but had you disobeyed it a thousand months' retribution. The second is more to be avoided than the first is to be had."

(3) I have left this night unidentified that the seeker may pursue his search and gain the reward of his diligence.

(4) If the servant is not certain which is the night of power he will maintain a careful obedience through all the nights of Ramaḍān, saying hopefully to himself on each: "This may be the one." And God Most High boasts of them to His angels and observes: "You said of them that they would corrupt in the earth and shed blood.[1] Now see man's carefulness and well-doing in the night of which he does not know for certain. What would it be if We had allowed it to be known?" Thus is made manifest the hidden meaning of God's word: "Verily I know that of which you are ignorant." '

These thoughts, however, do not preclude much conjecture as to which night it might be and whether it is perpetually the night of power at every anniversary. Numerous suggestions are tabulated with supporting argument.[2] But an equally complex question is how the

[1] The reference is to the angels' demurring at the creation of Adam as God's *khalīfah*, or vice-gerent, in the world. See Surah 2: 30.

[2] It is thought that there are at least eight possibilities, perhaps the most ingenious

night of power can be said to be better than a thousand months, and in what manner the angels and the spirit come down. It is hard to detect any inkling of what might be thought to have been the obvious clue to any contrast between one night and a thousand months.

> '(1) The first issue here is the exegetical import of these words as variously understood. One is that in saying: "Better than a thousand months", months which lacked this night must be meant. For it would be impossible to say that a thousand months containing this night were better. The sense, then, has to do with the supreme benefits and benisons that God packs into it.'

After finding 'weak' several theories based on the comparison of time in Islam and periods in other peoples or cults, Fakhr al-Dīn goes on to wonder if it is meant as an undisclosed enigma, or simply the affirmation of God's free decree as happens in all kinds of spheres, moral and social and 'the intent is the pre-eminent virtues of this night'.

As for the angels coming down, may it be that it marks the evident dignity of men implicit in their being objects of revelation. In a fascinating passage, the commentary argues from the angelic disquiet at the creation of man the creature.

> '(1) . . . They repudiated you when they saw how despicable you were at the beginning of things, when you were just a drop of sperm, nor did they accept you as a blood-clot. Rather they showed every sign of aversion, finding your sperm and blood-clot mean and squalid. They washed their hands of you and tried in various ways to upset and nullify man.[1] Yet when the Most High gave you a handsome form and the dissident angels saw this, they accepted you and inclined your way. Thus it was that when the angels saw your beauty of nature and how it consisted in the knowledge of God and His obedience, they came to love you and descended to you, apologizing for what they had said at the first. This is the import of the passage about "the angels descend". When they come down and *see your spirit* in the dark of the womb's night and the dark of the

being the suggestion that the night is the twenty-seventh of Ramaḍān, since the Arabic phrase *lailat al-qadr* has nine letters and occurs thrice in the Surah, which multiplied gives twenty-seven. It could be the last night, because, while the first night is like Adam the last is like Muḥammad. Fakhr al-Dīn can find eminent advocates for each guess.

[1] See Chapter 6, below, for a discussion of the Qur'ān's repeated allusions to man the embryo in the womb and man the creature in the world, holding a divinely given dominion, man both creature and procreator.

sexual powers, then they excuse themselves for what they earlier said . . .'

The striking depth of this passage, to which we will return, quickly gives way to an exegetical imagination of a very different vintage.

> '(2) . . ."The angels come down" seems at first glance to embrace all the angels. They are, however, so very very many that the earth could not accommodate them all. . . . There are those who say that all the angels together descend to the lowest heaven, though doubt must persist about this. For heaven is full, since if there were places lacking angels where would be the awe? How then can *one* heaven hold them all? Our view is that the generality of writers do not favour this account of their coming to a single one of the heavens, seeing them rather as coming down in troops, some descending with others ascending. Then it might be compared to the pilgrim throng—the whole host enters the sacred house (the *Ka'bah*) but some are coming and others going. For this reason it goes on until the rising of the dawn, as the word "they descend" is meant to convey, meaning "time after time".'

That they descend to the earth itself is given as the prevailing opinion. But with what motives do they come? Perhaps to observe men's worship, to vet their deeds, or out of sheer love for mankind, or simply by divine mandate. But the two last may not be mutually exclusive.

> '. . ."By leave of their Lord" surely indicates that they seek permission and have it granted, and this would imply a very deep love, seeing that their whole desire was towards us and they sought to be with us. Even so, they awaited permission. If it is said that the verse: "We are truly those who stand in obedient array" (37: 165), contradicts the words: "The angels descend", we would say that two different times are intended.'

The phrase 'upon every behest' is taken in several ways, but clearly includes the 'fates' for a year ahead as they are given on that mystic night in Ramaḍān. But, further, angels have many missions.

> '. . ."We have not come down to the earth" we can imagine them saying, "for some whim of our own, but for the sake of every errand involving the well-being of men in their obligations to God". . . . As if some

> questioner were to ask: "Whence have you come?" and the angel should reply: "What do you want with this curiosity? Say rather. For what errand have you come?" For this is your true interest.'

Finally come the implications of 'It is peace until the breaking of the dawn'.

> 'The peace meant is security from evils and calamities. For men, as the proverb says, are always beset, things are back and forth, to and fro, like a man who goes on pilgrimage and has to watch out for the raiders . . .'

After a paragraph of intricate grammatical discussion turning on whether 'the dawn' is a thing or a time or a place, a verbal noun or a noun of location or duration, Fakhr al-Dīn concludes:

> 'God, to whom be praise and majesty, knows best. May the blessing and peace of God be upon our master, Muḥammad, and upon his people and companions every one.'

Here, despite some slight abridgement of the minutiae, we have the patterns of the exegetical mind in action on a crucial Surah. The passage is a fair index to a monumental figure in Quranic commentary. It exemplifies the salient characteristics. One finds the same painstaking erudition and exhaustive tabulation of grammatical matters in 'Abdullāh ibn 'Umar al-Baiḍāwī, of the seventh Islamic century (his death is variously given as AD 1260, 1286, 1293 and 1316), a native of Fars, and of all exegetes the most familiar and devout. There have been more than four-score commentaries on his commentary which was entitled: *Anwār al-Tanzīl wa Asrār al-Ta'wīl.* Its savour may well be had from the entire comment on the great Surah of Unity (Surah 112) which runs:

> 'In the Name of the merciful Lord of mercy. Say: "He is God, One, God the ever self-sufficing; He begets not nor is begotten; none is equal unto Him." '

Al-Baiḍāwī writes:

> 'The pronoun "He" is the subject pronoun fixing attention (*li-l-sha'an*) as when you say: "*he* is Zaid going away". It is in the nominative case

as the subject. Its predicate is the sentence. The antecedent to "He" is not necessary, since "He" is what the sentence is about. As for the question which might be asked, that is which you have asked, as to "He is God", it is narrated that the Quraish said: "O Muḥammad, describe your Lord to us, the One to whom you call us." It was then that these words were given in revelation. "One" here is in apposition (to "God") or may be taken as a second predicate. It indicates the manifold attributes of God's majesty and points to all the elements of (His) perfection. For the truly One is transcendent in essence above all seriality and multiplicity. For He has no need of these as physical, partial and participant entities certainly do.

Inherently unique to God is necessary existence, might in Himself and perfect wisdom divinely accordant with Himself. "He is God" is read with a terse: "Say", since it is fully agreed that what is meant is: "Say, O you who are unbelievers." Perhaps this is because the Surah of the *Kāfirīn* (109) was the arena of the Prophet's struggle (peace be upon him) with the gainsayers. It was there that the decisive break with them came and his remonstrance with his uncle with whom it was unfitting for him longer to remain.

However this may be, the affirmation of unity was often on his lips and he was enjoined to call men to it.

"God the ever self-sufficing" means the Lord who is recoursed to (*al-maṣmūd ilaihi*) in all needs. The word here is *ṣamad*: God alone is so described. For He is completely and absolutely adequate, non-contingent, whereas all that is other than Him is in need of Him. This is so from every angle, in view of His knowledge of all and their knowing by virtue of His self-sufficiency answering to His Oneness. The repetition of the word "God" here is because of the awareness that only what is truly divine is capable of being so characterized. It may also be for the sake of keeping the sentence free of a conjunction. The sentence anyway is consequent upon its predecessor and points back to it. "He did not beget" because He is of a totally other realm than man (lit. "not homogeneous with"). He was not in need of that which would complement Him or follow after Him, seeing He is beyond the reach of want and transitoriness. Perhaps the sole use of the past tense here is due to its coming as a reply to those who said that the angels were daughters of God and that Messiah is the son of God, and also to correspond with the further words: "He was not begotten."

This clause is so because God is not in want of anything. Nothing precedes Him.

"There is none equal to Him", that is, none is comparable to Him or may be likened to Him, as a consort or otherwise. The sentence is inverted, with the subject coming at the end after the adverbial sense of "in" or "as" an equal to Him, which is the predicative clause.

But, in that the intention is to negate the idea of likeness to the being of the Most High, the more important thing was given precedence.

It is possible that *kufuwan* ("equal" or "match") is a *Ḥāl* construction, that is, the accusative denoting "state", so vowelled because the weak radical letter is given "strong" value. Otherwise it may be taken as the predicate of *yakun*, or else as *Ḥāl* to "One".[1]

Perhaps the three sentences here are to be taken as one unit by their conjunction. For the import of all of them is to deny the practice of avowing similitudes (for God). It will then be seen that the one sentence is made the more striking by its threefold form.

Hamzah and Ya'qūb and Nāfi'a read *kufu'an*, turning the weak letter into a *hamzah*. Ḥafṣ has *kufuwan* with the vowel on the "*waw*" in its own right. Others take that letter as simply the seat of the *hamzah* (*kufuw'an*).[2]

In view of the inclusiveness of the Surah—for all it is so brief—comprehending all that may be known of God and as a reply to all those who deny the knowledge of God, it is related in Tradition that it is equal to a third of the Qur'ān. The purposes of the Qur'ān are concentrated on making clear the beliefs, directives and stories. This Surah is equal to the whole for its having to do so evidently with the very essence of God.

It is said that the Prophet (peace be upon him) heard a man reciting this Surah and he said: "It was your bounden duty." It was said: "O apostle of God, what is due has been done, how so?" And he said: "You have Paradise due to you." '[3]

From a modern perspective it seems odd that a brief comment on a Surah confessedly so central to the whole book should be so disproportionately concerned with the niceties of grammar alone.

The work of Al-Baiḍāwī rested largely on the achievement of a still earlier exegete, also of Persian birth and author of the great *Al-Kashshāf 'an Ḥaqā'iq al-Tanzīl*, completed in the year AH 528 (AD 1134). This was the Mu'tazilite thinker and rhetorician, Abū-l-

[1] The technical points involved here, having to do with how a weak final radical affects the form of a preceding syllable in various syntactical situations, requires a more extended translation than the Arabic strictly allows.

[2] Again technicalities, but included because the care for readings serves to illustrate the meticulousness of the commentator.

[3] Something of a play on the double sense of *wajabta*, as to what is 'due from' and so 'due to' the doer.

Qāsim al-Zamakhsharī (1055–1144). It was, in fact, to rescue his exegetical labours from the taint of 'heresy' that Al-Baiḍāwī undertook his own commentary, while relying heavily on the earlier work. Al-Zamakhsharī's mind had a strong poetical strain and he relieved his painstaking grammatical and philosophical observations with numerous quotations in verse.[1]

An almost entire translation of his commentary on Surah 90 will complete the concern of this chapter for the feel of the classical exegesis.[2] The Surah, entitled 'The Land' is an early Meccan deliverance alive with the atmosphere of confrontation between Muḥammad and the lords of the city.

> 'Nay! I swear by this land, this very land of your right, by father and fathered. Surely we have created man in trouble. Does he consider that none have power over him? I have consumed wealth abundant, he says. Does he think he goes un-noted? Have We not given him two eyes, a tongue and two lips. Have We not guided him on the two highways? Yet he has not essayed the steep climb? What idea do you have of the steep ascent? It is the freeing of a slave, or giving food on the hungry day to an orphan near of kin, or to a needy one in his distress. And thus to be of those who believe, those who each counsel patience and mercy to the other.
>
> Such are the companions of the right hand. Those who disbelieve our signs they are the companions of the left hand: over them is a confining fire.'

Al-Zamakhsharī begins:

> 'He to whom be all praise swore by the inviolate land and by what follows. Man was created liable to the throes of hardships and distresses which he has to endure. God inserts between the two parts of the oath the saying: "You are free prey in this land", with the meaning that it was part of what Muḥammad had to endure that despite his great sanctity it was allowable he should be hunted down albeit in that sacred country—just as the chase is permitted in ordinary territory. We have it on the authority of Shuraḥbīl that they were forbidden to kill there in the

[1] See the edited collection, tracing the sources of the poems and adding a commentary *Tanzīl al-Āyāt 'alā Sharḥ Shawāhid al-Kashshāf*, Cairo, 1864. The collector is Muḥibb al-Dīn.

[2] Chosen, in part, for the clause that supplies the title for Chapter 6 below. Translated from the edition of 1859, Calcutta, edited by W. Nassau Lees, vol. 6.

hunt or to lop off a tree there. Nevertheless "they count themselves free to harry you and kill you".[1]

Confirmation of this can be seen in that the Apostle (God bless him and his people and give them peace!) prayed for the will to bear what he had to endure from the people of Mecca, as well as in his puzzled surprise at the degree of their enmity against him.

God consoled the Apostle (the peace and blessing of God be upon him and his people) by this oath in the name of the land. For man cannot be free from hardships to be undergone. God gave voice to the promise of the conquest of Mecca, thus adding substance to his comfort and cheer. He said: "You are free of this land", meaning "You will be in control of it in the future, when you will do as you will, killing and capturing." For God was to open Mecca to him and authorized him thus.

Not to any one before him was the city given into his hand nor rendered lawful in this way. So he legitimatized as he would, and anathematized as he would. He killed Ibn Khaṭal when he was clinging to the curtains of the *Ka'bah*, and Miqyas ibn Ṣubābah and others besides these two and he proscribed the house of Abū Safyān.

Then he said: "God made Mecca inviolate on the day He created the heavens and the earth and it is made inviolate till the hour comes. It was not thus made free to any before me and never will to any after me. It is only free to me for an hour in a day. Let no tree there be lopped, nor its open country changed. Nor let its prey be pursued. It is not permitted to exploit its treasures...."

Al-'Abbās said: "O Apostle of God, surely its resources are exempt? We need them for our smiths, for our tombs and our houses." And the Apostle of God said: (the peace, etc.). "Its resources are exempt." To the question whether there is anything comparable to such a saying as: "You are free of this land" with this future import, I would reply by noting such inclusive sayings in the words of God (let His glory be exalted) as: "You are mortal and they are mortal" (39: 30). You say to one to whom you do great honour and reverence: "you are held in great esteem and love". This kind of thing is frequent in the words of God. For future circumstances are with Him like the known present.

What can suffice you as a categorical proof that this clause relates to the future and that its exegesis as an actuality is impossible is the fact that the Surah, by common consent, is Meccan. Where was the *Hijrah* at the time these words were sent down and the conquest was not in mind?

[1] *Hadhā-l-Balad* might be translated 'this city'. It is not clear what extent of territory is in view. There is a single Arabic root within the words for 'liver' and 'endurance', namely *kabad* and *mukābadah*, awkward to achieve in English.

As for the intended sense of "by father and fathered", my view is that the Apostle of God (peace, etc.), and he whom he begat, is meant. God swore by the country which was his, his birthplace, and by the shrine of his father Abraham, and the place of nurture of his father Ishmael and by his progeny and him begetting. As for the repetition we have here, take it as arising from the hidden springs of praise and wonder. To the question why it does not say: "Whom [*man*] he begot", my answer would be in line with the sacred text: "God knows well what she had given birth to" (Surah 3: 36; Mary, mother of Jesus and herself child of the wife of 'Imrān) that is to say, a progeny (or subject) of wonderful significance.

There is a view that the phrase means Adam and his son, or, again, every father and his son.

As for the *kabad*, we go back to the remark that a man's inside gives him trouble, and since it has this liability to pain and distress the word has acquired an extended use to cover all toilsomeness and trouble, including the hardship of endurance. . . .[1]

The pronoun in "Does he think . . ." refers to one of the lords of the Quraish from whom the Prophet (peace, etc.) suffered. The meaning is: "Does this strong chief of the people with their lordly airs towards the believers, suppose that there will never be a resurrection? that there will never be a power to requite him and bring retribution on all that he is?" Then the passage rehearses what he said that day: "I have consumed wealth abundant." The reference is to the ample expenditures of the people of the *Jāhiliyyah*, their self-styled grandeur and their lofty pretensions. "Does he think he goes un-noted?" when he thus indulges and consumes, enjoying the glory of men? God indeed sees him and has been keeping him under surveillance.

It could be that the pronoun above is actually man's in the sense that he swears by the noble land and its excellency that you are free, or absolved, in it of all that its people do there by way of crime and iniquity, from which you have kept yourself innocently free.

This would accord with what follows, namely "Verily We have created man in trouble", that is to say "in sickness, sickness of heart and inward corruptness". This meaning would relate to those among them whom God knew when He created them that they would not believe nor do the right.[2]

. . . "Have We not given him two eyes?" by which to see the visible world, "and a tongue" to give utterance to his innermost thoughts, "and

[1] The sentence that follows plays on the theme of *kabad* and *mukābadah*. See previous note and pp. 95 f. below.

[2] Here are nice grammatical points about the vowelling and implications of *lubad*.

two lips" with which to call out for help, to take food and breath and drink and much else.

"Have We not guided him on the two highways?" that is, the two ways of good and evil. Religion is thought to be meant here.

"He has not essayed the steep climb." That is to say, he has not thanked those instruments and graces by good works in freeing the slave and feeding the orphans and the wretched, by the faith which is the source of all obedience and the foundation of all good. Instead he has disdained the gifts of grace and belied their Giver. To expend in this way is the thing that is pleasing and profitable with God, in contrast to the wasteful consumption that goes in for pomp and excess. For their likeness is "like a freezing gale that smites the tillage of a tribe . . ." (3: 117). . . . "Then to be of those who believe." This refers back to the meaning of "essaying the steep ascent", equated thus with "he did not believe." For that venturing is an entering upon a difficult thing and pursuing it with vigour and drive. For God made good deeds an upward ascent on a rugged way because of the toils involved and the personal endeavour. God knows it is a hard path. A man has to struggle with himself, with his passions and with the enmity of Satan.

The freeing of the slaves means their release from servitude or other ills. Tradition has it that a man once said to the Prophet of God (peace, etc.): "Show me the deed which will get me into paradise." And he said: "The freeing of the slave and the liberation of those in bonds." The man said: "Are not the two things the same?" The Prophet said: "No! freeing them means that you take the initiative personally and liberation means that you maintain help to make good their rescue from retaliation and extortion. Giving freedom and giving alms are the finest of deeds." Abū Ḥanīfah held that setting slaves free was finer than acts of charity. With the other two [authorities] charity is finer.

The verse here supports Abū Ḥanīfah, in his opinion . . . .[1]

The saying: "What idea do you have of the steep ascent?" is a protestation, meaning "You will in no wise understand its difficulty to yourself nor how utter is its value before God".

The three words "starvation", "near kinship", and "distress" derive from their corresponding verbs. . . .[2]

"And thus to be of those who believe" *Thumma* ("thus" or "then") here is not a time sequence, since faith is always antecedent to anything else and there is no good work without it. It refers to how far removed from the work of emancipation and charity he had been when faith was at a low ebb and virtue so remote.

[1] Certain traditions follow on the relative merit of acts.

[2] There is, for English, a certain tautology in the omitted sentences here, deriving nounal significance from verbal origins.

Mercy is as mercy does. "They exhorted each other to patience", in faith and fidelity, or to patience against the evil things, patience in well-doing and in the trials the believer has to undergo. They exhort themselves to show compassion and loving kindness towards one another and all that conduces to the mercy of God.

"The right hand" and "the left hand" stand for what is "right, good" and what is "sinister". That is to say: "Those who are right with themselves in good and those who bring the omens on themselves."[1] . . . The Apostle of God (peace, etc.) said that whoever recited: "Nay! I swear by this land" God would give him security from His wrath on the day of resurrection.'

From these three renowned leaders of Quranic reading and their handling of three vital Surahs, we may take such honest stock as space allows of the long, sustained traditions of commentary. It is *this* exegesis which represents the faith-community's scholarly and authoritative possession of its document of revelation.

Yet it poses many questions for the contemporary mind, asking as it must such different questions and possessed in heart of so many deeper urgencies than those of grammar and citation. For all the eminence, and the undoubted cares, of this classical exegesis, the external reader is bound to turn back, from them, to reflect on the original question with which Surah 97, and Fakhr-al-Dīn al-Rāzī, begin: 'Would that you knew . . .' with its hint of an irony in the very effort after comprehension. Do we not perhaps have to conclude that there is a poetry—which has been almost missed here—calling for an imagination that kindles to a different dimension of awareness? Do we need to ask, for example, how a certain single night in the year could possibly be better than a thousand months since those thousand months (being in fact over eighty-three years) would be bound to contain a thousand occasions of the night itself? This misses the use of the quantitative to indicate a measure of intangible quality.[2] Are we really in need of the assurance that there is no contradiction in angels 'standing' in obedient array, and their 'descending'? What should we make of the attitude of mind that worries about the nature of consis-

[1] The double sense is hard to render. The 'evil' and 'the left' are synonymous. There follows a brief linguistic point about *mu'ṣadatun*, translating here 'confining' (fire).

[2] One does not, for example, assume an arithmetical intention when the psalmist declares: 'One day in Thy courts is better than a thousand.' That would be churlish indeed.

tency in this regard? Surely *qadr* and *amr*, glory and the divine *fiat*, power and its energies, authority and will, as the Qur'ān knows them, are greater than, other than, the pre-occupations of the exegetes?

Occasionally, it is true, a Fakhr al-Dīn will let the poetry prevail. That 'God would not set something in train and fail to see it through' is a sentiment much nearer to the heart of 'the night of power' than an obtuse searching for its date. There seems only a dim awareness of the deep meaning in an angelic misgiving about the creation and the dignity of man, with its underlying mystery of whether or not God is 'justified'. When the embryo comes to the full stature of manhood and the creature is seen to be the sphere of revelation, the angels—save for Iblīs—apologize. But he remains obdurate, insisting, against God Himself, that man is an improper risk. He sets himself to prove it so. Thus the very lordship of God is set at issue in the theme of man. There could hardly be, in mythical form, a more elemental statement of the mystery of history than this. But the exegesis glimpses it only to lose it in more mundane inquiries.

Nevertheless, classical commentary is one of the massive institutions to which Quranic contents have given being and is therefore a repository of the religious experience which the Qur'ān reader today must be set to recognize and possess. His problem is how to do a different kind of justice to the great original.

What, it might be asked, of modern twentieth-century commentary? The study is a large and detailed subject,[1] which it is no part of the present purpose to attempt. But by way of a single appendix to this chapter it may be useful to take one random sample, mainly with a view to testing the inter-play within it of the Qur'ān itself and awe of the classic masters of its elucidation. For there lies the main issue of, and for, what we are calling the Quranic mind.

Dr Ā'ishah 'Abd al-Raḥmān, better known by her pen-name as Bint al-Shāṭī, affords a useful guidance. Her treatment of a crucial Surah (93) may illustrate a different approach to what text and reader might expect of each other and so form a prelude to our own reflections. She is one of the most popular of women writers in Cairo. In *Al-Tafsīr al-Bayānī li-l-Qur'ān al-Karīm* (Expository Commentary on

[1] See, for example, J. Jomier, *Le Commentaire Coranique du Manar: Tendances Modernes de l'Exégèse en Egypte*, Paris, 1955; and J. M. S. Baljon, *Modern Muslim Koran Interpretation (1880–1960)*; Leiden, 1961.

the Holy Qur'ān) she comments on seven Surahs, all chosen from the early Meccan period.[1]

That fact of selection calls perhaps for initial consideration. Given the bulk and pattern of the Qur'ān it is a natural device. Yet any selection involves a decision about meaning and relative 'value' and could be a means to the actual, if not deliberate, neglect of other areas, thus contributing to a possible shift in the received consensus of the Qur'ān. The practice of 'selecting' for commentary only focuses and sharpens the inescapable element of responsible initiative in the reader. It symbolizes that, whether we select or not editorially, the fact is that all reading is in some measure decision—decision as to significance and impact. Inasmuch as this is inevitable it had better also be conscious and alert.[2] Surah 93 is as follows.

> 'In the name of the merciful Lord of mercy.
> By the morning light, by the brooding night,
> Your Lord has not abandoned you,
> Nor are you disfavoured in His sight.
> The ultimate will far excel the present.
> With all your Lord has in store for you
> You will be satisfied.
> Did He not find you an orphan and proved your refuge?
> A wanderer and was your guide?
> A destitute and became your ample succour?
> The orphan, then take care not to distrain,
> Nor the suppliant to deny:
> Rather give currency to the grace of your Lord.'

After an initial discussion of the occasion of the Surah, Bint al-Shāṭī comes at once to the invoking of the light and of the night. This 'formula of the oath', as she calls it, relates to some trying abeyance of

[1] Cairo, 1962. Surah 93 occupies pp. 13–43. Bint al-Shāṭī has published studies of the Syrian poet and sceptic, Abū-l-'Alā al-Ma'arī (d. AD 1058) on whom her doctoral research centred. She has written imaginative works on the mother and the wives of Muḥammad, *Umm al-Nabī*, Cairo, 1961, and *Nisā' al-Nabī*, Cairo, 1961, and evaluations of recent Arabic writing in *Qiyām Jadīdah li-l-Adāb al 'Arabī*, Cairo, 1961.

[2] Selective commentary has a long history. There were, for example, *Al-Tafsirāt al-Aḥmadiyyah*, of Aḥmad ibn Abū Sa'īd, (d. 1717) who dealt only with the *Aḥkām* of the Qur'ān, as he listed them, and *Shu'ūn al-Munazzalāt*, by 'Alī Mutaqqī (d. 1568) who treated only those verses about which there was reliable information as to the 'occasion of their revelation'. These are both criteria on which a selecting interest might concentrate.

inspiration in Muḥammad's earliest days of prophecy, in which he deeply needed reassurance. She develops Muḥammad 'Abduh's thought (d. 1905) of 'celebration' and quotes his observation:

> 'The oath by the light refers to the excellence of the power that gives light . . . Its aim is to turn our thoughts to the fact that light is one of God's great mysteries and sublime blessings. . . . The oath "by the night" has to do with its awe inspiring effect upon you, its peremptory restraint over you from movement and activity, its ineluctable inducement of your soul to silence. The fear night inspires has an indefinable power, elusive and intangible in its impact. It resembles the divine majesty in besieging you from all sides in imperceptible ways.'

She herself sees the formula as 'an artistic usage to serve the meaning through the things of sense', and she continues:

> 'When we examine successively the oaths of the Qur'ān we find they have to do with some metaphorical purpose, utilizing concrete experience and visual vividness to conjure up a kindred intangible realm that is unseen and elusive.'

The sequence of day and night does not allow

> '. . . at all the notion that heaven has abandoned the earth and given it over to darkness and barbarity. . . . What cause for surprise, then, is there, if there should follow the Prophet's gracious illumination and insight an interlude of silent abeyance, such as enveloping night brings over the brilliance of day?'

She regrets that no older commentator known to her has taken the Quranic oaths in this natural and satisfactory way, preferring what she finds remote and far fetched in such subtlety as that of Fakhr al-Dīn, for whom the seasonal lengthening and shortening of daylight or darkness parallels the varying frequency of inspiration and its intermissions.

Moving on to the significance of 'the morning' and 'the night', she reviews at length the numerous intricacies of the old commentaries and, on literary grounds, discounts them. Why ask: Does 'the morning' mean the day as a whole or an hour of the day? Is 'the pouring night' night approaching? Or night fallen? Or night in full career? Or night ended? Or is it, as 'Abduh thought, a synonym for believing humanity 'quiet as a nun'? She reaches her own conclusions only through a long excursus into dictionary cognates of 'morning' (*al-ḍuḥā*), and its connections with 'sacrifice' and the pilgrimage ceremonies and the forenoon prayer. All these bring her back to the sense of 'that which reveals or discloses' as the intention of the formula. She takes further time to dismiss—to her—fanciful theories that 'the morning' and 'the night' are, respectively, Muḥammad's face and hair, or the males and females of his household. She rejects exegetical speculations as to the circumstances in which it was necessary for God to assure the Prophet that he was not in fact abandoned.

In all this, Bint al-Shāṭī's commentary stays in a certain awe of old authority even when breaking free of it. This may well be a tactical necessity, lest those she means to persuade should be too quickly deterred by her independence of mind. As for 'the ultimate which will far excel the present', she rejects the prevailing idea that the eternal future is meant, insisting that the word *ākhirah* has to do with the terminus of Muḥammad's mission. The satisfying thing the Lord has in store is success in preaching, the surrender of the Quraish, the adherence of droves of believers and the great expansion of Islam, as well as the bliss of heaven.

As for the final interrogatives which have been the sphere of much questioning, they are meant to be taken, she believes, in a direct and immediate sense. Subtleties about 'orphanhood' and compunction about 'wandering' are unnecessary. The latter (*ḍāllan*) has to do, not with the metaphorical sense of unbelief, but with not knowing the way. Tedious debate about 'immaculate' prophecy is ill-conceived. on the point of the enrichment Muḥammad received, Bint al-Shāṭī is clear that it should not be seen as the material resources of his wife, Khadījah, or of his uncle and protector, Abū Ṭālib. Such a monetary sense would run counter to all we know of the prophetic biography. The refuge, guidance and succour all have to do with the gift of prophecy. This must be understood from the correspondence of those three clauses with the ones that follow. The final command: 'So discourse of it', or 'give currency to the grace of your Lord', points her to the single duty of proclamation.

She concludes:

'By carefully noting the order of the verses we recognize another remarkable element (in the Qur'ān), namely that God alerted His apostle to the realization that the reform of society had first priority and importance, in thus rehearsing for him the sum of his mission. This was to relieve the plight of the destitute, the needs of the indigent, the oppression of the orphan and the bewilderment of the wistful. Such was the mission of reform and guidance. The Prophet was enjoined to proclaim it and achieve it. . . . Has the Apostle any responsibility but this of clear transmission of the word?'

There is a directness of interpretation about *Al-Tafsīr al-Bayānī* and a refusal to be deterred by the pious overgrowth of sacrosanct authority. There is a refreshing freedom from inventive subtlety and a will to see the text steadily and naturally. It does not scrutinize metaphors with the chronic instincts for mystery that Fakhr al-Dīn exhibits. It is ready to judge by literary criteria intelligently applied. It takes the Qur'ān with an evident reverence and discipline, but yet with a liberty of mind that reads for itself. Some may feel that its careful disengagement from traditional niceties is too lengthy and deferential. But the logic of the writer's emphasis does point to an imaginative reckoning with Quranic meanings.

Can its intuitions be carried even further? It is for their ordinariness, rather than for any special eminence in this field enjoyed by their author, that they are cited here. Can the modern reader within Islam, and—a still more exacting question—the reader today outside Islam, hope to know and possess the Qur'ān in its essential reality in a truly religious reading? Can such a readership take it, in its full immediacy to Muḥammad and his Arabia, and yet also in the larger idiom of the centuries and the cultures beyond? What, in a word, are the inherent truths which address us from its pages? What is the ultimate reading concord with the text?

Chapter 5
'PERHAPS . . .'

The previous chapter and its review of traditional exegesis left us in hope of 'a different justice to the great original', the way to which must lie through the essential realities—vocation and prophethood, the rule of God and the order of men, the relation of power to truth and of truth to power, preaching and society, the natural world, the human dominion and the moral tribunal of history. To read within the elemental bigness of all these is to require, and find, the imagination tuned to the local and temporal conditions, but capable of transcending them and reckoning with the whole, in the inclusive framework of humanity and religion.

This, it would be fair to say, is the ultimate 'perhaps' of the Quranic reader in his reading. The word so translated (*la'alla*) is one of the most frequent in the Qur'ān's own usage.[1] It relates, among other things, to its reception in the mind of the community and in the wills of hearers. 'Perhaps your (their) wits may be alert', 'perhaps you (they) may comprehend', the phrases—run. They would seem to sustain the claim that the book is looking for the right recognition, for a hearing—and a readership—with a due perception. There are clues in the text awaiting their realization by the listener, a kind of reading by which the reader, as it were, is right with the Qur'ān, attaining a true concordance of his thoughts with the intention of the text.

The phrase *Kitāban mutashābihan mathānī*, as noted in Chapter 3, points the same way, with its implication of recurring significances—if we may so speak—in a book expecting a lively relation between the vital purport of the words and the intuitive sense of the hearer.

[1] See below, Chapter 9, 'The Sacramental Earth', where it is studied in relation to the natural order and the 'signs' there discernible. For its use in our present context of a true cognizance of the Qur'ān itself, see, for example, 12: 2, 21: 10, and 43: 3.

What, we might ask—taking *la'alla* seriously—is the Qur'ān expecting of the reader and what should the reader expect of the Qur'ān?

These are plainly formidable questions, the more so if we are registering an incompleteness in the ancient forms of commentary, where text and intelligence would seem to be joined in a manner alien to the integrity of the contemporary mind, if not also insufficient to the relevance of the meaning. We cannot avoid the responsibility of decision and interpretation. Even those who prefer to rely entirely on traditional commentary do so in the judgement of their own will. They presumably proceed upon the asumption that their reliance on sacrosanct authority is the right response. But they do so within their own option. To decline independent thinking is, nevertheless, to exercise an individual choice. There is clearly no denying the principle of reader's responsibility: the book is in his hands. It is *Al-Hudā*, 'the guidance'. Yet it is so only in the terms in which he lets it guide him.

This necessity to read the Qur'ān with a lively sense of who and where we are in time and culture means an exercise of reading responsibility both ways—to 'hear' the relevance of the Qur'ān without distorting its own time and setting. Both the will for, and the possible temptations of, such 'timely' considerations—both the reader's and the book's—may be illustrated in a frequent aspect of current commentary. It is the facile assumption that the Qur'ān can be made to bear, indeed to anticipate, the findings of modern science. Though laudable in its will to be alert to current pressures of thought, this form of initiative is unhappy and misguided. But it is well to note it briefly, since a dismissal of it may be a useful preface to more responsible attitudes.

For perhaps the last half-century the pseudo-scientific school or, perhaps better, trend, of commentary has been ingenious and persistent in reading modern meanings in, or into, Quranic terms and words. The book is seen as a scientific text, foreseeing, often in uncanny detail, the discoveries of recent knowledge. Chance connections or subtle potential significance in words or incidents are cited and elaborated as intending or denoting the discoveries and creations of the modern laboratory and its techniques. The desire to have the Qur'ān abreast of all modernity despite the anachronisms such exegesis involves overrides a proper loyalty to the place and time of the Prophet's own hearers and readers. One has to assume that they were unaware of the full, or true, import of what he said, which had to wait for its sophisticated audience after long centuries and the arrival of the technological age.

For its practitioners this type of exegesis seems persuasive enough. An early example can be found in Ṭanṭāwī Jawharī[1] (died 1940), who drew a variety of findings in astro-physics, radiology, biology, metallurgy and social theory from Quranic verses. *Nūr al-Islām*, since 1930 entitled: *Majallat al-Azhar*, official publication of the Azhar University, carried frequent contributions from an early date, deriving from the Qur'ān, for example, the use of alloys in metals, the techniques of photography and the telescope, the cutting of the Suez Canal, the use of radio and the invention of the submarine and the aeroplane.[2] On the story of Solomon and the ants (Surah 27: 16 f.) it comments:

> 'We are told by entomologists of the ingenious and ordered ways of ants and of astounding feats which they perform, facts which highly delight the heart of every Muslim thus to find established in his holy Book long before science had revealed them to the world.'

Or again, on 53: 50, 'He is Lord of Sirius', the same journal notes:

> 'We were not aware of the magnitude of Sirius, to which the Qur'ān refers in this verse, until the natural sciences disclosed it. . . .'

by the power of modern telescopes.[3]

Muslims with their Qur'ān are by no means unique in this kind of exegesis. It recurs in some patterns of approach to other Scriptures. In every case it betrays an attitude that misconstrues both the real onus and the true resources of faith. This kind of 'forward' significance is in danger of neutralizing the sense of the text for the original audience. It is in danger of turning a supremely religious mission into a sort of esoteric encyclopedia awaiting the lapse of centuries to be understood. It bears all the marks of special pleading—a pleading which has missed the real character of what it would espouse. It disserves the authority of the text, an authority in no way diminished

[1] Cairo, 1920. See the useful survey of exegesis bearing on this and other modern fields in J. M. S. Baljon, op. cit.

[2] Cf., for example, vol. 2, no. 2, 1931.

[3] *Nūr al-Islām*, op. cit., vol. 3, no. 9, 1933, p. 112.

by the fact that it ante-dates things scientific. The writ of the Qur'ān in a technological age stands in its interpretation of man and his dominion as set under God. By its very nature this covers and governs all that man can ever do, or invent, or achieve. But it does so by virtue of a sure insight having to do with the abiding man-in-nature situation, not by obscure anticipation of technical development in the mechanisms of it. Dr Muḥammad Kāmil Ḥusain in a spirited essay has given effective rebuttal to these inventories of inventions. He insists on the spiritual nature of the Qur'ān's content and relevance[1]. Professor Muḥammad Nuwaiḥī, likewise, rejects as 'a folly' and 'a nuisance' the views that find the Scripture prescient of all technology ages before its actual currency. Ingenuity of this kind, he urges, cannot convince us that finger-printing and the atom-bomb, and the like, are really intended in the Qur'ān's words. For these dealt with things as they were in its own time and dealt with them religiously. It is that religious dimension, more urgent now than ever, which is its real and abiding significance for man as (now) technologist come to his incredible kingdom.[2] The 'perhaps . . .' of the Qur'ān, clearly, is not of this inventive kind. The intelligence it is looking for is not a facility for imaginative detection.

The force of that religious awareness of man in the natural order may be felt in the 'oaths' of the Scripture, so far removed in their sublimity from the easy notions we have just reviewed. These invocations serve to speak the morality of the universe itself. We have seen the reference, to 'the formula of the oath' with which Bint al-Shāṭī began fromSurah 93. Such invoking is no mere verbal eloquence. It is a conscious setting of the obligations of men within the majesties of God. Or, conversely, it is a deprecation of human ways by the context of the divine. It is greatly to hallow, because it is greatly to reproach, the earthly scene. Unless we align ourselves with the fidelities of nature we turn them to death in our own treacheries and the open questions they present to us become the answers of damnation. Then the very heavens are defied and the land is blighted.

'I have planted a false oath in the earth
And it has brought forth a poison tree . . .
I have taught the thief a secret path into the house of the just

[1] In *Mutanawwi'āt* (Miscellany), vol. 2, Cairo, 1960, pp. 29–37.
[2] In an unpublished essay in Cairo: 'Problems of Modernization in Islam', 1969.

I have taught pale artifice to spread his nets upon the morning:
My heavens are brass, my earth is iron, my moon a clod of clay,
My sun a pestilence at noon
And a vapour of death in the night.'[1]

William Blake was nearer than he could have known to the temper of Muḥammad's early preaching. In the awe of nature was a voice demanding to know 'for what sin the buried babe was done away' (81: 8–9). For the earth cannot eternally hide infanticide. These nature invocations were the constant setting of Muḥammad's ethical summons. For the same reason natural convulsions were the *mise-en-scène* of final judgement (cf. 82: 1–8 and 99). All, in the words of 85: 3, is 'by the witness and the witnessed', 'by the beholder and what is beheld'.[2] Man is a sentient being. The world waits on his interpretation of its meaning. But it only allows him to make it as all the time the crisis of his own. So 91: 1–10 joins in one solemnity the macrocosm of the universe and the microcosm of the soul. If we will not learn how to bless, we shall learn how tragic is the curse.

Learn how to bless, the Qur'ān reader certainly does, if he is alert. For there is a steady theme of praise. The refrain *Al-Ḥamdu li-'llāhi* or *Laus Deo* opens the *Fātiḥah* and the book. Some twenty-three times it occurs with *Allāh* and a score more with the pronoun, or with *Al-Rabb* (the Lord), while *Al-Ḥamīd*, the kindred adjective, occurs in fourteen verses. 'As I come,' wrote John Donne in *To my God in my Sickness*, 'I tune the instruments here at the door.' He was viewing the approach of death and himself beyond it as a musician of eternity.[3] But life is no rehearsal, if it be rehearsal alone. 'Let us tune our instruments' is the readers' chorus which the Qur'ān inspires. It gives an insistent call to praise, to celebration, as the proper employment of the powers of men. 'We do not know how to celebrate because we do not know what to celebrate', writes an analyst of the modern theatre.[4] The Qur'ān is in no doubt about either.

[1] William Blake, *The Four Zoas, Night ii*, in *Complete Writings of William Blake*, edited by G. Keynes, New York, 1957, p. 290.

[2] The clause is usually taken to mean either, 'Muḥammad and Islam', or 'angels and men'. Can it be also conscience alerted and conscience convinced, the awesome, real and realized?

[3] The thought is not un-Quranic. 'They shall be guided in the path of the all-praisable', says 22: 24 of the blessed in heaven.

[4] Peter Brook, *The Empty Space*, London, 1968, p. 47.

> 'Sing in the praise of your Lord, when you arise, and sing in the praise of your Lord in the night and at the setting of the stars' (52: 48–49).

For

> 'Do you not see that God it is whom all things praise, in the heavens and in the earth and the birds also on wings of flight? Each truly knows its prayer and its praising and God knows their every deed. For to God belongs the kingdom of the heavens and of the earth and unto Him is their becoming' (24: 41–42).

Such celebration of life in gratitude is the point, of course, of the invocations. The themes of praise are the pledges of the preaching: 'By the night enveloping and the day in splendour' (92: 1–2): 'By heaven and the night star' (86: 1): 'By the elements of wind and storm and rain in full cry, reminding, absolving, or warning . . .' (77: 1–6).[1] They give universal range to the Qur'ān. The will to praise is the deepest, the most hospitable, activity of faith. Sometimes it is the only form that faith can take. To hear the Qur'ān in this dimension and to heed it is to counter the drabness in our modern souls, to water the parched ground of our affairs, to kindle the mystery of being alive and to end the starvation from wonder.

Praise is also the likeliest context of compassion. In adoration we learn how to take our relationships. The recognition of God reverses the calumnies of men. It allies us with goodness. We have love more surely as a bond in the mundane when we celebrate it in the transcendent. In blessing the Lord we have a livelier benediction of our own towards our fellows. Life in the world is purified and simplified, silenced in its malignities and livened in its mercies, by the will to give God praise. We might say that 'O ye holy and humble men of heart, bless ye the Lord', is a command which actually generates the quality it addressss. It may seem to some a mere illusion, a transcendentalizing which ends where it began—in man. But the will to praise knows its own music and finds itself in knowing it.

That the acknowledgement of God should dominate man and his doings is the crux of all Quranic themes. It is the central element in the study of Quranic vocabulary. Take the term *qadr*, so pivotal to the

[1] A venture in translation of the well nigh untranslatable phrases of 77: 1–6, taking five active participles and conflating them into one noun, three possessives and the 'full cry' phrase. The probable sense is there, the eloquence gone.

business of Fakhr al-Dīn al-Rāzī with Surah 97 in the previous Chapter.[1] The 'measure', or 'given dimension' of anything, it comes to be the authority or 'determination' that made it so, and thus, by evolution, the glory and sovereignty within the divine design and the revelation which expresses what they ordain and dispose. Then, in turn, the right recognition of the divine in relation to man constitutes what religion means. Hence the telling comment, for example, of 6: 91,22: 74 and 39: 67 about men who 'did not esteem God a right esteeming' (*mā qadarū Allāha ḥaqqa qadrihi*), 'they did not reckon with God as He is', or, 'their thoughts of God did not correspond with Him'. When this happens the human concept is too small, too remote, too sanguine, too anxious, too monopolistic, too defensive, too partisan, too solicitous for majesty, too ecclesiastical, too patronizing. Within a single phrase, the reader can discern the varieties of religious perversity, all latent, for him, in the original controversy with the scorners and the jealous of Muḥammad's day.

For those who assume some mutual patronage between God and themselves is the question of 46: 4. 'Have they taken out shares (*shirk*) in the heavens?'[2] Let them know that 'diversities of language and colour' are 'among God's signs in the creation of the heavens and the earth' (30: 22). 'Your hearts were in your mouths', says 33: 10 in another context, '. . . and you supposed suppositions about God'. The immediate factors in these issues, at the time and place of the Qur'ān, are far removed from a sophisticated age. But a right recognition of God abides as the crux within all changes.

'O man, who has beguiled you from your generous Lord, who created you and fashioned you and wrought you in symmetry and shaped you after the form He willed?' (82: 6), was one of the earliest questions asked by Muḥammad. Its substance stays, within a deep humanism, even without the premise of creation, as does the crisis or nemesis in human history noted in the words: 'Be not like those who forgot God and God caused them to forget themselves' (59: 19). For, as will be argued more fully in Chapter 8, it is around the significance of man that the present relevance of Quranic theism is most readily discerned.

[1] See the exhaustive contextual discussion in Daud Rahbar, *God of Justice, a Study in the Ethical Doctrine of the Qur'ān*, Leiden, 1960, pp. 108–19. This pioneer study is a most valuable documentation of Quranic vocabulary, with tabulation of usages.

[2] Arberry has: 'Have they a partnership in the heavens?' The emphasis is God's sole creativity, but with a hint of patronage expected.

Man in religious decision, as the oaths and doxologies of the book regard him, comes into clearest focus in the *Fātiḥah* itself, the great opening summation of the whole Qur'ān. All that belongs within the recurrent *la'alla* phrases is already there. Its theme of praise, its deliberate resolve, its plea for guidance and its sense of destiny, epitomize the Quranic mind. It is imaginative to preface its study with the symbol of Muslim prostration in the ritual of *Ṣalāt*, or prayer, at which the *Fātiḥah* is recited. For symbolic, even sacramental, those postures of the *Rak'ah*, or prayer sequence, assuredly are, using the body to convey to the self its own submitting and solemnizing the personal house of life in the ordered movements of its own physique. There could hardly be a religious pattern more intimate or more intent, independent as it is of all external aegis, and reinforced by the solidarity of the community and the mystique of the mosque. *Sujūd*, or prostration, needs no priesthood and the *Qiblah*, or direction of *sujūd*, though it enlists geographical direction, requires no subtlety.

Perhaps most significant of all in the usages of Muslim prayer ritual is the erect-prostrate-erect sequence in the several movements of a single 'prayer',—movements repeated two, or up to five, times, variously, in the five daily 'hours'. Man in erect posture has ever been a sign of his *imperium*, and indeed, biologically, its condition. 'The human form divine', as William Blake called it, is ready for, and invited into, authority over nature. Erectness, freeing the hands from grovelling or mere propulsion, enables the conquest of the earth, tooling the manual dexterity as the basic circumstance of all technology, while the open, upturned countenance is lifted out of mere animality into the sense of the horizons and the heavens. It is this dignity, in all its liabilities, that man brings to the act of worship, bowing his face earthwards in submission and resting his hands in surrender from their tasks. He makes a gesture of creaturely dependence and utter gratefulness on the very soil he exploits and fructifies. It is to erectness that he returns when the *Ṣalāt* concludes.

For man, by this symbol, does not stay crouching and supine. Its meaning fulfilled, the prayer returns him to his feet, to translate into activity the meaning of his great gesture, which he must repeat before its summons fades or his erectness is betrayed. He salutes his surrounding society in an expression of human community and disperses to 'occupy his business'. The mosque, so to speak, is meant for the market and the *takbīr* ('God is great') for technology. The proudest part of him is most abased that its activity may be exalted. The brow touches the earth in order that the mind may work and will its hallowing. There has to be a steady alternation of the confession of liability and the pursuit of dignity, between *orare* and *laborare* in their deepest mutuality.[1]

It is with this active sense of things that the reader should take the familiar verses of the *Fātiḥah*—the sevenfold *āyāt* often linked with the *mathānī* already noted in 39: 23, 'the oft repeated' (compare 15: 87).

> 'In the Name of God, the merciful Lord of mercy.
> Praise be to God, the Lord of all being, the merciful Lord of mercy,
> Master of the day of judgement.
> Thee alone we serve and to Thee alone come we for succour.
> Guide us in the straight path—
> The path of those whom Thou hast blessed, not of those against whom there is displeasure, nor of those who go astray.'

There are seven terminal rhymes in the Arabic, four with the 'n' and three with the 'm' consonant, closing the long 'i' (*een eem*) syllable. No translation can hope to register the force of the original in its literary and emotive quality. Inasmuch as it is the only place where the Qur'ān 'prays'—save in narrative situations of the patriarchs and prophets where there is address to God—it serves perfectly to represent the deep 'perhaps' of human devotion and destiny. All the chapters that follow here take their direction from its awareness of God in mercy, judgement, unity, guidance and will.

It is noteworthy that all the human pronouns, participles and verbs are plural. The only singular pronoun is the emphatic *iyyāka* 'Thee it is . . .' twice repeated in v. 5, avowing an undeviating worship of, and reliance upon, God. Whereas elsewhere, in the *Shahādah*, or confession of faith, the faithful use the singular: 'I bear witness . . .' here in the *Fātiḥah* everything is corporate. '*We* worship, *we* look to as suppliants . . . guide *us*. . . .' Theology here is always doxology. God, as existent, is believed, not argued and all, therefore, is vividly relational. *Rabb al-'ālamīn*, 'the Lord of all being', is reality, not a tenet.

[1] There is an intriguing reference to this dignity of man by the divine endowment in Fakhr al-Dīn al-Rāzī's *Al-Tafsīr al-Kabīr* at Surah 25: 2 where he comments on *fa qaddarahu taqdīran*: 'He [God] made each thing as it specifically was to be', remarking: 'He gave man being, as you see him have, with the capacity to exploit and pursue to advantage all that is given into his hand (*al-manūtah bihi*) in the sphere of both the religious and the temporal (*al-dīn wa-l-dunyā*)', Cairo edition, 1890, vol. 6, p. 300.

The meaning of this *Rubūbiyyah*—as the theologians term it—is all-embracing, an utterly exclusive relationship, a monotheism of the will and the imagination, and not merely of the idea and of the word. The fact of God precludes all multilateral attitudes of trust or dependence and so doing subdues all relativities of tribe, or power, or kin, or place, to the inclusive sovereignty.

'Ponder', writes Abū-l-Kalām Āzād, 'the limitless *Rubūbiyyah* of Almighty God.'[1] He understands in 'the Lord of all being', or, more literally, 'the Lord of the worlds', both the creating authority and the sustaining providence by which the divine is known. There is no doubt that the Arabic term *Rabb* belongs with the Semitic themes of rule and dominion, absolute and transcendent. But much contemporary study is linking it with broader concepts of an ordered, even an evolutionary, realm of nature, with a beneficence of process and of law. Whether the etymology involved in this understanding can be firmly upheld is a matter of debate. But it plays a central part in the border relations of current Islamic theology with the scientific and the philosophical, especially as expounded in the subtle but adventurous thinking of Muḥammad Iqbāl (1876–1938). Certainly 'the worlds' within the *Rubūbiyyah*,[2] being more and more given—or taken—into human knowledge, provide an ever-sharpening, never-staying, focus of the theological sense of wonder and, with it, the human liability.

What the *Rubūbiyyah*, understood in this way as the will behind and within the order of the worlds, effectuates and sustains is, from another angle, the reality of *Raḥmah*, or divine mercy. The two terms have been variously related.[3] But, broadly, they point to the whence and the how of the ground of our experience. What Lordship achieves, *Raḥmah* conceives. The beneficence men greet in the *Bismillāh* is a merciful authority, a provenance that is merciful. The *Fātiḥah* is thus, essentially, and confidently, a 'human' theology, a sense of the divine rooted in the central relevance of God to man. It

[1] In *Tarjumān al-Qur'ān*, translated by 'Abdul Laṭīf, Bombay, vol. 1, 1962, p. 20.

[2] The plural is of course significant. A simple earth/heaven, time/eternity, material/spiritual contrast would have required the dual. The plural term admits of everything in the macrocosm/microcosm totality—universes, stars, planets, atoms, histories, societies, psyches, in the endless manifoldness of reality.

[3] See, for example, *Abū-l-Kalām Āẓād*, op. cit., pp. 20–7, and Muḥammad Iqbāl, *Reconstruction of Religious Thought in Islam*, London, 1934. *Raḥmah* is more fully discussed in Chapter 7 below.

might be said that there is, indeed, no other possible theology, since man cannot escape his human-centredness. Yet there are 'theologies', notably from Asia and, strikingly, from within Islam, which call upon him to do so and, in the name of absolute monism, urge a surmounting of the 'dualism' in which devout awareness of God always moves.[1] Not so the *Fātiḥah*. It speaks throughout in the accents of human relatedness. Muslim humanity, in its verses, is saying in the solidarity of the *Ummah*, or faith-people-hood: 'We are Thine', not the self-disavowing: 'I am Thou' of mystical religion. This is not to say that the *Fātiḥah* cannot be borrowed—as indeed it has—to speak a mystic's *Islām*, but then only by the liberty with language so characteristic of the mystical temper. Such liberties apart, the 'concentrated version of the Qur'ān clenched to the full form of it'[2] in the opening Surah is undeniably a theology of humanness, a summons to the religious acknowledgement of the whole seriousness of man, of man under God and unto God.[3] It is for this reason that we have set it here under the theme of the Quranic 'perhaps'. Its words are, immediately, worship, praise, encounter, crisis, in the awe of the divine.

This sense of the *Fātiḥah* brings us to the petition of v. 6: 'Guide us in the straight path', a prayer which may be said to hold within its nine syllables the whole ethic of Islam. The grammatical construction is itself intriguing. English needs to supply a preposition 'in' (preferably not 'into' which would, or could, imply that the petitioner is not yet within the sphere of the revelation, as, of course, every Muslim is). But in the Arabic, the verb 'to guide' in the imperative, *ihdinā*, has the pronoun object 'us' and the accusative of place, a sort of second object. In the guiding, the path and guided belong together. *Dīn*, in other words, is as explicit as *īmān*. As the theology is unarguable, so also is the ethic. Revelation is in hand, in being, in control. Speculation is no more necessary for conduct than for belief. The phrase *al-ṣirāṭ al-mustaqīm* occurs some thirty-two times, though almost everywhere outside the first Surah it is indefinite in form. Al-Baiḍāwī in his commentary records the prayer:

'Guide us in the way to go in Thee, to banish the dark shadows of our

[1] See, further, Chapter 10 below.

[2] Āzād's phrase, op. cit., p. 6, if the translator has it well.

[3] Not, of course, in the sense of any crude anthropomorphism, nor implying 'a theology of men's making', but simply, within the revelatory form, a framework for surrender, a theology of worship.

state and take off the concealments of our bodies that we may be illuminated with the light of Thy holiness and in Thy light see Thee.'

He adds that the imperative here, and the petition it makes, are one in speech and in intent and serve to distinguish what draws upwards to the truth and what drags downward to the worthless.[1] For 'the straight path', the undeviating road, is known by and in the *furqān*, or criterion, which is one of the Qur'ān's titles for itself (25: 1, cf. 3: 4). The transcendental lawgiver ordains the human order, establishes the due constitution of society, and communicates it in the final revelation. *Al-mustaqīm*, 'the upright path', as Al-Baiḍāwī tersely explains, is the level way; the intended sense is the way (*ṭarīq*) of truth, which is understood to mean the *millah*, or community, of Islam.'

Hence arises the firm distinction of the final verse. '. . . not the path of those on whom displeasure rests, nor of those in error wandering', but 'of those on whom Thy favour rests'. The two parts of the negative clause might be said to tally with the double sense of *Raḥmah* and *Hudā* (or *Hidāyah*), of mercy known and guidance followed, in contrast to wrath and wandering. There are more specific interpretations of these excluded people, idolaters, probably, on the one hand and errant monotheists, perhaps Jews and Christians, on the other, or possibly some relevance to these last only, whose tensions with the claims of Muḥammad and the fashion of his emerging success were so marked in the hinterland of the Quranic scene. Other, and more recent, exegetes tend to connect these clauses with elements in human society that make for disintegration and contention—elements which reap their own reward of frustration and divine disavowal. The disfavour then comes to stand for an inner nemesis by which history disowns those who flout its moral laws and despise its inner logic. Islam is traditionally confident in a retributive principle manifestly at work in the historical order, and is, therefore, by the same token, instinctively set for, and expectant of, the vindication of the good.

[1] He follows this with a conjecture that involves an interesting reversal of the usual western metaphors about 'swallowing' and 'truth'. His point is the variant *sirāṭ*, instead of *ṣirāṭ*, saying that if '*ṣ*' is read, rather than '*s*', it is because it allies better with the heavy '*ṭ*' at the end of the word. *Sirāṭ* means the oesophagus, the path of swallowing, the throat's habitual pathway. The path might then be paralleled to a diet and its 'taking' to the habitude, finality and quick assimilation of the food-taking process. Lane's Dictionary adds the thought that 'he who goes away on it (*al-sirāṭ*) disappears like food that is swallowed.'

In our present context this posture of spirit is of great importance. Leaving aside aspects of it which, though fascinating in themselves in relation to the tragic mysteries of suffering and redemption, are not for reflection here, the point of vv. 5, 6 and 7 of the *Fātiḥah* ushers us into what might be called the instrumentality within 'the great perhaps' around man in the Qur'ān. There are, as we are due to see in subsequent chapters, these great question-marks of human decision and destiny. Truth and error, grace and disowning, the blessing and the curse—these are real, cumulative and sure. Beyond them is 'the Master of the day of judgement'. Standing, in the Quranic scheme, at the heart of the flux of the historical, where the issue is determined, is the prophetic. The mentors of men on behalf of God, are the prophets, and subsequently the writings in which their missions are sealed and still pursued. What then is the nature of the prophetic charge in respect of the human crisis? What role does the prophet have in resolving the great human question?

The answer requires some discrimination between the major and the minor mentors of society under God. Some are merely warners and spokesmen and messengers with limited audience and partial insights, contributory rather than definitive. Others, however, notably Abraham and Moses, gave their message shape in acts and forms more tenacious than words alone. In measure, by iconoclasm and vigorous action, they initiated what they affirmed, and moved by human institutions of tribe and polity, in corroborating service to the spoken word.

With Muḥammad above all prophecy emerged into power and witness into statehood. The human 'perhaps' was understood to entail the political. What might be called a mutual sanction arose between the means of power and the ends of religion. The narrative in the *Sīrah* of Muḥammad has often been told and its impulses explored.[1] The issues ramify bewilderingly. The clue in this context is, rigorously, that of the Qur'ān's own *la'alla* in its several elements belonging to man in nature, in revelation, in gratitude, in mortal

[1] The heart of the matter is whether the ultimately political form of Islam in the years after the *Hijrah* is to be seen as implicit from the beginning and simply awaiting its ripe occasion, or whether it is more truly interpreted as a decision fashioned out of the (apparent) logic of the hard and humiliating years in Mecca. If the latter, then does the 'decision' represent a declension or a true consummation? On the power theme in Islam reference may be made to the present writer's *The Privilege of Man*, London, 1968, Chapter 5.

making. Man is everywhere invited to a verdict of worship and of surrender, understood in its giving or withholding as a verdict on himself. Can prophecy constrain, conduce, concert, his answer?

A verse in 26: 3 (cf. 18: 6) gives the sharpest of urgency to this issue. It uses the same *la'alla* particle, in the singular, Muḥammad himself being the one addressed. The question focuses, perhaps more than any other passage in the book, the persistent problem of its reception in the Meccan world. 'You are actually wasting away with grief, are you not, in that they are not believing?'[1] The phrase *bākhi'un nafsaka* is customarily used for suicide, for a self-destruction, either deliberate or cumulative, arising from the adversities of life. The immediate context has to do with the 'signs of the open book' and the acrimonious obduracy of the Meccan populace. The title of the Surah, *The Poets*, recalls the invective of the unbelievers in scorning the Qur'ān as mere poetics—a charge which called in question the whole seriousness of prophetic mission, as well as compromising the sources in *waḥy* of the Qur'ān's literary quality. As everywhere in the book where this controversy of pagan Quraish with Muḥammad is mirrored, the precedents of earlier prophets are recalled both for warning and for vindication. The force of 26: 3 is that Muḥammad's experience of the emotional and spiritual hazards (and physical dangers) of prophetic calling had reached a point of dire intensity, where the very life was being wrung out of him.

Prophets, as in some sense the spiritual genius of their time and place,[2] become in this way the symbol of what is at stake in human history. Their words and their very presence dramatize the claims of God. Their encounter with men is a catalyst of all that is implicit in human history. They move at the point of decisive climax and have their prophetic being in its inner tensions and its outward conflict. In them the *la'alla* of humanity, the 'whether' of response or non-response, comes to culmination. Public and personal reaction to the prophet then emerges as the explicit form of reaction to the God whom

[1] The interrogative form of translation here does justice to the force of *la'allaka* as a statement. Arberry has: 'Perchance thou consumest thyself that they are not believers', and Pickthall, 'It may be that thou tormentest thyself because they believe not.' It is not, however, that the anguish is in doubt. It is, rather, that there is a great burden in its unresolved tensions. The passage would seem to be interpreting to Muḥammad the significance of his own anguish, as the focal point of the truth/world encounter.

[2] 'Genius' is loosely used here and is not meant to beg any dogmatic questions. To comprehend those around whom history moves is to learn what was at stake in and for the inarticulate and the 'masses'.

he serves and for whom he speaks. Thus his reception in the world becomes a test case of the human relation to the divine will.

As such, it is deeply alive within the prophetic experience. The Biblical prophets, especially Jeremiah, read in their own inner history the mystery of the divine sovereignty and the divine patience *vis-à-vis* the actual world. In certain senses that inner crisis of 'representing' the divine summons to men was most acutely present in Muḥammad. It is the largest of the themes that are latent in the Qur'ān. Yet, perhaps surprisingly, there is little direct intimation of its interior nature in the text. It emerges, rather, in the decisions involved in the *Hijrah* as the pivot of the narrative.[1] One verse, on which modern thought has often fixed in this connection, is that in 2: 97: 'He brought it down upon your heart' (*'alā qalbika*). The context has to do with the sceptics about the Qur'ān, depicted as being thereby 'at enmity with Gabriel', under whose wing Muḥammad is alerted to the sequences of the Scripture.[2] 'Upon your heart' is often taken to denote the quality of travail and "existential" yearning entailed in prophetic vocation, as distinct from intellectual apprehension or verbal facility alone. It is also contrasted with the passivity of reception frequently implied in the way Muḥammad's illiteracy has been understood.[3] Traditional views of a purely inactive recipience on his part belong, of course, with the corresponding way in which the *I'jāz*, or 'miracle' of the Qur'ān is understood, as a wholly supernatural phenomenon answering to the speaker's literary incapacity. Contemporary thinking, however, taking its cue from 2: 97, and from the clear implications of 26: 3, is encouraged to recognize a deep dimension of active emotion and spiritual quest in the experience of Muḥammad with the Qur'ān. Whatever is finally the fact behind belief in an entire verbal inbreathing of words it must surely not exclude the heart's own urgent pressures as these arose out of the context of the time and place and the prophetic sense of a revelation to it.

[1] See *The Event*, Chapter 8. Some aspects of the power-context of Medinan Islam after the *Hijrah* will arise in Chapter 11 below. The point here is what must have been the inner burden of the situation from which emerged the outward 'logic' of emigration.

[2] Cf. the title of Annemarie Schimmel's perceptive study: *Gabriel's Wing*, Leiden, 1963.

[3] See *The Event*, Chapter 3. Al-Baiḍāwī observes on 2: 97, that 'the heart is the first receiver of *waḥy* and the place of understanding and of *ḥifẓ*. The truth was indeed in his heart, but it came by the relating words of God directing him: "Say what I have said, by permission of God and by His command and mandate".' This view would see the heart as simply the storehouse of the given word, not the crucial factor in its very receiving.

It is surely in this realm of personal travail in the *charisma* of the Prophet that the reader must look for the deepest measure of the mind of the Qur'ān. The surest justice to the book will be a worthy cognizance of what was at stake in prophetic vocation and of how that experience, interpreting its own meaning, issued into rulership. For this is what the Qur'ān's being 'on the heart of Muḥammad' must be seen to involve. The truth of the unity, as he believed himself entrusted with it, came to be identified with its effective vindication in his own status. It was not to be, as with other prophets in another tradition, a truth that might be for ever linked victoriously with the prophet's unbroken suffering. By contrast it was to be bound up successfully with a political structure giving effectuation to the divine claims. Muḥammad's message in prophecy and his identity in prophethood became a single cause, with the state for its criterion. Hostility to him, in the trust of the divine word was read, in the texture of events, as an enmity to the divine will. The vindication of either was the vindication of each.

The whole Qur'ān revolves around this decision as to the destiny of prophetic travail and its issue in the human *la'alla*, its task in the order of time. It gives point and urgency in the book to all the patriarchal precedents, drawn unanimously towards the same goal and the same logic of success. As the definitive crisis in Muḥammad's biography, it is perpetuated as the central quality of Islamic history.

There had been moments in the early years when vocation had been detachable from vindication and the call distinguishable from any necessary issue—as, indeed, it must be with truth within history. One passage, in particular, is notable in this connection. Surah 10, which is a Meccan Surah, has to do with a typical confrontation between the Prophet and his Meccan foes (vv. 41–43). It continues with the grim hint to Muḥammad that he might even die an apparent failure in mission. 'Whether We let you see something of what is coming to them [the unbelievers], or whether We bring you to the point of death, to Us is their returning. God is witness against all their deeds' (v. 46). The word here 'We cause you to die' (*natawaffayannaka*), used invariably of God, is emphatic.[1] It speaks a deep reassurance in the event of death in an unavailing vocation. This is the hazard which

[1] It is the term used in participle form in the passage about Jesus in 3: 55: 'O Jesus, I am causing you to die . . .'

is no doubt in mind in the dark tribulation of 26: 3 *bākhi'un nafsaka.*

Muḥammad survived. The experience was read, in its cumulative significance, as both the prelude and the case for 'manifest victory'. The post-mortal reckoning of the adversaries would, indeed, come at 'the returning unto God'. But the vindication would be established unmistakably in mortal history. Surah 10: 46 is the closest the Qur'ān comes to the unrequited sufferer as the ultimate service of the prophetic to its mission. Islam was not given, in its founding history, to the treading of that path. The Qur'ān does not move with the momentum of a prophethood walking through the valley of the shadow. Suffering in the Qur'ān is a circumstance to be endured until it can be reversed, rather than a travail itself yielding the victory of redemption. When this other dimension emerges in Islam in the Shī'ah experience of tragedy, it happens beyond the confines of the Scripture and with no explicit support from the major emphases, or even the minor terms, of the Qur'ān. Shī'ah Islam furthermore, is a minority verdict.

Yet the possibility of a prophetic ultimacy that stands in the power to suffer, though it never ripens into fact, was in essence a present option throughout the Meccan Surahs. That consideration only sharpens the inclusive criterion as to how prophetic vocation fulfils itself, in and with the trust that makes it. It is determined in political authority. From that inner decision of prophethood comes the outer shape of the community. The human question we have been studying as the great 'perhaps' of the Qur'ān reader has its answer unequivocally. The answer is representatively given in the resolution, within Muḥammad's biography, of the central issue of prophethood. It is there institutionally in the consequent structure of Islamic polity.

Perceptions closer to the human tragedy will find it religiously sanguine and politically naive. For it assumes a humanity amenable to God by state expression, communal habitude and patterned piety. Yet its realist philosophy of society and its resolute handling of the theme of power give it a sturdy direction which minds alert to the darkness in man must acknowledge with respect. But here are questions which had better stay until, in the concluding chapter, some effort is made to see the bearings of Islamic convictions on the wider ecumenical discourse of contemporary faiths.

Meanwhile there are aspects of Quranic reading, of critical terms and emphases, which require more direct attention, aiming af that sort of long perspective and close intimacy which Thomas Fuller caught in his quaint way when he remarked: 'A man knows his companion in a long journey and a little inn.' For humanity has long been on the one and the contemporary world is very much the other.

Chapter 6
THE TROUBLE OF MAN

'Have you realized what you do in procreating?' asks Surah 56: 58, or, in more literal translation, 'Have you considered the seed you spill?'[1]

> 'What is the substance whereof you are made,
> That millions of strange shadows on you tend?'

There is, for the Qur'ān, a strong fascination in the mystery of birth and in the power of sexuality by which it happens. Life is the constant procession from the loins to the wombs for their travailing, from the wombs to the earth for its travelling and from the earth to the eternal for its deciding.[2] There is the sequence of the generations into life and

[1] This second rendering is Arberry's. Others run: 'Behold the semen you discharge' (Dawood); 'Have you seen what you emit?' (Pickthall); 'What think you of what you emit the germs of life?' ('Abdul-Laṭīf); 'Do you then see the (human seed) you throw out?' (Yūsuf 'Alī); 'Have you considered the life germ?' (Muḥammad 'Alī). The words *a fā ra'aytum mā tumnūn* have to do, in the direct manner of the Qur'ān, with sexual orgasm as the genesis of each generation within the creative gift of God. The force of the indicative verb is simple, direct and reverent. The interrogative verb has to do with 'seeing' and 'thinking', with the same sort of double intention belonging to the English: 'view', that is, both sight, and opinion or estimate. Our more idiomatic translation is, therefore, right. The concern, clearly, is not with literal seeing, but with responsible awareness, even though the effective agencies are not visually discernible. Here in sex is the focal sacrament of existence, of the begotten begetting. Perhaps one might recall, in very different vein, the opening sentence of Laurence Sterne's *Tristram Shandy*: 'I wish either my father or my mother, or indeed both of them, as they were in duty equally bound to it, had minded what they were about when they begot me . . .' Or the lines of the poet:

> 'The night my father got me,
> His mind was not on me.'

[2] Commenting on Surah 55: 29: 'Active is He, day in and day out', Jalāl al-Dīn Rūmī observes in the *Mathnawī* (1.3069–73): 'His least act every day is that He despatches three armies. One army from the loins of the fathers towards the mothers in order that seed may grow in the womb; one from the wombs to the earth that the world may be filled with male and female; one army from the earth to what lies beyond death.'

their exodus out of mortality. 'Unto God is your becoming' (*al-maṣīr*), 'unto God is your returning' (*al-marjiʿ*). The purpose of this chapter is to ponder the humanity which the generations take and give and so to reflect on some contemporary bearings of the Quranic portrait of man.

It can hardly be denied that it is a stern and sombre picture. Every sensitive reader soon perceives that the Muslim Scripture is a book of dark shadows. Despite the strong assurance, the celebration of light and victory, its perspective of human history is grave and anxious. Past civilizations are mirrored in the ruins they have left.

> 'How many a city given to evil have We made to perish and it is fallen on its own towers: how many an abandoned well, how many a fine palace.'

So runs Surah 22: 45. Archaeology is thus a lesson in retribution. For these wrecks are not merely the vestiges of time and of decay. They are the requital of folly and perversity. Time, it is true, overtakes all mortal things in the reckoning of frailty. But, within it, is the accusation which may overwhelm it in the reckoning of doom. This grim quality of history belongs with the Qur'ān's vision of a humanity poised between prophecy and disaster. The good of obedience proceeds within the conflicts of evil. Rebellion ripens for apocalyptic judgement and the sure nemesis of God.

Throughout in the narrative of the prophets runs their urgent, but often unheeded, contention for the truth. Obduracy dominates the human story. 'Most of them never give thanks.' 'In their hearts there is a sickness.' 'Most of them do not know.' The duty of truth is, therefore, unremitting, ever urging its cause against the irresponsive and the irresponsible. The prophetic tenacity is everywhere exemplary. But in its vindication the evil is subdued rather than transformed. Minor prophets, minor tribes, major prophets, major tribes—the pattern tallies. The human habit of inertia and resistance repeats its cycle of indifference, ridicule and enmity, and moves on to doom. Judgement is re-assuring in that it makes good the *Tauḥīd*, or unity—the indefeasibility of the divine power, though there remains here a deep paradox.[1] In the Qur'ān the polarity of law and judgement, over against lawlessness, terminates all questions.

[1] It is the question whether judgement alone is not a sort of divine defeat, frustrating creation in condemning man. We return below to this issue, in assessing how far we

How gravely, then, does it move in 'the trouble of man!' It is odd that Islam and its Scripture have been sometimes claimed for optimism. There is, it is true, an instinct for success and triumph. God is sought and found in vindication. Yet there remains within its pages the most forthright indictment of mankind.

> 'When the earth casts forth her burdens and man cries: "What ails her?" on that day she will tell her tidings' (99: 2–4).

Humanity through history has lain heavy upon the good earth, wasting her beauty, polluting her bounty, raping her treasures, and flouting her covenants in hard defiance of her Lord. The 'burdens', in the context of Surah 99, are the bones and bodies of the dead summoned from their graves. But these, in their generations, were parties and victims in the passions and struggles of exploitation.[1] The earth that holds their remains has borne grievously with their deeds. The thought is repeated in 84: 4, where the earth is rid, or freed, of what is in her. The resurrection of the dead and the disclosures of mortal history are seen as one event, liberating the soil from the moral, as well as from the physical, interments of the ages.

Is this the setting in which we should understand the saying of 90: 4: 'We have surely created man in trouble'? *Fī kabad*, the phrase here translated 'in trouble', occurs in the same context of procreation and seems to relate to the twin factors of birth and territory, and to the pitfalls of wealth and poverty. These, with the accompanying demands of mercy and compassion, make 'the steep ascent' of which the Surah

can truly speak of the 'tragedy' of man in the Qur'ān. The urge to avoid paradox, in the interests of uncomplicated sovereignty, is deep in Islamic thinking. Cf., for example, Ismail Ragi al-Faruki, *Christian Ethics*, Montreal, 1967, especially p. 11, where non-paradoxicality is a main criterion of the author's exposition of Islam as it contrasts with the Christian liability to the paradoxical.

[1] Hishām Amīr 'Alī, in *The Student's Qur'ān*, Karachi, n.d., p. 22, takes *athqāl* (burdens) here to mean 'great ones', that is tyrants or economic oppressors and exploiters, so linking it with warnings against the pride of abundance and the menace of worldly wealth in, for example, Surahs 102 and 104.

In a different vein, we might venture a parallel with William Styron's words from a father to a son in *Lie Down in Darkness*, 'Always remember where you came from the ground is bloody and full of guilt where you were born', op. cit., New York, 1951, p. 74. In *The Miracle Play of Hasan and Husain*, collected from oral tradition by Lewis Pelly, revised by A. N. Wollaston, London, 1879, there is a similar passage, in which a traveller, camping on the ground of Karbalā' is said to find blood around her tent pegs from the 'abiding' of the massacre which once hallowed the soil, op. cit., vol. 2, no. 35.

speaks, the *'aqabah*, or rugged upward path, the hard going of the steadfast soul in a strenuous world. *Kabad* is also the seat of the affections, the interior 'heart' of man, where the springs of his being rise. These, confronting the real world, must 'bear it out even to the edge of doom',[1] if they would come through in patience and fidelity, with eyes and tongue and lips unbetrayed and still beneficent.

The odds are heavy. For 'man is created with a restless anxiety', as 70: 19 observes. The 'unease' meant in this phrase belongs with both his propensities for love and his capacities for evil. The word *insān* (man) is tied with *uns* (sympathy) in a way curiously like the English connection of 'kin' and 'kind', and 'kindliness' with one's 'kind'. It is from the very quality of yearning within relationship that procreation and society alike derive. The *'alaq* (clot) of the many procreation passages may well refer, not simply to the physical sperm or embryo, but to the generating desire, the love and 'clinging affection', by which sex both expresses and achieves itself. But this ardour in man's making turns readily to fear and dismay.[2] Its clinging passion grows destructive, acquisitive and wild. Thus its benedictions are forfeit. Frustration and wretchedness supervene. Men are then an easy prey and in their restlessness are prone to evil ends.

We might almost say they are 'commandeered' for wrongdoing by forces that take over their wills. Such is the sense of a phrase in Surah 12: 53, in the Qur'ān's narrative of the incident of Joseph and the wife of Potiphar. The latter, confessing that the guilt was hers in soliciting him, reflects on the impulse she now disowns, with the

[1] The line is from Shakespeare's Sonnet 116. The whole of Surah 90 fills out these meanings. Al-Baiḍāwī in his exegesis takes *kabad* in a literal sense. It is for him 'the toil and grief of man in his ceaseless troubles, beginning from the darkness and straitness of the womb and closing in death and what lies beyond it'. The passage, he adds, was to 'comfort the Prophet, the peace and blessing of God be upon him, over what he was enduring from the Quraish'. See Chapter 5, above.

[2] The phrase in 70: 19, *khuliqa-l-insān halū'an*, is often translated 'man is created fretful', or 'impatient', 'anxious', or even 'inconsiderate' and 'rash'. Some translators relate it to the 'hasty' of 17: 11 and 21: 37. Al-Baiḍāwī argues simply from the context to see in it the watchfulness that characterizes the hoarder and the impatience of those who are baulked by circumstances. But a deeper import can well belong to the word, if the sense of *halū'an* is taken, in the way suggested, into the larger dimensions of *insān*, and of man in creation. For the procreation passages, see below. Hishām Amīr 'Alī, op. cit., translates 96: 2 (*'alaq*): 'created mankind from mutual attachment'. Mirzā Abūl-Fazl has: 'Humans made from love for love.' Whether these renderings commend themselves or not, *halū'an* in 70: 19 seems to imply something much more than circumstantial worries.

words: 'in truth the soul of man is prone to evil'. 'Under a bias towards evil', is the exact sense of the construction.[1] 'Man', as 4: 28 remarks, 'is created weak', with a liability, that is, to pervert and distort the powers that belong with his positive dignity and privilege. He is, we might say in the double sense of the word, a 'liable' creature—responsible to yield account, yet conniving against his own good.

These phrases about weakness and 'bias' towards wrong do not suffice as a basis for any final Quranically argued philosophy of human nature, isolated as they are. They suggest no elaborate doctrine and they are early in the Prophet's mission. But their realism persists, as we must see, within the more confident pragmatism of the later political years, and there is no mistaking its urgent quality. The passages about birth are so frequent and striking that the reader must let his imagination respond to their pre-occupation. In the current world of human flood-tide, so different from the precarious human tenure that found insurance in frequent pregnancy, there is new force in the Quranic reverence for birth. The main verses are 22: 5, 23: 12–14, 32: 7–9, 35: 11, 36: 77, 40: 67–68, 53: 46, 56: 58, 76: 1–2, 77: 20–22, 80: 18–20, 82: 7–8, 86: 5–7, and 96: 2. They see the womb and the embryo as God's mercy in man's gift. Surah 23 is perhaps the most explicit.

> 'Truly We created man as a progeny of clay and set him as a living seed in a secure lodgement. The seed We created into an embryo and the embryo into tissue and the tissue into bone and the bones We garbed in flesh, so bringing forth another creation. Blessed then be God, the fairest Creator.'

From this beginning in awe the human creature is launched into the world with the self he can frustrate or fulfil, in the empire of environment and the converse of society. Surah 56, inviting man to a sense of his procreative force and his embryonic mystery, continues in the same vein: 'Have you considered your agriculture?' 'Have you considered the water you drink?' 'Have you considered the fire you kindle?' (vv. 63, 68, 71). Tilling the earth, drawing the water, striking

[1] The crucial word here is *la ammāratun*, from the verb 'to command'. It is the emphatic, intensive participle. Hence the point of 'bias'. One might literally translate: 'The soul is indeed obliged evilwards', or, 'the self is under a conducing towards wrong'. There is in man, it says, an inner, ruling tendency which makes evil the easier option.

the fire—man's dealings with the familiar elements that house and furnish his life and serve to his dominion—are symbols as well as instruments of his nature. Earth is his fruitfulness, water his security, fire his friend. There are parables of meaning between the womb and the world. In both there is tenancy, cycle and termination. Comparably and contrastedly—there is also travail. One can be sure of nothing after birth and 'no soul knows in what land it shall die' (31: 34), just as no soul knew in what womb it would come to life.

Ambiguity pervades all mortal existence. 'The life of the world is a game and a sport', we read in 6: 32, 29: 64, 47: 36 and 57: 20. The phrase intends 'the life of the worldly world', which will fall away into 'child's play', in the retrospect of eternity. 'God', nevertheless, 'has not created the world in jest' (or sport) as we read in 21: 16 and 44: 38. Those who trifle with it, and with their religion in it, will discover their grievous delusion (6: 70, 7: 51). Had some divine plaything been intended, heaven would have kept the jest to itself. So highly fraught an enterprise as the creation and *imperium* of man is no celestial pursuit of amusement (21: 16). If men, for their part, toy with existence they grossly distort what they should truly read in it. Whatever incentive existence may seem to give to notions of futility, to proceed upon them is to misread the tokens of eternal meaning.

Yet, blandly and sadly, the tokens *are* misread. Men falsify their calling. Crucial decisions accumulate into destiny. 'Has there ever been over man', asks Surah 76 in its opening verse, 'any flux of mortal time within which he was of no importance?' The question is perhaps enigmatic.[1] It seems to mean that there are no intervals of exemption from the issues and the pressures of his being. Surah 76 goes on to speak of birth, faculties, guidance, response and final destiny. In the

[1] Translations and interpretations are various. Arberry has: 'Has there come on man a while of time when he was a thing unremembered?' Dawood ventures: 'Does there not pass over man a space of time when his life is a blank?' Palmer and Rodwell have a sense similar to Arberry, with 'a portion' for 'a while', and 'nothing worth mentioning'. Pickthall has 'period' for 'portion'. 'Abdul-Laṭīf has: 'Surely hath there passed over man a period of time of which nothing is recorded', while Muḥammad 'Alī prefers: '. . . a thing that could not be spoken of'. If it is only the insignificance of the embryo that is understood, it seems to do less than justice to the question. 'Flux of mortal time' meets the force of the verb 'to come upon', and of *dahr* here as temporality. I have taken the concluding words as idiomatic for 'negligibility'. It would seem to mean, then, that man, from the beginning, whether in personal or in collective terms, has had an unremitting seriousness. This certainly gives due force to the rhetorical question and it coincides with the sequel in the Surah.

well-doers God's mercy is displayed: in the evil-doers his righteousness is vindicated. If, with the English poet, the external 'world is charged with the grandeur of God', the Muslim's world is 'charged with the greatness of God', and in that awareness 'the world of all of us' is truly understood. Mankind is laid under the authority of an entire Lordship and a conclusive judgement.

There are, in particular, two aspects of this theme that call for study, by virtue of their repeated emphasis and the centrality of the terms that define them. The one is *ẓulm*, or 'wrong'. The other is *nifāq*, or 'hypocrisy'. The trouble of man might be said to lie in the situations these basic concepts describe.

The derivatives of the root *ẓalama*, verbs, nouns and participles, are among the most frequent of all Quranic terms. Their usage is exceeded only by the most central of all words, like *Allāh*, *Rabb*, and *Rasūl*.[1] The basic sense of *ẓalama* is to do wrong, to treat wrongfully, to deal unjustly, with or without an object. It is the act of falsifying in not according what is due, whether to things or to people, to truth or to trust. It means distortion and perversity, tyranny and evil will. *Shirk*, or idolatry, says 31: 13, 'is great *ẓulm*'. It is wrong against God done by the idolater in denying the true worship and so distorting what is due to God and what is true about God, namely his indivisible, inalienable sovereignty. More frequently *ẓulm* denotes wrong against fellow humanity—injustice, deceit, fraud, slander, treachery, calumny, robbery and the rest. Most eloquent of all is the re-iterated notion of *ẓulm al-nafs*, the wrong of the self against the self. 'It was their own selves they wronged', we find in numerous passages (for example, 2: 57, 3: 117, 7: 160, 177, 9: 70, 10: 44, 16: 33, 16: 116, 20: 40, and 30: 9. Compare also 3: 135, 4: 64, 11: 113, 14: 45 and 34: 19). Sometimes the accent here is clearly on the contrast: it was not God but themselves they wronged.[2] The concern is with the divine immunity rather than with the human diagnosis. But, even so, the very desire for the divine to be inviolate concedes the force of the human rebuke. Whether or not we can finally exempt the divine realm from the human

[1] Quantitative measures are dubious, no doubt. But it is interesting to note that *Allāh* has 70 columns of the Concordance, *Rabb* 27, *Rasūl* 15, *kufr* 15, *'abd* 8, *shirk* 5, *islām* itself as a term with related derivatives 4. *Ẓulm* and its derivatives fill 9 columns.

[2] For example, 11: 101. 'They did not wrong Us but it was . . .' Here we are close to the concerns of Chapter 8. The most careful study, within the Qur'ān, of divine justice is that of Daud Rahbar, *God of Justice: A Study in the Ethical Doctrine of the Qur'ān*, Leiden, 1960.

crisis, there is certainly no *legal* indifference. On the contrary, God's is understood as the sort of righteousness which does not allow the human waywardness to get away with evil. The sequel to wrong-doing will be there in the forfeiture of true being, in the despite done to the soul itself. There is nothing human or material that can compensate for the inward consequences of the evil done. There is nothing in the whole world one can exchange for oneself (compare 10: 54, 13: 18 and 39: 47). This is the sort of world in which evil-doing corrupts the evil-doer and distorts his being, so that he stands self-condemned and self-betrayed. This is a fact of the situation, quite aside from the related issue as to what the divine relation to this self-destruction of man is understood to be. But we are studying the Quranic 'trouble of man', not the trouble of God about man.

This aside, *ẓulm* is never to be laid against God in active dealing with men. All the verdicts of heaven proceed according to the strictest justice. 'Your Lord is no inflicter of wrong upon his servants' (3: 182, 8: 51 and 22: 10). This principle can be brought, it is true, within a sphere of assertive inscrutability, so that whatever eventuates is simply taken for what the justice is. Or it may hold within itself a real response to the sort of questions about justice that human frailty and perplexity and tribulation continually generate.

The phrase about self-wronging, significantly, is usually in the plural. *Ẓulm* has frequently a collective character. It obtains in solidarity. Individual guilt, in its personal entail for the self, arises within the pressures of a whole society and from the forces at work in what we may call the larger dealers in *ẓulm*—nations, races, systems, structures, ideologies and other establishments, social and political. We are all deeply involved in the selfishnesses built into our corporate existence by history and by society. 'Each of us is responsible for all', as Dostoevsky often noted. But, by the same token, the all conditions each. The individual is liable in part for the greater evils that can destroy humanity. The universalizing of guilt does not exonerate the individual in the specifics of his own activity.

To counter *ẓulm al-nafs* is not, therefore, a simple search for a private rectitude or a personal acquittal. It requires also a will to righteousness within the wider whole. If there is no diagnosis that can rightly isolate the individual, there is no merely individual escape from *ẓulm*.[1] Rather the countering must be that of an active goodness

[1] Fuller discussion of this theme of evil, personal and collective is taken up in Chapter

committed to the world and militant within society against its deceptions and its tyrannies.

The theme of *ẓulm* lies close to the Quranic sense of men's eternal destiny, and here some of its sharpest puzzles arise for the non-Quranic mind. Despite the plural nature of evil, just noted, doom is inexorably personal. Since the evil-doer anyway is self-condemned, there is no injustice involved. The final state is simply a condign conclusion. Hell itself need not be questioned, nor its denizens, once—after interrogation—they have become such. Quranic doctrine of the end-things has a strongly absolutist, static quality, that seems to be sharply at odds, for some readers, with the dynamism that characterizes the Quranic sense of sovereignty in God. If *ẓulm al-nafs* matters and if it happens, as we have seen, in a world where the person cannot be isolated, can it be so entirely finalized in the solitariness of judgement and in the total hopelessness of hell? Quranic teleology needs to be asking its theology bigger questions, in both directions. If *ẓulm* is so deeply relational in its temporal workings, can heaven be so blissfully secured in serenity, or damnation be so adamantly perpetual, and both be so roundly individual?

We have already noted earlier, in Chapter 3, how some exegesis has been minded to emphasize local and circumstantial factors allegedly belonging with seventh-century Arabian mentality, to explain the Qur'ān's form of presentation of the future state. Orthodoxy has always been wary of this stance, with the freedom it implies to re-interpret where sophistication exists. But may the modern reader, for his part, take the clue of intention, thus historically argued, deepen it to the full measure of human *ẓulm* and read the picture of the final state simply as a symbol, as it were, of the earthly crisis? On the Qur'ān's own showing it is a picture about a conclusion: it does not obtain while life continues. It belongs with warning and with prospect. Whatever be its ultimate relevance, its immediate significance is about this life, and for the here and now. What is happening in life, it urges, has the character of a moving crisis in which the soul's stake *is* the very soul. The self is charged with the self. To the issue there is a climax which will neither lie nor fail. For 'God is not mocked'.

While *ẓulm* is a concept which has to do with human exchanges through all their broad range, social, moral, economic, *nifāq* belongs

7, on *istighfār*. For a more technical study of *ẓulm*, see *The Muslim World*, vol. 49, no. 3, 1949, pp. 196–212.

squarely with the religious realm, even when it takes political form. It is a much rarer term and occurs, mainly in the participle form, and then invariably in the plural, namely *al-munāfiqūn*, or (fem.) *al-munāfiqāt*. It has to do with the issue of sincerity which emerged in the political days of Muḥammad's mission.

The word *nāfaqa* means 'to play the hypocrite', or 'to be of dubious reliability, a suspect character'. It may be linked also with the idea of selling—in this case one's conscience, so becoming a dissembler or a cheat. The Prophet's forceful policy *vis-à-vis* the Quraish meant a deliberate and determined invocation of power in the interests of an ultimate peace. His logic seems to have been that an effective pacification required a unity with sinews of strength, capable of enforcing and maintaining itself, and that this was a goal fully justifying the strong measures needed to achieve it. Breaking traditional truces was not reprehensible in this logic, since truces were merely the palliatives of a chaotic pattern of strife.[1] It was better to master, once and for all, the sources of faction. But, inevitably, mastery, when it came, drew to its cause a purely time serving and prudential allegiance. As Muḥammad prospered, it became impolitic to impede or resist him, and wise to fall into line. Some tribes and persons temporized, feigning an enthusiasm they did not feel. Others pledged a dubious commitment they did not mean, and might well revoke if pressures eased or odds shifted.

Had this been purely political it could have been countered by just the sort of vigilant suspicion that suspects engender and deserve. But it was also a religious insincerity. The two could not readily be disentangled, since the masterful cause itself, which brought political capitulation, did so in the name of creed and prayer. So the deceivers did not merely cheat a ruler. They feigned a credence and so, in a sense, they sold a prophet. Pseudo loyalty is one thing: treacherous confession another. The danger, of course, was latent in the very pattern of Quranic policy and continued so through all the years of its success. One cannot recruit force successfully and stay innocent of hypocrites. It is the success of force which makes or draws them. This situation is implicit in the double sense of the words *islām* and *muslimūn*, to surrender to power and to submit to truth. Hence the distinction, for example, in 49: 14:

'The bedouin Arabs say: "We have believed." Say: You have not believed.

[1] See, more fully, the author's *The Event*, op. cit., Chapter 3.

You should rather say: "We have submitted (*aslamnā*)." Faith has not entered your hearts. . . .'

The Prophet was impelled by his own logic to take no risks and spare no watchfulness. But sharper vigilance tended only to accentuate the problem, and put the religious criterion of faith the more at risk. The very sanctions that watched against subterfuge could work to engender an empty conformity. The more surely they succeeded the more likely they were to fail.

Thus it was that Islam within the Qur'ān itself found its religious quality deeply involved in its political necessities. It had, therefore, on its hands in acute form one of the perennial problems both of religious establishments and of personal religion. It suffered in the sharpest form the penalties of its own success and thus raised for itself—and for all religious history—the focal question as to how 'success' is identified. It involved itself in an experience of the dynamic of all evil which, the more it is detected for what it is, the more subtly it disguises itself. The power that aims to deter it in the open, incites it in the hidden. Where force operates on behalf of beliefs it may reach the attainable securities, but probably only at the cost of those that are ultimate and spiritual.

Most of the Quranic occurrences of *nifāq* are in the political context. Surah 68 has the title: *Al-Munāfiqūn*. It deals with the wiles and plots and pretexts of the dissemblers, whom it likens to 'propped-up timbers'. In 3: 167 we find them a menace to military discipline, in 8: 49 quislings under pressure, and in 4: 138 f., 5: 57, and 33: 60–61, vacillators guessing at their shifting fortunes.

Behind these outward disloyalties of the *munāfiqūn* and their manoeuvrings lay the deeper questions of heart. Four times, in apposition to *nifāq*, is the phrase: 'those in whose hearts there is sickness (*maraḍ*) (8: 49, 33: 12, 33: 32 and 33: 60), which occurs elsewhere also in the context of unbelief, hostility and perverse dealing (see 2: 10, 5: 52, 9: 125, 22: 53, 24: 50, 47: 20, 47: 29, and 74: 31). In the main the classical commentators do not read the phrase with any great intensity. They assume it to refer to incredulity and impiety, or, in some cases, the disease of carnal lust. It is a shiftlessness whose symptoms are lip-service and dissimulation.

Disease, however, is hardly a realm of metaphor which fits with entire condemnation. The thought of a sickness in hypocrisy might be expected to check somewhat the vehemence of a denunciation that reckons only with guile. There are references in scattered passages to healing, but they do not reach as far as the hypocrites. Surah 10: 57 speaks of 'a healing come . . . for what is in the breasts', and 17: 82 and 41: 44 make it clear that what is intended is the Qur'ān. The phrase 'what the breasts conceal', which is a frequent one, undoubtedly relates to the inner secrets and the hidden springs of action, where *nifāq* develops. To think of these, even if only in part, within analogies of sickness, is to see them more realistically than a mere countering caution would allow. It is characteristic that Islam finds the remedy in revelation itself. For its confidence throughout, in this problem of human waywardness, is that knowledge suffices in reply. And since guidance, as the known revelation affords it, ought to be followed, even the 'sickness' remains blameworthy.

It is in this area of 'the trouble of man' that the Islamic Scripture leaves a sensitive new-comer ill at ease with his thoughts. It is not simply that the religious liabilities of power are sharply at issue: these are inescapable. It is that the 'sickness' within sinfulness is not more gently, more patiently,[1] treated. If there is a *maraḍ* in *nifāq*, the hypocrisy is more than a deliberate disloyalty to the community. It is a malady in the psyche. The sick are those who spurn the remedy itself. The vigilance that may neutralize the social menace will not heal the inner state. 'Disease', in the last analysis, is not a political phenomenon. Almost unanimously, the commentators seem to wish to make it so, concentrating as they do on those areas of the parallel which suit their case, for example, that the condition is chronic, infectious, dangerous to others, and having symptoms that need to be exposed. In consequence they do not probe into those depths of human soul-distress, of the psychic wronging of the self, of bondage to fear and pride, which are the final reaches of the human tragedy. It is this situation in text and commentary which, as well as any other, illustrates the reliance of Quranic religion on the efficacy of the political in the search for true, human being. It may well be that the *munāfiqūn*, in the Qur'ān, were, in fact, a political party, organized and vigorous.[2]

[1] In both senses of 'patient'.

[2] The lack of capital letters for distinguishing 'proper' nouns in Arabic makes this question harder to determine. 'Abd Allāh ibn Ubaiy, ally of the Qaynuqā', figures prominently among them. See Surah 3 for his dubious behaviour at the Battle of Uḥud and 59: 11 for his later dealings with the Jews.

Even so, their 'sickness'—if the term applies—was more than opposition! How to understand the 'more' and how to meet it—this is the perpetual calling and burden of 'religion'.

It will be the work of two succeeding chapters to explore further the Qur'ān's response to human evil by a study of 'forgiveness-seeking', and of *kufr*, or 'the exclusion of God'. The sickness and healing analogies, anyway, are not prominent. Quranic metaphor turns far more readily to the juridical sphere, to the scales of reckoning and the court of judgement. *Nifāq* brings us to the same terminus as our reflections on *ẓulm*. Here, as elsewhere, the accusatory element in the Qur'ān lives in the awe of its own climax. The issue of all issues is resolved in decision eternally binding.

There is an oppressive pathos in the prosecution of man in the Scripture. The indictments are necessary to the diagnosis of the world and to the Quranic sense of the divine. They are set to warn. And to warn may be to save or not to save. No alert reader can miss the urgency with which the book solemnizes our mortality.

But alertness here cannot be other than perplexity. The gulf in the Qur'ān between the fire and the garden is so wide, the contrast between the condemned and the blissful so absolute. *Bi's al-maṣīr*, 'a painful doom', 'a woeful state'—the term with which the Qur'ān denotes damnation—reads in its re-iteration like a hollow echo in a cavern of despair. The very sovereignty which it vindicates it seems also to accuse. A gulf yawns between the creative authority and the destroying eternity. The paradox that is inevitable between sovereignty and evil is here at its most desolating. Since that paradox is in any event inescapable, need it be so sharply negative? How are we to think of 'the fairest of creators' (23: 14, 37: 125) and of his ends in the end? Where the human is so vitally at stake, how, in the Qur'ān's own phrase, do we rightly 'esteem' the divine?

It is not that these questions can escape, or dissolve, the mystery of evil: it is that they search it more profoundly. Their greater expectancy is a greater acknowledgement of the divine rule. It is, therefore, irreverent, and so un-Islamic, to silence or exclude them. They are not involving God unwarrantably in what He transcends. They are asking the meaning of his transcendence. Through creation and revelation, through law and providence, God is 'involved in mankind'. The truth, of which Islam has been so jealous, of his otherness to man has to be consistent with this involvement. The ends of creation must be there at the end. The 'trouble of man' must be neither betrayed nor discounted in its climax.

It falls, of course, to Islamic exegesis to decide what it understands, and means others to understand, by the great Quranic divide of eternity. Can it be wisely read, even by the outsider, except in commentary, as earlier suggested, on the living present? This is not to presume a solution to the larger question of eschatology which faith cannot evade. But it is to seek an immediate realism, and some abeyance of rigidity as a help to tender spirits.

'How the past perishes', wrote Alfred Whitehead, 'is how the future becomes.'[1] There is a continuity of personal being through a life-span, where self-identity is known from within and may be presumed from without. A man is successively responsible and cumulatively made. All moral accountability—not to say social experience and artistic creation—pre-suppose this constant of the person through the years of biography. We bear in us and with us the marks of our having thus far been. What we now are is all our history at its present point. Each present is the immediate terminus of the past—a fact which repeats itself into the available future.

The Qur'ān is very eloquent about the singular and serious quality of this personal continuum between birth and death. It knows well that what is being suffered physically as flux is being made morally as content.[2] Is not this constancy what we mean when we speak of the person? Even when it is 'inconstant', in that it is shiftless and unreliable, there is a 'constant' whose shiftlessness is registered. There is, moreover, a law in sinning by which it cannot be 'unsinned'. Evil has its entail, wrong its momentum. We cannot elude the cumulative character of time. Biography is reckoning. Only in the sense of evil is there reality in hope. When Hamlet says that 'something is rotten in this state of Denmark', and adds in apprehension, 'it is not and it cannot come to good', he speaks a conviction vital to integrity. If rottenness were to come to good, all would come to chaos. Only through condemnation is there salvation. It is forgiveness, in fact, rather than requital, that constitutes the real problem of an eternal future.

[1] *Adventures of Ideas*, London, 1933, p. 305.

[2] In his poem 'Personality: Musings of a Police Reporter in the Identification Bureau', Carl Sandburg writes: 'Out of the whirling womb of time come millions of men and their feet crowd the earth . . . and among them all are not two thumbs alike', *Collected Poems*, New York, 1950, p. 18. There is only one of each of us, known and to be known.

The Quranic picture has all this very clearly focused. Nor does it elude or blur the issue by withdrawing the continuum of the self at death into the sort of 'objective immortality', of which poets and others have dreamed, which is garnered into nature and wrapped around with rocks and stones and trees. There may be meaning in such abiding in departing. African humanity speaks its fascination, as indeed did William Faulkner in a poem on his own demise.

> 'If there be grief, let it be for the rain,
> And this but silver rain, for grieving's sake: . . . for where is any death
> While in these blue hills slumbrous overhead
> I'm rooted like a tree? Though I be dead,
> This soil that holds me fast will find me breath.'[1]

The peasant and the ploughman, the architect and the musician, the poet and the craftsman, may think such a staying with the world where they wrought and loved. Or, any man, having lived awesomely 'noting such things', may be imagined by his successors, lingering there.

> 'Slowly he climbs the familiar path . . .
> . . . halts awhile, and then in the lane
> Is lost in the last of the dying chimes.
> But while sorrow remains, and chance, and war,
> His loving wraith will return again.'[2]

Yet, for the Qur'ān, these 'immortalities' leave the core of death untouched. They belong, on this earthly side, only while memory lasts and they tell only of an absence and the mystery of a presence gone. Actual mortality is a real dissolution, and Islam believes that the ultimate meaning of death cannot be answered in less than personal terms. It is an event in, not after, personality. The Qur'ān is vivid in its comment on the physical disjuncture of death. A man's soul leaves his body under the very eyes of his friends (56: 83–86). The burden of the passage is that these, though grimly aware that suddenly a man has become a corpse, are quite unable to restore him. This body, thus distenanted, is yet the very house of life, the place of all things spiritual,

[1] William Faulkner, *The Marble Faun and the Green Bough*, New York, 1933, p. 67.

[2] Clive Sansom, *The Witnesses and Other Poems*, London, 1956, p. 56. The poem is about Thomas Hardy and echoes his own will to be remembered as 'one who noticed such things' as birds on the wing and lovers in the lane.

where personality was active, recognizable and self-expressive. So the Qur'ān will have nothing to do with the notion that the corpse, admittedly discarded and corruptible, is the final fact about the body and its tenant. On the contrary, leaning with a Semitic intensity on the parable of nature's sleep and spring and harvest, it anticipates the resurrection of the body as an integral part of the central conviction about personality as significant. 'Unto God', it insists 'is our returning. For, to God, verily, we belong' (2: 156 and many parallel passages), and that, not as some kind of residue in disembodiment, but as persons, known, judged and—in the archaic sense of the word—achieved.

So solemn and decisive is this conviction that it returns us powerfully to the residue of our living years. What is beyond death, as Emily Dickinson has it,

> '. . . is a different thing
> Conjectured and waked sudden in.'[1]

'Waked sudden in' exactly describes the Quranic picture of post-mortal experience. Waiting there, are all the 'forwardings' of man's vital span. In perhaps the gentlest of the many passages on eternal destinies we read:

> 'O you who believe, hold God in awe. Let a soul look to what he has forwarded for a morrow. Hold God in awe. God is cognisant of all you do. Do not be like those who forgot God and God caused them to forget themselves. These are the wanton with life. The denizens of the fire are not as the denizens of the garden. The denizens of the garden theirs is the triumph.'[2]

Here is the essence of the Quranic reading of life—faith, identity, awe before God, cumulative destiny, unfailing known-ness to God, the danger of self-loss, and the final sequel.

Standing, as we are, within the mortal range—albeit the mortality with these dimensions—the question stays. Can the sense of contrast—these and those, the triumph and the tragedy, the winning and the wasting—be so static and so absolute? *Lā yastawiyā*, says the verse.

[1] *The Poems of Emily Dickinson*, 3 vols., Cambridge, Mass., 1958. Poem 172: ''Tis so much joy'.

[2] Surah 59: 18–20. 'Wanton with life' translates the more usual 'evildoers', *al fāsiqūn*, aiming to capture the idea of waste, deviation, negative 'forwarding' of the dissolute.

It sounds a strange under-statement with which to distinguish heaven and hell.[1] Yet perhaps in that very modesty a wiser one than the utter sharpness of pictorial contrast. Certainly the things we forward through the web of years are always wrought in ambiguity. Scales cannot sift. But nothing can be truly weighed unsifted. Even our virtues we may not call our own. In our sins are the schemes of a thousand factors beyond our birth and choosing. Islam has always been close to realism. It does not find virtue merely in asceticism. It has never disengaged evil from the necessities of power and of the state. Virtues may in part be rightly blamed and vices have their just causes. All is tangled and contorted in its earthly incidence. To find it tidily adjudged beyond death must surely be taken as a profound conviction of divine justice—a justice to which to entrust all things including the very pictures under which we think of it.

The fire and the garden, then, must be seen to dramatize what they cannot simplify. If they suspend ambiguity it can only be to illuminate more starkly the elements that comprise it. The trouble of man is not that he has no destiny to reach but that reaching it takes him through the enigma and the paradox, through the struggle and the crowd. And all of these, with himself, stand within the summons of God. That summons, the Qur'ān assures us, begins and ends in justice and mercy. More than this, about the divine relation to his answer, it will not say.

There would be no trouble, if there were no summons. Were there no summons, there would be no men. Of the final reckoning the Qur'ān says, in words it is wiser not further to interrogate: 'Truly the good deeds outweigh the evil deeds.'[2] This suffices both for fear and hope. The Qur'ān has no word for yesterday. Mortality is this vale of soul-making, the shaping of the personal eternity.

[1] *Lā yastawiyā* means 'they are not on the same level', 'they should not be held alike'. It is a very different note from the frequent and dramatic contrasting.

[2] The verb *yudhhibna* means to over-master, to nullify, to annul, to cause to go. 'Make amends for . . .' (Dawood) is a limiting translation. 'Outweighs' keeps within the imagery of the Qur'ān—though this particular passage does not use it. In another realm of metaphor we might say that the good deeds are left in possession of the field.

Chapter 7
THE SEEKING OF FORGIVENESS

'Candidly to admit where one is in candour before God', wrote Kierkegaard, 'is the first and the last.' Only the sense of unworthiness truly crosses the threshold of worship, and that, 'not in dread and fear and despair' which 'are of no avail', but in 'the consciousness of sin' which alone is 'the expression of absolute respect'.[1] To seek God is by the same token to seek forgiveness.

It is natural then that in the Qur'ān's theme of worship the will to be forgiven should be a constant exhortation. 'Seek forgiveness from God' runs the repeated command. *Istaghfir Allāh*, the Arabic verb, employs the root which yields, in three variants, the divine Names that relate to pardon (*ghāfir*, *ghafūr* and *ghaffār*) and does so in the grammatical form that means the desire to have the action done to which the descriptives point. *Istighfār*, the verbal noun, denotes this explicit quest for pardon, with God always understood as the object. The study of the significance of this usage and of the instinct within it takes us into a deep measure of contemporary relevance in the Qur'ān and of the nature of Islamic devotion.

There would seem—if we may anticipate—to be several vital meanings implicit in this recurrent phrase.[2] Forgiveness has to be sought. It cannot be had unless it is wanted. Pardon must be a yearning before it can be a transaction. It is provisional to the state of the heart. But, further, it must be sought from God. Before Him, all wrongdoing, whoever the intermediate sufferers and victims, is radically known and manifest. To know that it is God against whom we have sinned is the deepest element in the knowledge both of God and of our

[1] S. Kierkegaard, *Training in Christianity*, translated by Walter Lowrie, London, 1941, pp. 70 and 72.

[2] The verb *istaghfara*, in various persons and tenses, occurs forty times. The original root, *ghafara*, 'to forgive', is found sixty-five times, the adjectives ninety-seven times and the noun *maghfirah*, 'forgiveness', twenty-eight.

selves. But if, further again, there is a command that forgiveness be sought, then forgiveness must be feasible. For it cannot be a command to ask, as the philosopher, Kant, used to note, what it is inherently impossible to receive. Forgiveness from God is our most essential hope because it is our most elemental need, and always the one because the other.

If, moreover, as in the Qur'ān, the injunction to make the seeking of forgiveness a directive to others is laid upon ourselves, then can *we* rightly withhold the thing we bid them seek? Forgiveness from God as a correlative of the forgiveableness of the penitent, is thereby also a bond of association, binding men to the same relationships. To urge the vital penitence is surely to be committed to heeding it ourselves. As both enjoined and heard, the command to ask forgiveness of God cuts at the root of the obstinacy of enmity and forbids all adamant irreconcilability. *Istighfār* would seem to be at the heart of all social existence. For it has to do with turning the human condition, collective and personal, through self-accusation towards mercy, liberty and peace.

These ready anticipations must first be tested by a careful study of the Quranic occurrences of *istighfār*. Surah 47: 19 says:

> 'Know that there is no god but God and seek forgiveness for your sin and for the believers, men and women.'

The singular verb is used again in 40: 55:

> 'Be patient, then, for the promise of God is true. Seek forgiveness for your sin and occupy yourself in the praise of your Lord at evening time and at the dawn.'

The personal prayer of forgiveness is thus set in the context of the *Shahādah*, or confession of faith, and of daily adoration. It is the practice of the divine presence that most surely constrains the will towards purity of heart.

This, however, means no idle piety. It concerns the central realities of life and history. In Surah 11: 61 the (minor) prophet Ṣāliḥ enjoins the tribe of Thamūd to serve God and continues

> 'You have no other God but He. He has given you being from the earth and established you in it. So ask forgiveness of Him and repent before Him. For my Lord is near to answer.'

Here the impulse to penitence is made to spring from the gift of existence itself and from the human exploitation of the earth where men are tenants and farmers and so, by implication from the arts and the evils of civilization as a whole.[1] No less crucial is the command of Surah 110, which sees in the very success of religion in the world urgent occasion for the exercise of critical self-judgement.

> 'When God's help comes and victory with it and you see men thronging into God's religion, then occupy yourself in the praise of your Lord and seek His forgiveness. For He is ever cognisant of repentance.'

There could hardly be more complete and inclusive realms than these, standing as they do for the economic and the political, in which to set the relevance of penitence to society. In 51: 14 f., comes an eloquent expression of it in the most direct of terms. The passage has to do with the blessed in paradise. In their mortal days they are described as those who 'prevented the night watches' to pray and 'in the mornings sought forgiveness'. The comment follows with an uncomplicated directness: 'and the needy and the destitute had a share in their goods'. Could this sense of a human compassion as its consequence have been in Luther's mind when, in the first of his famous Theses at Wittenberg, he affirmed the divine intention 'that the whole life of believers should be penitence'?

The same Ṣāliḥ of Surah 11 appears again in 27: 45–46, where he asks the question that is at the heart of all prophetic interrogation of humanity.

> 'Lo! there were two factions contending together and he said: O my people, why do you hasten after the evil rather than the good? Why do you not ask forgiveness of God that haply you might find mercy?'

The answer, in part, doubtless lies in the continuity of evil and in the entail of collective tradition. Forgiveness is a new departure, whereas strife is 'the way of the ancients' (18: 55), prejudicing men against the guidance that has come to them, and against its urge to a seeking of forgiveness before retribution overtakes them.

The re-iterated call of the messengers is to this sense of the need of

[1] The verb here could be translated 'made you to colonize the earth'. *Ista'marakum* yields the modern Arabic for 'imperialism'.

pardon. So Muḥammad in 41: 6, Hūd in 11: 3 and 52, Shu'aib in 11: 90, and Noah in 71: 10. God, says 3: 135, loves 'those who having committed evil and wronged their own souls, remember God and seek forgiveness for their wrong doings. For who shall forgive sins but God?' But they must abandon the things they know to be evil. Forgiveness-seekers always find God merciful, declares Surah 4: 110. Surah 8: 33 lays down the principle that as long as men sought forgiveness God did not requite their transgressions.

Numerous passages describe the prophets asking forgiveness on behalf of others, Abraham in 19: 48 (cf. 60: 4) for his father and his family, Jacob for his sons responding to their request (12: 98), and Muḥammad, who in 3: 159 is commended for an act of gentleness which he is to follow up by *istighfār* for the same persons who, otherwise, would have been lost to him. Angels around the throne of God are likewise forgiveness-seekers in the name of men who believe (40: 7 and 42: 5).

But no such concern for penitence in others can avail without the response of their own repentance. Mere nearness of kinship affords no vicarious righteousness. Where men persist in unbelief, be they the closest relatives, *istighfār* for them is forbidden (9: 113). Though it were attempted seventy times, it would be pointless as long as men deny faith and go on in evil (9: 80). There is no power in external relationships to reverse evil and turn men to truth without the inward turning of the will itself where the wrong belongs. The battle for the good in the world must be won in the heart. Thus Surah 63: 6 f. indicates that the Prophet's asking forgiveness would be immaterial, one way or the other, in respect of evil-doers who, in this case, are themselves contemptuous anyway of the whole matter.

In circumstances that present this kind of impasse between the claim of repentance and the obduracy of evil, *istighfār* becomes almost an act of dissociation from those with whom the wrong is identified. The theme, as we will argue later, carries us deeper than this, as the witness to good cannot *merely* repudiate the evil and maintain its own integrity. The responsibility must be perpetual. For if the good assumes an indifference to wrong, even though it be for its own protection, it fails its own antiseptic duty in the world. For 'there is no discharge in that war'. Nevertheless, as part of the courage and the resources of its own conviction, the good must hold to a steady disavowal of the false, and this sense comes to attach to *istighfār*.

Thus in 4: 105–107, the passage, after noting that God has sent down the book by which judgement may be determined between people, continues:

> 'So do not take the side of traitors: seek God's forgiveness: surely God is forgiving and merciful. You shall not plead the cause of these who betray themselves.'

The second directive there can hardly be read as having the deceivers for its object, since the disowning of them is so explicit. It can only mean an act of conscious repair to God against them, a kind of spiritual shudder in the presence of enormity, an instinctive turning to that which is holy where the unholy is so oppressively close, as some medieval Christian would cross himself at the mention of the devil.

Deferring a larger possibility of exegesis here, it is useful to note that a context such as this gives rise to the view that *istighfār* means 'to seek protection', rather than 'to ask forgiveness'. It has been suggested frequently within Islam, not least in modern commentary, that the sense is often protective and prospective, an invocation, as it were, about possible, future wrong-doing rather than actual, present culpability. To a considerable degree controversies about partiarchal or prophetic sinlessness have contributed to this desire to avoid the implications of guilt that are inseparable from the direct sense of *istighfār*. The several passages we have reviewed, and parallel ones, seem, however, to concern real occasions of wrong and temptation and to concern them so deeply that attempts to reduce the meaning from pardon to protection quite unwarrantably distort or diminish the sense. Nor are such efforts seriously or sensibly assisted by claiming for the root verb *ghafara* the meaning of 'to cover' with the force of protection ahead, rather than of 'hiding' evil done by remission present. Forgiveness, in the Qur'ān, can only be rightly seen as forestalling or thwarting potential wrong, as a consequence of, and in fullest duty to, its actual pardon and defeat.

The aura of commendation and almost of benediction does, nevertheless, attach in certain cases to the phrase *istaghfir lahum*—'ask forgiveness for them' as a kind of solicitude for the morrow. Thus in 24: 62 there is a directive about Muslims in the Prophet's entourage asking his permission to depart for private business, which runs: 'Give leave to them as you [i.e. Muḥammad] please and ask God's forgiveness for them. Surely God is forgiving and merciful.' Here there is no wrong or evil in view or at stake: the phrase plainly has to do with a general amity and goodwill expressed in term's of God's forgiveness, as perhaps also a kind of assurance for their well-being in absence, against anticipated temptations or possible dangers. But the usage in this manner is rare. It would, of course, be quite inappropriate in such cases as Potiphar's wife in her guilt over Joseph (12: 29) or David in his 'great offence' (38: 24). The prospective, as well as the retrospective, sense may well be intended in 60: 12, where the Muslim women who have made full allegiance and undertaken the whole moral obligations of belief are the subject of a directive to Muḥammad to 'seek the forgiveness of God' for them. The reader may understand an inclusive pardon for what they have been, or an invocation over what they are and shall be. It is, in any event, unnecessary to try to isolate the two intentions. It may likewise be the same double possibility we should understand in 48: 19, where the nomads ask Muḥammad to 'ask forgiveness' on their behalf in respect of their failure to join in battle in the cause of Islam. Was it genuine pardon they sought, or reinstatement in favour? Either way, their insincerity disqualified their plea.

Perspective requires that the derivative meaning of *istighfār* as protective conferment should be noted, so long as it is allowed to be derivative. It is the sort of interpretation which could neither obtain, nor develop, without the primary and dominant meaning. The latter belongs deeply in the very texture of the Qur'ān and relates to all the duties of Islam. In the concluding verse of Surah 73 Quranic recitation, prayer and alms are together sealed with the exhortation: 'Ask the forgiveness of God.'

Perhaps the most telling passage of all is 2: 198, where the context is pilgrimage to Mecca and the directives have to do with right Muslim behaviour in ritual acts and ceremonies the traditions of which lay deep in earlier paganism. After certain practical matters about provender and attitudes to trading, pilgrims are bidden to 'remember God at the sacred waymark (*al-mash'ar al ḥarām*)' as they 'move forward *en masse* from 'Arafāt'. *Afaḍtum*, the verb here, has the sense of speed or urgency. Some translations read: 'pour forth', 'press on', 'run swiftly', or 'come running'. But it combines with these the idea of multitude and throng. The picture here is that of a tide of humanity straining forward in the accomplishment of pilgrimage. The next verse repeats the verb in the imperative (*afīḍū*). 'Hasten forward where the people hasten forward . . .' or, more prosaically, 'Go out from the place whence the people go out'. Then it adds: 'And seek God's forgiveness; for He is forgiving and merciful.' There are points of topography and history here over which we need not linger. One suggestion is that the Quraish desisted from the pilgrimage before reaching 'Arafāt in a gesture of superiority over others. The 'standing before God', as the phrase goes, in the great plain of 'Arafāt marks the furthest point outward from Mecca that the pilgrims reach. It concludes with their great and ardent surge back to Al-Muzdalīfah, prior to the 'stoning' in repudiation of the devil.

Beyond these details of the matter which cannot be readily assured in the minutiae of exegesis, there lies without doubt an intense religious climax and it is this the command for *istighfār* concerns. Here are all the elements of religious fervour—pride of identity, crowds, expectancy, emotion, the momentum of ceremonies and the flush of action, all heightened by nocturnal vigilance and collective zeal, and, in many cases, achieving the ambition of a life-time, the supreme prospect soon to become the proudest retrospect of one's existence. All this has to be covered by an inclusive plea of forgiveness, habitual no doubt and in its simplicity familiar, yet potentially assuming, in this context, the most profound significance. If it is necessary to be forgiven where one is most devout, penitent where one is most proud, accusatory where one is most 'religious', are we not, by that very token, close to the heart of the divine Lordship? Such are the temptations of the religious institution, of whatever allegiance, that we are never in greater danger of evading God than when we traditionally approach Him, and that even our service, public, orthodox and proper by the criteria we assume, may be no more than the admiration of ourselves.

The prosaic critic will insist that to reflect in this way is to take the passage too finely, that the *istighfār* here can bear no such relevance, since it is normal, even perfunctory, a piece of common parlance saying no more than a general caution. At a ritual high-point, one must be watchful and duly solemnized. As with a taboo, there is need of protection and alertness. One has to tread circumspectly in the holy place and invoke a divine insurance over one's performance of the rite.

But this, though in some eyes and on one level it may be realist, is to miss the deeper meaning behind that very sense of a situation fraught with special quality. The feeling of the awesome, where it would be wise to incur no risks, where the holy is also unpredictably hazardous, as supersitition supposes, is no more than the crude and vulgar fashion of an encounter with power and with glory—the encounter which Islam finds in the sanctity of pilgrimage in the larger framework of the Quranic faith. The 'seeking of forgiveness' cannot there be read aright except in the whole context of revelation, law and mercy. These lift the dim and calculating apprehensions of the pagan into the full measure of moral responsibility and religious reverence, where what a man is before God, in the conscious transactions of ritual and beside its hallowed 'waymarks', takes in the essential criticism of himself. Such ultimate criticism learns to ask forgiveness, in the presence of the religious climax, not to ensure against the vagaries of the mystery but to acknowledge the certainties of the revelation. Of these none is more certain than the claim of 'the majesty of high' and in its light the grandeur and the misery of being human, the high calling and the tragic reproach. It is faith in God which has the largest criteria of human judgement and so the furthest measure of what forgiveness means and so, in turn, the greatest need of it.

'Seek forgiveness', then, may be rightly claimed as one of the most elemental precepts of the Qur'ān and a pointed theme in its contemporary study, both as a direct imperative to each and a constant posture about all. 'Ask it for yourself,' says the book, 'ask it for others.' The precept is inseparable from consistent conviction about divine sovereignty. What denies or defies the divine will must be identified for its real character, forsaken within oneself and disavowed outside oneself. Repentance is the only proper temper of the acknowledgement of God, whether a private penitence that foreswears the evil of its own, or a public sense of wrong about the world that strives also for the penitence of others. These are the twin directions of the Quranic *istighfār*.

This is the clue to the only effective honesty about evil. It is the will, as we saw, for example, in discussing 4: 105–107, to dissociate from wrong, by personal confession, by the urge to be forgiven made social in the world. But confession within and dissociation without, though properly mutual, are liable also to be in paradoxical relation. For while repentance detaches me inwardly from responsibility for evil, it cannot of itself undo the entail of my part in it. Nor can I make private the evil of which I repent. The separation from it which my penitence affirms and, in measure achieves, remains only an interior salvation as long as its social wastage and tyranny persist. The paradox deepens with the realization that repentance in one quarter may be the very occasion of hardness of heart elsewhere. Evil thwarted or defeated in one sector intensifies in another. Thus, by my repentance, with its inward liberation or 'justification', I am the more deeply involved in the tensions and conflicts of the wrong around me. The dissociation I will to have from evil takes me into it more deeply, not, now, thanks to my repentance, as an abettor or participant, but, thanks to my new will for goodness, as one who cares and struggles and means to redeem. We will occupy the rest of this chapter with the reflections to which this leads, to prepare the way, as they must, for the theme of the divine recognition in Chapter 8.

When we begin to seek forgiveness we discover that the need to do so enlarges. Begin to think penitently and the range of reproach widens. Break away, in personal evils, from callousness of spirit, and the resulting sensitivity perceives liabilities it cannot delimit or foreclose. The desire to be forgiven, even within a private world, learns to look questioningly at what it customarily thought were areas of innocence. 'Seeking forgiveness' requires for its sincerity an open-ended will. It were more prudent to refrain from any *istighfār*, if we are unready it should grow upon us to include the world.[1] Is it not precisely for this reason that it is so insistently a command?

Istighfār, we may say, is essentially a desire not to side with evil. It is a will to extrication from the sinfulness of life, from the reality of a guilt we acknowledge. As such, it avails in the mercy of God. For He is *ghafūr* and *ghaffār*, forgiving and Forgiver. But, in other senses, the extrication cannot happen. We are inextricably part and parcel of the world that does the wrong, lives by it and approves it. By our very penitence as seekers of exoneration, we confess a conscience. But it is a conscience which, therefore, cannot stay content

[1] It is almost, in a much deeper key, what W. H. Auden sees to be the business of the novelist who cannot describe unless he participates.

'For to achieve his lightest wish he must
Become the whole of boredom, subject to
Vulgar complaints like love . . .
. . . among the filthy, filthy too
And in his own weak person if he can
Must suffer dully all the wrongs of man.'

For 'dully' read 'deeply'. How much less can we care and aspire, as penitence does, unless we participate and 'become the whole of' man?

with a righting of evil that is only retrospective and particular to ourselves alone. Just by wanting to be forgiven, we are the more quickened to register the evil that persists. We are the more aware that the collectives of which we are part are still impenitent, still unwanting of forgiveness and chronically unforgiving—nations, for example, profits, interests, passions and powers of every kind, political, economic, cultural and even religious.[1]

So there is no innocence: only an inward pardon for what we can effectively confess and an outward duty to serve and quicken such wider *istighfār* as may be in our power about the larger evils and the stronger demonisms of our society. In that duty, we must not allow a private 'peace with God' to confuse or stay the task of caring for the peace with Him of the world around.[2] For such moral apathy would mean a death of the heart within us and the forgiveness it sought would be an empty thing. *Istighfār* cannot rightly live with indifference to evils it does not choose to know or understand. The forgiveness it asks is not an escapist release into an irresponsible existence. In the world of the oppressed and the embittered, of the exploited and the broken, there can be no private salvations.

Right as it is, then, to seek our own forgiveness, the will for it leaves us squarely with the evil things we disown in asking it. Penitence has to be the more, not the less, alert to the tangles of society and alive to the ubiquitous ways of human selfishness. It needs to resist the instinct to find innocence in the fact that evil may often be diffused so widely as to be nobody's responsibility. For blame that is everywhere can readily be said to be nowhere. Or the effort to trace the ramifications of ill-doing leads to an inconclusive jungle where nothing decisive can be incriminated.[3] Or, again, the complex is so bewildering, the guilt so elusive, that there is always a shelter in the crowd, an

[1] The theme of conscience and the collective character of wrong have been imaginatively treated by Muḥammad Kāmil Ḥusain, in *City of Wrong*, Cairo, 1952: English translation, by the present author, Amsterdam, 1959. Dr Ḥusain explores the Quranic concept of *ẓulm* and *istighfăr* and the dilemmas of private conscience *vis-à-vis* the vested evils of society and 'establishment'.

[2] One may compare James Baldwin's devastating comment. 'Your grandfather . . . was defeated long before he died. . . . This is one of the reasons why he became so holy', *The Fire Next Time*, New York, 1963, p. 15. Piety, here, equals capitulation and saintliness is taken to be the guise of timidity.

[3] As, for example, in John Steinbeck, *The Grapes of Wrath*, New York, 1939, where the passionate search for the thing to be blamed leads only to a brass plate on a bank wall.

extenuation in the mass. Or there are always external expediencies we can invoke to justify ourselves.

All these evasions the meaning of *istighfār* forbids. It makes us to know that though egoisms may be socially diffused or economically approved, they are none the less our own. To leave them unquestioned is to let them gather greater condemnation. The sense of the judgement of God is the first condition of their correction and the only safety from their menace. It is thus that asking forgiveness is the one security from the distortions and disguises by which we justify ourselves, and from the excusing and the accusing of partisan opinion.

Lest this posture of spirit should be thought a morbid or a pessimistic thing, it is well to insist on the inherent hopefulness of such thoroughgoing *istighfār*. The seriousness of evil from which it proceeds is only the other side of the blessedness of life. Where evil is minimized, life itself is devalued. Unless sin matters, nothing matters. We do not fully esteem, except we deeply reproach, ourselves. Seeking forgiveness is not some dispirited gesture. It is the vivid cognizance of how surely and mercifully God reigns. If we know no condemnation, we have no destiny. 'Be merciful to me, a sinner', is the only language that joins honesty and hope.

Just as dishonesty here tends towards a final despair. Not to face ourselves as truth and mercy find us is to dismiss the dimension of forgiveness from our future as well as from our past. To let penitence die is to die within ourselves. It is to take what the psalmist called 'the way of the ungodly', which descends from 'consenting' to 'frequenting' and ends in 'the seat of the scornful'. Antisepsis ceases and contagion wins. From the absence to the atrophy of the will to be forgiven, man moves towards the disowning of himself. The Qur'ān, in its graphic way here, describes what we may call the efficient parts of man bearing witness, in the end, against his final personality, against the will that made them serve those purposes. It sees the limbs and members of a man, his feet and hands and tongue, accusing his biography, telling in dismay the things he had them do (24: 24, 36: 65).

'Who then shall blame
His pester'd senses to recoil and start,
When all that is within him does condemn
Itself for being there?'[1]

[1] William Shakespeare, *Macbeth*, Act 5, Scene 2, lines 22–25.

Or, in the different idiom of 17: 14: 'Read your book. Your own soul is enough this day as a reckoner against you.' The passage, after the Semitic manner, ignores the intermediate factors and fastens on the final issue as if it had always been there—'the bird of omen tied about his neck' (17: 13). But the inevitable is not so till the end. Otherwise *istaghfir* could have no place. 'Will you not turn and ask forgiveness?' (5: 74) is the constant option of the living. The finality of the last things, as the Qur'ān sees them, is consistent with the conditional character of all mortal existence.

The call *istaghfir-Allāh* is therefore the present sense of the ultimate claim. The force and urgency of the Quranic picture of the mortal verdict at the grand assize belong antecedently with daily life. 'Only our concept of time', wrote Franz Kafka, 'makes it possible for us to speak of the day of judgement by that name: in reality it is a summary court in perpetual session'.[1] The evil which it arraigns reaches beyond ourselves, beyond the social order, into the ultimate reckoning of the rule of God. It is undone, therefore, not in a mere psychic therapy designed to restore some mental poise, nor in apology to a human neighbour, nor in the re-assertion of a law by which society is satisfied. It is fully answered only where it is fully measured—in the forgiveness of God. Where there are no more alibis to plead and all evasions fall away, there the mercy of God is fully known.

Our final study, then, must be the Quaranic sense of *Raḥmah* in God, the quality of mercy responsive to man's forgiveness-seeking. The term, in all its derivatives, is fundamental. It is best studied in the setting of the *Bismillāh*, or divine invocation, which prefaces each Surah of the book (save, for no significant reason, Surah 9): 'In the name of *Al-Raḥmān al-Raḥīm*'. These two derivatives of the R Ḥ M root can be understood in a progressive, rather than a merely repetitive, sense. *Al-Raḥmān* denotes the divine 'property' of mercy, the abiding 'quality' within all the divine activity, while *Al-Raḥīm* has to do with the operative expression manward of the nature of *Al-Raḥmān*. There is that by which God is merciful in Himself and that by which He is proved to be merciful in our experience. There is, we might almost say, the music's musician and the musician's music: the one is a 'who', the other is a 'how'. Mercy *does* (*Al-Raḥīm*) as mercy

[1] Quoted from 'The Notebook of Franz Kafka,' by Philip Rahv, *Literature and the Sixth Sense*, London, 1970, p. 185.

is (*Al-Raḥmān*).[1] Or, conversely, that which we may believe of the divine nature is that of which we are aware in the divine dealings.

That sequence, however, in Quranic understanding, must always be thought of as a prerogative wholly within the divine will. 'God particularizes (*yakhtaṣṣu*) with his mercy whom He wills' (2: 105). Part of the thrust in the concept of forgiveness-*seeking* is that the divine response is in no way pledged. Man has no viable claims on the divine. The transcendent remains in sovereign decisiveness. Omnipotence has not brought the bestowal of mercy within any humanly assured pattern of action, or redemption, or grace, where men could dependably look for heavenly transactions of pardon responsively to their penitence and faith. Prerogative taking counsel only with itself has ever been the characteristic Islamic understanding of divine mercy and *istighfār* must always be seen in those terms. 'He makes whom He wills enter into his mercy' (42: 8, 48: 25 and 76: 31).

Nevertheless, these and kindred passages, of great frequency, are always closely associated with moral issues and religious criteria. As Surah 7: 156 has it: 'My mercy embraces (co-extends over) all things', and the sequel assures the faith-keeping, alms-doing, truth-serving people that mercy is 'prescribed' for them. This striking phrase, echoed in 6: 12 and 54 (*kataba 'alā nafsihi al-raḥmah*: 'He has [lit.] set down for Himself mercy'), does not violate the sovereignty in its untrammelled quality but goes far to characterize the framework of its operation.[2] The will to be forgiven, corroborated by the evidences of a Godward piety and a manward sincerity, stands—albeit without assurance—on hopeful ground.

The 'rule of mercy', if we may so translate the 'setting down for Himself mercy' passages, is certainly evident in the awesome providences of external nature. These, indeed, are the immediate context of the phrase in 6: 12: 'To whom belongs all that is, in the heavens and the earth? Say: "It is God's."' The natural order is the first realm and the constant parable of the divine *Raḥmah*. The fact of revelation,

[1] Simple distinctions are made by the classic commentators by which the one term refers to heavenly mercies and the other the earthly, or mercies extended in nature to both believers and unbelievers and mercies relating to believers alone. But these are conjectural and it seems best to argue, as here, a sense-progression that fits both the word forms and the theological situation.

[2] See the analysis in full in Daud Rahbar, *God of Justice, A Study in the Ethical Doctrine of the Qur'ān*, Leiden, 1960, pp. 158–71. He is ready to translate 6: 12 and 54 with the phrase '. . . imposed mercy on Himself'.

the gift to humanity of messengers and mentors and prophets, is the other vital mercy. Both nature and history, religiously apprehended, teach the *Bismillāh*, the invocation of their 'merciful Lord'. It could, therefore, be said that the forgiveness-seeking of Islam is the steady counterpart of its adoration. For God is named in praise as He must be named in penitence. The double root of the divine address has within it the double sense of the human response. The glory and the hope meet in the same vocabulary.

We conclude with a reflection on a rare Quaranic comparison of mercy in this context. God is described 23: 109 and 118 as *khair al-rāḥimīn*, 'the best of the merciful', and in 7: 151, 12: 64, 12: 92 and 21: 83 as *arḥam al-rāḥimīn*, 'the most merciful of those who show mercy'. It is no doubt possible to translate in a sort of rhetorical sense that does not involve any comparing.[1] Yet there is a profound theological reason for not doing so—a reason which the grammar certainly sustains.

The thought of any analogy between a divine forgiving and a human has generally been a matter of extreme reluctance to the Muslim mind.[2] Al-Baiḍāwī comments succinctly on 7: 151, 'You are more merciful with us than we are on ourselves', and on 21: 83 he remarks that Job described his Lord as having the utmost mercy, when he recalled his own duty and the sequel to his fortitude. But, with and beyond these descriptive superlatives, is it not possible to understand the comparative form more tellingly? The force of the construction *khair al* . . . suggests 'the good of . . .' or 'the quintessence of. . . .' Men, in the practice of compassion or the exercise of mercy, reflect in their behaviour that in which God surpasses and excels. Comparison, indeed, is impossible. But affinity remains. To speak of God as 'the most merciful of those who show mercy' is to allow that there is an inter-human quality fit to be analogous with the transcendental—and not only fit, but also called, to be. The *khair* of anything is where the inherent benediction of it comes to fullest flower, to richest form. It is the ultimate which both rates and draws out the lower levels—but only within the common theme.

[1] As, for example, does 'Abdul-Laṭīf in 7: 151. *Al-Qur'ān*, Hyderabad, 1969, p. 127. 'And who is there who can show the mercy that Thou alone canst show?'

[2] One might cite the issue sometimes aroused over the clause in the Lord's Prayer, 'Forgive us . . . as we forgive. . . .' This is often read by Muslims 'proportioning' divine forgiveness to the human (rather than the affinity between being forgiven and forgiving) and thus rejected by them as a poor and quite inappropriate parallel.

If this reading is sustained, as one which there is ample ground to state, then it clearly bears strongly on the scope of *istighfār*, as we have already measured it. A compassionate society lives by the conviction of a rule of mercy. Unless there can be penitence there cannot be hope. Penitence is futile unless there can be pardon. For Quranic religion both penitence and pardon belong with the submission of man to the sovereignty of God. From that transcendental relation they draw their meaning and must have their authority in the human world. In the heat and urgency of the first Islamic encounter with the human scene, compassion was very closely tied to the exigencies of the conflict of the faith itself. Good will moved with right faith and discriminated according to its own *jihād*. Belief was a prerequisite of obligation. Yet, even so, and for present thinking, the mandate of mercy abides—of mercy needed, mercy sought, mercy practised, and mercy eternally enthroned. It would be right to see in the *Bismillāh* and in *istighfār*, so pondered, the surest word of Islam to contemporary history.

If so, how apposite it is. For to take as sacred or to find absurd would seem to be the human alternatives about the present world. Existing itself is somehow, as it were, an act of faith, an acceptance of liability, a necessity for decision. If we opt for evasiveness we have given a verdict about what we evade. If we choose to circumscribe our liability in personal exemptions,[1] we acknowledge what we do not undertake. If, contrariwise, we wish our existing to be fully open to its whole nature, we are at once involved in the whole bewildering manifold which baffles intelligence and 'puzzles the will'. In that complex of things, political, scientific, social, racial, moral, religious—potential, passionate, or perverse—there is at least a way in, if not a way through. It is identified, prior to all 'solutions' and even without them, by the clue of compassion, by the sense of a mercy needed and given, by the will to forgive and be forgiven. By these we may set the compass of relationship. The realist will say that this returns us to the gnawing problems of institutions, structures, societies, ideologies, establishments and revolutions. To be sure, it does. Yet these peren-

[1] In the sense, for example, of the remark of André Gide about the characters in Henry James's novels that 'they never seem to exist except in relation to each other'. (One might say the same of Jane Austen's.) It is the evident incompleteness of such islands of privacy which should give us pause when we are told that 'God is known only in personal relations'. There are, after all, the stars, the centuries, the poets, the mosques, the cathedrals, the nations, of history.

nial areas of our confusion, our strife and our experiment, will more likely yield the approximate answers of which they are capable, if the primacy of compassion is heard in the flux of their argument.

For only so are the protests that generate the dynamic against the static saved from the absolutizing of their own demands. Modern history has seen so much of the revolt that has become a new tyranny, of the emancipators who bring a fresh enslavement, made the more total by their impetus of initial indignation. This is the place to set the sense of *istighfār*. It is passionately to identify evil by the clues of inhumanity, but never, so doing, to assume the exoneration of the will that does so. Every outward indictment has an inward liability, if not to present blame, then at least to present temptation. 'Be ye angry and sin not.' To accuse alienation is to seek forgiveness for it. Every prosecution of evil has to have 'the quality of mercy'. If we are moved to say with William Styron: 'We'll bring back tragedy to the land of the Pepsi Cola . . . something to clean out their tiny souls',[1] we may well be caring for a right cleansing of a self-debasing world, but only if we cherish mercy learned from the affronted God.

It is probably here that the deepest themes lie between Islam in its Quranic theism and the mind of the Marxist. For the latter proceeds, emotionally if not conceptually, from a cry of pain and anger at the human scene materially constituted. 'The opium of the people', in the famous phrase, was damnable, in Marx's view, as an anodyne. It was authentic as a symptom. It was the indictment of a total situation drugged by it—a situation which Marx proposed to remedy by economic diagnosis and correction, attacking the soporific as an enemy. He diagnosed religion as the ground of apathy only because he measured the pain and intended a cure. 'Religious distress', he wrote, in the same paragraph as the 'opium' conclusion,

> '. . . is at the same time the expression of real distress and the protest against real distress. Religion is the sigh of the oppressed creature, the heart of a heartless world. . . .'

'Thus', he continued, 'the criticism of heaven turns into the criticism of earth.'[2] In other words, the wrongness around them which men register when they pray—whether their prayer is for vindication, or

[1] In *Set This House on Fire*, New York, 1960, pp. 118–19.
[2] Karl Marx and F. Engels, *On Religion*, Moscow, 1957, p. 42.

respite, or compensation, or resignation—has to be laid at the door of the 'things' which breed and inflict it, and these things are susceptible of historical, economic correction. The 'heartlessness' being in this way removed—since it is a structural phenomenon in society—the 'heart' can settle down in unalienated satisfaction. The transcendent ceases to be necessary. The heart beats well under an empty heaven, because the earth is now well organized into classlessness and communism.

Perhaps, in its own way, this is the ultimate secularization, at least diagnostically, though it is corroborated by many forms of thought and conduct having contrasted theories of society and wealth. In its utopian naivety it forecloses the diagnosis of evil and thus betrays its own passionate emotion about wrongs that are seen to be violating man. In its own self-absolute methods and claims the heartlessness returns, whether in the total exigencies of party discipline, or the ruthlessness of state tyranny. Then its brusque dismissal of the religious dimension turns into a new dimension of ultimate blasphemy. From banishing thoughts of heaven as an incubus on urgent human struggle, it passes to banishing thoughts of earth as a brake on the movement of its own absolute dialectic. Neither the original impulse—for all its deep passion—nor the developed drive, reckons with the rule of mercy. That rule is, in the end, more realist than all the realists without it. 'The criticism of earth' stands accused before 'the criticism from heaven', in the sense that historical frustrations prove again transcendent obligations. The appeal to the human emerges as the claim of the divine.

It may be significant in this connection that some recent Marxist thinking, in dialogue with theism, has understood its task in the historical order as 'this exigency in man . . . a never satisfied exigency of totality and absoluteness . . . This future, open on the infinite, is the only transcendent known to us atheists. . . . We do not name it God.'[1] Do we not read here a sort of 'accusation' of the human order in its actuality, a will so far discontent with the world as to be dedicated to changing it radically? It could not be described as a will to be forgiven, or to be forgiving, since these are not its categories. Yet it is a vast responsibility *vis-à-vis* the world, a responsibility based on human dimensions, stirred by human alienation, and sustained by

[1] Roger Garaudy, *From Anathema to Dialogue: The Challenge of Marxist-Christian Co-operation*, London, 1967, pp. 82 and 83.

human surrender to categorical obligation. It is, in those ways, a sort of active *istighfār*, a will to liability about mankind, in a *de facto* (but in no way *de jure*) acceptance of transcendent reference. It is 'religious', as it were, *qua* programme, not *qua* conviction. As such, a theist, as the Muslim is, must come to terms both with its sincerity and its incompleteness.

'The thing that defines atheism', Roger Garaudy declares, 'is the reducing of the religious fact to the human.'[1] What 'believers' call transcendence is simply authentic humanity. Everything turns then on the reach and nature of the humanly authentic. For the Muslim it is rightly, solely, 'under God'. But that submission speaks the language of a penitence *before* God *about* the human—the human one, and the human many. And this is *istighfār*, the invocation of the merciful Name.

'To forge in the smithy of my soul the uncreated conscience of my race', was the final resolve of James Joyce's figure for himself at the end of *A Portrait of the Artist as a Young Man.*[2] The novel's meaning is elusive and the author's self-exile a strange shape for his vocation. Yet even so, it comes near to expressing what the seeking of forgiveness deeply means—the sense of corporate and personal wrong demanding to be righted into truth.

The condition of that situation is a constant alertness. For the acquiescences that thwart it or dissolve it are so easy. The will to exoneration, the impulse to indifference, the logic of despair, are all so ready and so plausible. There is an imperceptibility about the encroachments of ill-will. In assuming what we think we are, we fail to register what we have in fact become. In his poem 'The Good Town', Edwin Muir imagines a 'decent' community musing over war and desolation in the world and asking:

> 'Could it have come from us? Was our peace peace,
> Our goodness goodness? That old life was easy
> And kind and comfortable: but evil is restless . . .
> How could our town grow wicked in a moment? . . .
> And we, poor, ordinary, neutral stuff . . .
> . . . we have seen

[1] Roger Garaudy, *From Anathema to Dialogue: The Challenge of Marxist-Christian Co-operation*, London, 1967, p. 95.

[2] James Joyce, *Portrait of the Artist as a Young Man*, definitive edition, London, 1968, p. 257.

Good men made evil wrangling with the evil,
Straight minds grown crooked fighting crooked minds . . .
Look at it well. This was the good town once.'[1]

It may be that forgiveness is the major theme in history and the will to it the largest proof of man.

[1] *Collected Poems of Edwin Muir*, London, 1963, pp. 186–7.

Chapter 8
'NO GOD BUT THOU'

Atheism, it may be said, is no theme for theologians. For it denies that there is a subject to discuss. But atheists are certainly their responsibility. They at least exist and their disavowal of God involves discussion with a subject. The issue ceases then to be an academic denial and concerns a particular decision, namely that of concluding the unreality of God. The negation may take place for a variety of factors —a loss of nerve, a protest of rebellion, a distrust of mind, or an indifference of will. The casual forms, it often seems, are more prevalent than the argumentative. It is in existing, rather than in debating, that the atheism really happens, and it is in a whole worship, not in a bare assent, that theism, such as that of the Qur'ān, truly lives and belongs.

We have come to this central question of God in the Islamic Scripture through the human themes of the two preceding chapters for a deliberate reason. It is that the Yes! or No! about God are always and everywhere decisions about man. The divine recognition, or its voidance, are a human choice. They turn on conclusions, implicit or explicit, about ourselves. The doctrine of God is a corollary, or a casualty—as the case may be—of the account of man.

The point of beginning this way in study of the Quranic understanding of God may be developed by help of a glance at a mood of modern, existential thinking as found in Jean-Paul Sartre. He carefully defines his view as

> '. . . not atheist in the sense that it would exhaust itself in demonstrations of the non-existence of God. It declares itself rather that if God existed it would make no difference from its point of view.'

That point of view depends, quite evidently, on a conviction about the self, as being itself, only in independence of God. The closed-to-God here is locked within a view of the human. 'Nothing', Sartre adds, 'can save a man from himself, not even a valid proof of the existence of God.'[1] Intelligent theism has never supposed that it could. For it is not the proof, but the relationship, which is decisive, and truly saves the man. Sartre is no doubt contending for the inalienable nature of human experience and for the fact that there is no arbitrary or external answer to the crisis within our being. So far so good. But he is doing so only by excluding what, for others, belongs with the same selfhood. That mere argument is superfluous and inward integrity imperative are proper principles. But, outside his point of view, they are not necessarily God-excluding factors.

Theism and atheism, then, are decisions by men and about man. The redundancy of the divine, if such it be, is proclaimed by an atheist interpretation of the human. A self-awareness in which there is no place for an awareness of God is understood to be the only properly human posture. What is believed about the self determines what is disbelieved as to God.

Quranic theism is emphatically the other way round. It stands in a conviction about the reality of God as giving meaning and existence to man. The first half of the Creed, or *Shahādah*, is the formal expression of the faith: 'There is no god but God . . .' But it becomes a more intimate confession when we pass from the proposition 'There is no god but He' (especially 2: 163). to the adoration 'There is no god but Thou' (21: 87) with the reciprocating 'Truly I am God, there is no god save Me: then worship Me and be at prayer in My remembrance' (20: 14, cf. 16: 2 and 21: 25).[2] The sense of God is overwhelming and 'makes' the Qur'ān, as it 'made' the vocation of Muḥammad.

This imperious theism we mean to link here sensitively with the modern instincts of doubt and disinterest. Hence this form of prelude to the study. For only so can we be realistic about a contemporary Qur'ān. Uncompromising and forthright as it is in its theology, Islam in the Qur'ān makes the faith about God a theme within man, as radically as any modern thinking. The difference between its jealousy

[1] In *Existentialism and Humanism*, London, 1948, p. 56. Translated from the French by Philip Mairet.

[2] 'No god but He' occurs twenty-seven times in all. In 20: 14 'Be at prayer in my remembrance' seems to be the best translation of what might be rendered: 'Perform the ritual prayer with mention of Me.'

for a true worship, and the current loss of one, has to do with the authority of the answers not with the human context of the questions.

Its steadfast affirmation of the divine, and its summons to due worship and religion, are most truly seen as a battle over men, between men, and about their humanity. Hence, of course, the powerfully corporate and, ultimately, the political, form the witness took. Like the earlier Scriptures, the Qur'ān takes God as utterly real and, therefore, in no necessary relation to 'proof', but in urgent relation to recognition.[1] He *ought* to be worshipped. The whole urgency of the book is to require and achieve the human confession of God as vital to being human. This is the ground of the constant anathema against idolatry. The human situation is bound in a proper order under God, yet free for its own frustration in the undoing which overtakes every false absolute. The Qur'ān sees man as disowning his true being in refusing the divine sovereignty. The crisis of the alternative lies within the determination of men.

A recurrent phrase on which we may well let exposition turn is the words '. . . God apart', or '. . . . to the exclusion of God'. The Arabic *min dūni-llāhi* occurs some thirty times and an even larger number with the pronoun denoting God. It is also found with *Al-Raḥmān. Min dūni* has a connotation varying in intensity and may simply mean acting or thinking in unawareness of God. But it also sharpens into wilful neglect or unconcern. In all senses whether casual or deliberate, it could be translated '. . . . to the exclusion of God'.

That very flexibility is fitting to our discussion. For current non-acknowledgement of God ranges all the way from a mere unexamined indifference to an insistent or militant repudiation, just as, conversely, there are theists of mild, of arduous and of combatant mind. In the Qur'ān the words *min dūni-llāhi* describe that state of human unrelatedness of mind or will towards God, whether calculated or ignorant, which was the dominant burden of Muḥammad's mission and of the Quranic word. Was the book not *al-Dhikr*, the great 'reminder' of men? (Cf. Surah 38: 1 and 7; 41: 41; see also 15: 6 and 10; 16: 45 and 68: 51.)

The prevailing sense of 'the exclusion of God' has to do with pagan idolatry and the plural worships of seventh-century Arabia. These

[1] The word 'necessary' here has a certain ambiguity. Islamic theology, it is true, sees the divine as totally independent of the human response. But speaking, as we now are, within the human world Islam would certainly say: 'God must needs be worshipped.'

were the *shirk*, or polytheism, against which the whole preaching and enterprise of Islam were directed, on behalf of that *Tauḥīd*, or acknowledgement of the divine unity, which was its goal, both in creed and practice. The emphasis throughout, to borrow from the Decalogue, is on '*having* other gods'. Oddly perhaps, the Qur'ān has very little mention of literal idols. The words one might expect in that connection come only seldom. *Anṣāb* (idols) comes in 5: 90 among 'abominations' which, as 'Satan's work', are to be shunned. An alternative plural, *nuṣub*, occurs in 5: 3, in a passage about idol meats. Four idols invoked at ritual slaughter are named in 5: 105 and three goddesses in a controversial context in 53: 19 f. *Tamāthīl* (images) comes in 21: 52, where Abraham interrogates his father and family and disowns their habits of veneration. The word is found again in 34: 13 only, where *tamāthīl* are made for Solomon from copper, and no prohibition is stated or implied, though the workmanship is a topic of admiration and grateful delight. Another term for idols (*aṣnām*) occurs in five passages (6: 74, 7: 138, 14: 35, 21: 57 and 26: 71). In each case there is a clear repudiation made by Abraham.

But if the specific mention of this or that idol is rare, there is no doubting the urgent case against what we may call the actual pluralism of the tribal world of the Qur'ān. Its concern is with the real displacement of God in the emotions, the imagination, the reliance, of men. This lies at a deeper level than particular shrines and their outward demolition. It is a struggle with superstition and animism in their active power in the heart and in society. What matters is not simply the different gods but the indifferent humans. In that sense, the *Shahādah* itself, 'There is no god but God', is not simply a proposition that negates but a disqualification that unifies. It does not proclaim itself as an idea but as a veto and a liberation.

This is the main point of the *min dūni–llāhi* verses. They decry pluralism as making a chaos both of phenomena and of society. 'Had there been other gods there beside God', says 21: 22, 'the heavens and the earth would surely have been a chaos.' 'Without God', (*min dūni-llāhi*) 'you have neither protector nor helper.' (Cf. 2: 107, 4: 123 and 173, 9: 116, 29: 22, 33: 17, 42: 31.) The twin terms here *walī* and *naṣīr*, are variously translated as patron, guardian, sponsor, master, ally, guarantor and partner. The roots have to do with victory, friendship, fealty, the authority to prosper. Taken religiously they point to the responsible situation in which, reciprocally to the order of nature, man finds authority which gives attainment to his capacities. The cosmos allows and serves his ends and so entails the obligation to consecrate and hallow his creaturely dominion. This ordered relationship, both in its intelligent mastery and its final reverence, the idolater lacks. His world is disordered both in the confusion of his worships and the ignorance in his ways. He is thus in a sort of conspiracy against himself.

This is the state of having 'neither reliance nor aid', in which, as Surah 29: 22 tells the polytheists, 'you cannot, in earth and heaven, get away with it'.[1] Nor do they see through their own deception. They 'serve what neither benefits nor harms' (for example 10: 18, 13: 16, 21: 66, 22: 12 and 25: 55), in the sense that both their hopes and fears are awry. They are mistaken about the real fabric of life, both as to submission and as to mastery.

Perhaps it is just here that we move, however tenuously it might seem to some, from the world of pre-Islamic polytheism to the complex world of modern self-sufficiency. Paganism violates a right theology. But, so doing, it vitiates a right humanity. It is not properly the creature of the creation, either as to dignity or as to duty. In that sense it has 'neither reliance nor aid'. The irony is unmistakable in that phrase. For it was just 'reliance and aid' that were being sought in the pagan patterns. The sacralization of natural phenomena and resources, the taboos and sanctions in the thought-world of the deifiers, were all expressive of fear-conflicts. They spelled the self-insurances of tribes and causes and persons, and transcendentalized their besetting disorders. They demonized into obsessive competition the needs and passions of the mortal scene. As such they could not be dispelled or overcome by mere debating, but only by the liberating recognition: 'There is none save Thou.' 'Out upon you, you and your perversions. Do you not have minds to see?' (21: 67.)[2]

Contemporary demonism, it is true, is of a different kind. Man has 'reliance and aid' in incredible measure by dint of the organized

[1] The phrase is a favourite one. (Cf. 6: 134, 10: 53, 42: 31.) This translation of *mā antum bimuʿjizīn* is, of course, a colloquial one, but valid. The sense has to do with confounding, or disabling, an adversary, effectuating a superiority, getting one's way. The usual renderings are: 'You shall not escape in earth etc . . .' or: 'You are not able to frustrate . . .' with an object supplied.

[2] Again a preferable translation to the normal 'Fie!' or 'Shame!' *Uffin*, the initial word here, has the sense of the puff, or blast, of breath with which we remove what is annoying or disgusting to us. 'Out upon you', though a trifle Shakespearean, seems exact and right.

dependabilities of science. Through these he achieves self-help and self-reliance and is freed from pagan crudity. The pre-scientific pluralisms give way before a sure exploitation of the world. It is legitimate, with many recent Muslim writers, to see this technological competence as attaining, scientifically, what was latent in the religious theme of *Tauḥīd* or unity. For the sense of order upon which science rests and proceeds, which is indeed the core of its faith, derives from and grows with the sense of a single sovereignty such as Islam proclaimed.[1] The theology of a 'God who gives such power unto men' denies it to the plural divinizations of nature which the pagan mind assumes and, so doing, ensures it to liberated man. There is no doubt that the Quranic death to the idols contains the promise of the human science, however long delayed its historical realization. This fact, of course, is not diminished by the many extra-Islamic factors which contributed to the same end.

The Qur'ān itself, however, at least in the explicit, stays only with the religious rejection of the plural worships and does not formulate the claims of science. Even so, it has much to say about the dignity of knowledge and 'the use of the pen' (cf. Surah 96: 4). Its plea, 'Lord, increase me in knowledge'—the motto of the University of Kuwait (20: 114)—is apposite indeed in that place-symbol of applied techniques of man in nature. The context in 20: 114 is specifically religious and has to do with the Prophet's duty to await the Qur'ān's sequences patiently. But all its later implications may be said to lie within that first dimension, in the sense that a civilization like ours lives only in the desacralized order of nature where paganism, with its confused venerations, 'had neither reliance nor aid'.[2]

Yet the demonism persists in another and far more menacing sense. The very science which rides high on the amenability of nature to its will generates new idolatries more subtle than the old. It erects its very powers and structures into absolutes, into idols of the will. The strife within the old chaos of nature and of deities is replaced by the strife within the patterns of man's conquest. The seventh-century pagan was *min dūni-llāhi* because he had lost God in a welter of fears:

[1] This, of course, is a very different conviction from the pseudo-scientific anticipations of actual technology rejected in Chapter 5. The point is more fully made in Chapter 9 below.

[2] This debt of the scientific to the theological is not seldom forgotten. It was notably stated by the late Alfred North Whitehead in *Science in the Modern World*, Cambridge 1926, pp. 15–16.

the secular modern loses Him in a cosmos of pride and self-sufficiency. The one forfeited true humanity in a multiplicity of gods, the other puts it in jeopardy by an exclusion of God.

To think with the Qur'ān around this theme of man's secular isolation from the significance of the divine is to have at least one principle unmistakably clear. It is that we must be absolute for God alone, that all lesser loyalties be under divine submission. For, otherwise, all powers, wielded or suffered, are idolatries. To claim them or allow them is the most radical form of *shirk*, or deification of the false, which is, for the Qur'ān, man's cardinal temptation and his supreme sin. The call of Islam, within the modern crisis of man, is this for the right Lordship against all usurpation. 'There is no god but God.' The ultimate Lordship must be acknowledged ultimate. What is right in its place—science, race, nation, culture, power—is an idol in more than its place. If all these are to be rightly relative the final sovereignty must be effectively confessed. Only in such fidelity are all lesser fidelities secure. Only in such a sense of the divine, says the Qur'ān, can life be authentically human. For the perverse absolutes, the false gods, the modern idols, exact a forfeiture of the human meaning. Our liberties stand in our proper submission. This is the perennial relevance of the central imperative of Islam: 'Let God be God.' In its meaning the centuries, whether proud or primitive, fall into one perspective.

The reader finds it everywhere. Through all the vicissitudes of Muḥammad's mission this dominates and controls. It is the impulse in vocation and the imperative in preaching. The pattern of ritual prayer gives it personal, physical expression in the tribute of prostration, from which the believer must rise to erect posture and pursue his business in the world in its meaning.

> 'Say: "He alone is God,
> God the ever-adequate:
> He neither gives nor derives His being.
> Like to Him there is none." '[1]

The will to praise, which we pondered in Chapter 5, is simply the

[1] The Surah of Unity (112). The translation sees an apposition between line 2 and 3: *Al-Ṣamad*, used only here, means the One whose whole resources are within Himself. He is not like mortals in any chain of contingency, 'begetting and begotten'. Cf. Chapter 4 above.

music of this sense of the divine unity. All subsequent theology in Islam begins and ends in this *ikhlāṣ*, as the title of Surah 112 has it—this sincerity of unadulterated, uncompromised confession in which the purity of the truth of divine oneness finds true echo in the purity of the believer's word. All through, in Ezra Pound's vivid phrase, the concern, born of the Qur'ān, is to 'maintain antisepsis',[1] to keep at bay all disqualifying thoughts which might decry or obscure this *Tauḥīd*.

From what it believes God to be springs its demand about what man should be. He is *'abd*, or servant, to this sovereignty, subject under this Lordship. He must live and move ever in this transcendental obligation, careful for the right and only worship and vigilant against every pretension of idolatry. He must insistently relate all circumstance, all achievement, all intention, to this heavenly authority. He is to refuse to 'presume', not only as to what lies in the uncertain disposition of eternity, but over what seems securely within his will and reach. He is to boast no adequacy about which he is not utterly reliant upon God and expectant only from Him.

It might be said that there could hardly be a posture of spirit more categorically opposed to the instincts of current secularity, more wholly contrasted with the humanism of the age of cybernation and computerized culture. For these, in their quality, are just that self-ordering sufficiency which, in its own idiom, the Qur'ān decries as *istighnā'*. The verbal form *istaghnā* occurs in what is perhaps the earliest Surah of all (96: 6–7): 'Nay! presumptuous is man, thinking himself self-sufficient.' The term means that in his view he has all in himself and can 'dispense' (a root idea here) with God. He is saying in effect that 'the divine would make no difference from his point of view'. His wit or wealth or will suffice him, and in that sanguine, confident assessment of the human in him, he destroys the Godward sense of things. Surahs 80: 5 and 92: 8, which use the same term, show how deceptive such sense of 'wealth' can be to others (even to the Prophet in 80: 5) as well as to the 'wealthy', distorting all values. 'Man indeed transgresses, thinking himself his own master.'[2]

But does he? Or is there some distinction here we are bound to make and can the Qur'ān, with its downrightness against the human

[1] *The Cantos of Ezra Pound*, London, 1964, Canto 94.

[2] The translation of 96: 6–7 in N. J. Dawood's *Koran*, London, 1956, p. 26, cited here to help indicate that the passage involves more than material wealth, or simply 'getting rich'. Dr Syed Abdul Laṭif (translation of 1969) has 'presumptuous . . . that he regardeth himself as self-sufficient!'

pretension, serve us well in making it? How do we rightly think Islam and think secularity? This is the question which the confident Quranic theism compels upon the modern reader. There are aspects of the matter which we defer to Chapter 9, of a more practical kind. We mean here the God-awareness the Qur'ān enjoins and its viability, its intelligibility, in contemporary circumstance.

It seems clear that we have in this vital context one of the surest occasions of time re-interpretation. In its original pagan setting the claim for God could well be austere, rigorous, even strident and harsh. Its task was understood to require forthright negation of all that flouted it and its effectual establishment against all odds and at whatever cost. There is no mistaking the militant assurance of the Scripture of Islam as the text both of an apostle and a ruler. We can only respond to the 'excluders of God' in our day by acknowledging that mission in a different idiom. The Quranic vehemence against *kufr* and *shirk*, against the pagan refusal to 'let God be God', can be fulfilled in its current rejection of the false absolutes of men in their 'presumption' only by discerning the different time.

That discernment makes us aware that there are many secularizers whose reservations about faith have important bearing on the beliefs they question. They are not to be crudely denied or roundly rebuked. There is point in their interrogation of the theists and there are ugly things in the systems they disown. The believer cannot afford to be cavalier with their scepticism not unfeeling about their care not to be deceived. We do not serve truth if we suppose that all contemporary loss of the divine is perverse and superficial. Religious iconoclasm may well be the worse for being passionate. Its negations of *kufr* need a wise circumspection. It has to beware of its own vested interest in truth.

There is a perhaps significant incident in Surah 4: 94 that might afford us a precedent in point.

> 'O you who believe, when you are championing the way of God, be discriminating and do not say to him who offers you a peace-greeting: "You are no believer!" out of your designs on the goods of this world. With God there are goods abundant. You were that way aforetime but God has been gracious to you. So be discerning. For God knows well how you react.'[1]

[1] The usual translation is, either: 'You who are fighting', or 'You who are journeying . . .' ('in the way of God'). Physical *jihād* is meant. 'Championing' preserves this

In the context, the militancy of early Islam brought insincere offers of allegiance motivated only by a prudence that sought immunity from attack or pressure. Also conversion exempted the converted from confiscation of property and the like. On either count, there was a vested interest of the Muslims in non-conversion, whether by suspicion of the double-crosser or by loss of booty. This is clear from the passage, in its vigorous repudiation of such vested interest. The old hands were to be ready for every sign of response and to check in themselves any trace of reluctance to accept the newcomer inspired by self-advantage. The only authentic interest of the faithful was the other man's spirit.

Does the passage give us a basis for the case that custodians in religion must beware of vested interest of their own? Does it admit of the sense that suspicions of insincerity have to go first inward, that we are liable to misread what we accuse? Whether so or not, the keep-at-arms-length mentality seems to be condemned here. We must not, with secularism, assume perversity and find it damnable. It will be better to detect honesty, if not salutation, and let it be heard. If there is doubt the benefit of it must not always be supposed to lie with the establishment of belief. Much potential faith is in fact extinguished by insensitivity to its kindling.

So it is that the strong, even fierce, monotheism of the Qur'ān must be read today as a properly tempered passion speaking in a more subtle time. The fight now against the false absolutes must not obscure the puzzle and the search over the right loyalties. It is just such a mood of questioning and wistful confusion that underlies many a modern situation *min dūni-llāhi*. There are those who find no place for God in the vastness of the universe and the dark flow of history. Then it is that men are self-sufficient, not out of their repudiation of God, but in despair of His significance. In the deep stretches of stellar distance, under the suspended sentence of nuclear holocaust, they sense no place to pray. Then the human feeling of alone-ness or bereft-ness becomes either a defiance or an apathy in respect of God and those who speak of Him. What orthodox call 'presumption', might then be truly courage, or maturity.

The God of merely arbitrary power makes a travesty of faith. For it speaks only in despite of men and leaves them in a sort of valid

but also admits the larger logic argued from the passage. 'Be discerning' is certainly a significant command relating, as it does, both to what is met and to what is thought.

atheism. For it has given back all questions in the demand that they should be silent and submissive. So doing, it confirms itself redundant, no longer credible as God in the human world. That which abdicates meaning cannot command worship. Yet, on a slight reading, the Qur'ān seems so often to be taken in just these terms of arbitrary divinity. We have, therefore, to seek within it the deep corrective of its own traditionalists.

Its undeviating concern could well be defined as 'the right of the right-ful God'. In the first context this meant the negation of the right-less deities of pagan pluralism. It still means today the dethroning of every pseudo-worship and every guise of pride and pretension. But these negative missions of repudiation, old and new, must further speak the divine right-fulness in positive, present meaning so as to enable men to say: 'Thou art', to worship God on the further side of their defiance or their despair. The task which with pagans began with 'There is no god . . .' begins now with a negation it does not need to make. For it is already there—the existential negation in which belief would allegedly 'make no difference'. It has, therefore, a far sterner battle with nothingness than it ever had with pluralism. A world believed empty of God is a vaster, harsher, older, prouder, grimmer, place than a world peopled with gods. Its idolatries are the more massive by the very sophistication that educates its superstitions and discourages its reverence.

The perceptive reader of the Qur'ān will find light and succour, in a contemporary sense and service of the divine, from three fundamental features of its world. These might be loosely described as the concept of religion as submission, the dominion of man in nature and the poetry of human experience.

The first might seem at first a mere truism and axiomatic. Of course, *Allāhu akbar*, 'Greater is God'. 'Unto Him all things are surrendered.' But this vital demand of the Qur'ān includes religion itself. God is not an occasion, still less an excuse, for religion. On the contrary, religion is for the recognition and obedience of God. Islam exists to be *muslim*, to be surrendered. The claim of God must never be subordinated to claims on behalf of God. The institution, the symbols, the establishment, the prophethood—all are purposive and derivative. Even Muḥammad himself is only apostle and messenger. All is, that God may be all. Men can only be for Him under Him. The subordination controls the advocacy. For God is 'the First and the

Last', and knows all that the heart conceals. Worship cannot confer exemption from its fullest implications because its forms are being observed. The latter spell no indulgence, still less immunity, for the worshipper. He cannot escape from the God of worship in the worship of God. On the contrary, religion—in Islam perhaps most of all—is in perpetual theological liability. The transcendent must always be in control. To be right in the right-ful God is the only truly Islamic thing, judging all actual *islām*.

It is this Quranic Lordship of God which can be so significant for the modern scene. In one sense, of course, it meets irreligion head-on, in uncompromising antithesis. Yet it requires also a rejection of empirical religion (even Muslim religion) if it has settled for lesser deity, if by insensitivity it has withdrawn the real divine into a world of private devotion away from the full dimensions of divinity. To these unbelief itself often pays unconscious tribute by its distrust of actual religion. The Islamic trust of the greatness of God—if we may so describe it—is surely rightly seen as the ally, even the anticipation, of the current charge that much religion is not really about God, but about comfort, or illusion, or security, or cultural identity and that the God of a true worship is, and ought to be, greater than all these.

This is not to say that Muslims within the time of the Qur'ān, and since, have behaved with this lively sense of God, great beyond their actual worship of Him. Rather the contrary. Original Islam was iconoclastic and the iconoclast is always in a religiously dangerous position. He is only too liable to identify his militancy with the divine Lordship. There is ample evidence that this happens in the Qur'ān. Yet, beyond those immediate issues of repudiation and of negation in that behalf, the Lordship stays to witness even against the instrument that served it. The Qur'ān has no scruples about power, except the ultimate scruple that it be 'on behalf of God', and 'in His way'. In sanctioning force it also subdues its instruments. If 'Sedition (*fitnah*) is a bigger evil than war' (2: 217), and the extinction of truth a greater tragedy than strife for it, then truth is more final than its servitors, more sovereign than its forms of religious preservation.

That religion as a human phenomenon, historically institutionalized and personally confessed, is always 'unto and under God in His rightfulness' (as Islam insistently teaches and enjoins), may help in our time to check and reprove those aspects of religious faith which most impede the retrieval of modern unbelief—authoritarianism, complacence, insensitivity, formalism, obscurantism, and the other symptoms of the 'received littleness of God'. It may also teach a new temper of patience in the witness of belief, new and more worthy ways in which conviction may be its emphatic self in the world. If we find it so, will we not be thinking loyally with the *Allāhu akbar* assurance which is the sum of all Quranic faith?

The second theme, we said, was the dominion of man. The arrogance the Qur'ān reproaches in the attitudes of *istighnā'*, must not be confused with the legitimate *imperium* which man has been given to enjoy in the mastery of things. It was in fact the pretension that mistook and misconstrued such mastery. The tragic dimension of man which we have pondered in Chapter 6 is only such, as the distortion, the atrophy, or the frustration, of his proper dignity. The claims of pardon, as we have reflected on them in Chapter 7, hinge on the same fact of vocation and positive intent in the being of man under God. Thus, while the Qur'ān is emphatic in its rejection of pretentious (and in that sense promethean) man and so, by the same token, in its rebuke to his secularity, this is only so because it sees man as meant for power over things. His very status as *'abd* involves his competence as *khalīfah*. He has wherewith to offer in worship and in wonder, because he has wherewith to exploit and harness in the techniques of soil and city.

This conviction of man as vice-regent figures throughout the Quranic account of the creation of man and is inseparable from his creature-hood.[1] Surah 2: 30 and other passages dealing with the creation of man designate him as the deputy, or trustee-in-charge, on behalf of God. This 'caliphate' of Adam over nature is understood to define and hallow that status of due exploitation and authority which man exercises in the material world and which he has brought to such a peak of marvel in present technology. The role of man as *khalīfah* both validates his empire and expects his hallowing, and both in essential unity. For if he wielded no mastery he could bring no submission. He would have nothing to offer or to consecrate. His very culture and all his works are the substance of his Godward obligation. He is effectively over things that he may be responsibly under God. His worship is not an idle, extraneous, optional pursuit to which he

[1] The brevity of the discussion here of this important topic may be explained by reference to a fuller treatment in the writer's *The Privilege of Man*, London, 1968, Chapter 2.

might be whimsically inclined on occasion, but the prime quality, the pervasive obligation securing and symbolizing the moral law, and the poetic wonder, subduing things, scientific, economic, political and material, to a proper God-worthiness.

This is Islam and man understood as *muslim*. The angels, according to the Qur'ān, as noted in Al-Rāzī's exposition in Chapter 4, demurred at the evident risk divinely taken at creation. Man was seen by them as a dubious proposition in the divine counsels—too frail to be trusted, too arrogant to be thus empowered, too liable to 'shed blood and corrupt in the earth'. In this Quranic myth of man-the-liability history is seen as the sphere of the Satanic determination to prove the accusation valid and the divine risk discredited. The very theme of history is thus the question-mark of human worth, understood as a vital question-mark of divine wisdom and power. The wisdom of God is staked on the credibility of man as its supreme test and venture. Hence, of course, the law and the prophets, revelation and religion (*dīn*), as the focal points of that inclusive issue. The question for God, we may say, is the question of man. The human is in this way the sphere in which the divine is either acknowledged or belied.

This caliphal status of man meanwhile confirms the right of the scientific and other works he achieves within it. The God of the Qur'ān is not the anti-promethean sort of classical antiquity, needing to be defied before man can be free, jealously frustrating the human will to mastery. On the contrary, the sovereignty of God in Islam is such as to permit even the vital liberty of idolatry. Man is the sort of creature who has the option of the most inclusive rejection of the divine. The world of the creation is a world in which idolatry can happen, and men can live by choice *min dūni-llāhi*. The very urgency of the prophetic cry against the idols only makes this liberty the more impressive. The divine strategy—if the term is proper—is not to withdraw the privilege of creaturehood in reaction to the Satanic accusation of history, but to let the divine vindication stay where it first was, and where it will remain, namely in the response of human will.

Many a reader will no doubt find himself wondering how this tallies with the familiar assumptions of divine autocracy, of determinism and transcendent immunity to man, so often associated with Islam and the Muslim mind. The query is a large one and runs very deep. But, as agreed, we are thinking with the Qur'ān. Man as a being capable of preferring idols to God and God as creating such a creature in such a creation, are emphatically thoughts of the Qur'ān. We must concede that there are deep and insistent strains in Islamic theology, with feasible support from the Qur'ān, which withdraw divine sovereignty from the range of human power to impugn, which understand idolatry and anti-idolatry—and even for that matter the law of contradiction itself—as significant only for man and not really involving God.

This sort of exoneration of the divine from the liability of divine enterprises in the end makes havoc of the whole sphere of creation, not to say the religious situation and the moral urgency of Islam itself. But since it is widely current, as a mood or abstraction of Islam, it deserves to be faced.

We can possibly capture the issue best, in brief, by a phrase from the great Persian poet mystic Jalāl al-Dīn Rūmī (AD 1206–1273): 'The ugliness of the script is not the ugliness of the scribe.'[1] The immediate context in the *Mathnawi* is the problem of 'not being pleased with infidelity' and yet 'being pleased with every divine ordainment', of which of course unbelief must be one. The poet distinguishes between what God commands, namely anti-idolatry (or, better, the worship of Himself alone), and what God wills, namely the fact that this or that particular man or people is idolatrous. This distinction leads Jalāl al-Dīn to argue, further, that what is commanded of us by God does not really enter into His nature so as to characterize His will essentially and reliably. On the contrary, the imperative against idols bears only on the human sphere and comes from God only as a *diktat* for men.

We should perhaps refrain from saying here that by this logic God does not care for His own unity, but only for man's confession of it. For this would be a drastic conclusion. Yet it is one which the poet certainly intends. God's decree distinguishes good and evil, faith and *kufr*, *islām* and non-*islām*. But the distinctions belong only with the decree, and not with the will that makes it. The *fiat* displays the divine power but does not engage it. *We* are enjoined to deplore polytheism and to shun evil. But that divine behest need not, and

[1] *The Mathnawi*, iii, 1362 f., translated by R. A. Nicholson, London, 1925. Not the ugliness of the scribe as man, it is true. For calligraphic and personal beauty *are* different spheres. But surely it is the ugliness of the scribe as scribe? What the poet is saying might be paraphrased: 'Tragedy in the creation is not tragedy for the Creator'. 'It does not reach God; it is only as it happened'. But is such irresponsible sovereignty not a contradiction in terms?

must not, be understood as entering into the divine being. God remains free to contravene His own law. He is exonerated from its liabilities. We are judged and obligated by imperatives that are *from* Him but not *in* Him.

This, were we to accept it, might be, in an assertive sort of way, a metaphysical unitarianism. But it would point, in reality, to a deep dualism. *Islām* and non-*islām* cannot be taken in their Quranic seriousness as distinctions, if they make a contrast about which God is essentially neutral and only insistently 'partisan' where men are concerned. Nor is His power in the issue properly apprehended if it resides only in a determinism that arbitrarily divides the camps in order to display an inscrutable authority in doing so. Such an essential neutrality could never be dogmatized into goodness, into a goodness, that is, obtaining before and above the creation as well as in a code-making for the creatures. Divine goodness capable of the creation cannot be immunized from the historical shape of the struggles it sets up within creation. Nor can it relate to them as a will that is arbitrarily glorified simply in submissiveness.

For to think so would be to reduce all that we mean when we say: *Allāhu akbar*. Exoneration does not enhance the sovereignty: it cheapens it. 'God is not greater', confined to a formal status which precludes a real consistency within the will to create and legislate and rule. Or, reverting to Jalāl al-Din's metaphor, must we not believe that the creation, far from being a piece of penmanship casual about the way it is, is truly a work of authorship—of a consistent and significant integrity? There need be no doubt about which answer the Qur'ān would invite us to give and receive.

That confidence brings us to our third feature of the Quranic world which we made hold to describe as the poetry of human experience. It deserves the space of the whole chapter to follow. We simply note here, in preface to it, that the pagan exclusion of God in the Prophet's day, and in every form of plural superstition, derived from fear of the divine remoteness or unconcern. Islam did not invent the name *Allāh* or announce His existence. It declared the sole existence of *Allāh* already known as 'most high' in a pantheon of deities. So high indeed that the lesser deities made good, emotionally, for His aloofness or His immunity. The idols flourished because the real God was remote and dubiously disposed, a last resort perhaps and always on the farther side of intermediaries.

The pagan world, as it were, excluded Him by a curious kind of honour, by supposed delegation of power, not by negation. It revered Him in the avoidance of relations. The task of a monotheism of the heart and will was to proclaim and exemplify the great as also the accessible, the One as truly the One, the sovereignty as near and benign, as recognizable in the intimacies of daily life, in the common phenomena of mortal existence. So doing, it retrieved for a true worship those positive elements of pagan error, those ill-directed instincts of gratitude and awe, which in their blindness made the shrines and idols.

This is the whole realm of the signs of God in the Qur'ān. What the pagan mind associated with the gods many—life, haunt, birth, family, tribe, water, harvest, victory—and so dissociated from *Allāh* and His mercies had to be restored to their true context and so the veneration retrieved for a true worship. Only God is to be adored. But in that safe adoration, all things may be celebrated. When partializing superstition is at an end the true poetry can be heard. The very world of pagan vividness and sensitivity serves to refute the falsity of the pagan sacralization of natural events and rally to a unified worship the manifold reactions of the human spirit to the human scene. To this sphere of Quranic awareness we turn with the perhaps initially surprising title: 'The sacramental earth'. For the sacramental is not usually considered an Islamic category. For the moment such a negative assumption must be checked as premature. In retrospect it may be seen to be misguided.

What matters in the end about monotheism is not simply number, or arithmetical unitariness, or the numerical unification of the manifold in which we meet transcendent mercy. It is, rather, the wholeness of our worship, the fulness of our sense of God alone. It is, in the perceptive words of Martin Buber, 'to include nothing beside God but everything in Him'.

> 'It is not so decisive whether the existence of a unity exalted over all is assumed in one's consideration, but the way in which this unity is viewed and whether one stands to it in an exclusive relationship which shapes all other relations and thereby the whole order of life.'[1]

It all depends, as Sartre would say, upon 'the point of view'.

[1] In *Moses*, London, 1958, p. 10.

Chapter 9
THE SACRAMENTAL EARTH

> 'I always think that the best way to know God is to love many things . . . that is what I say to myself. But one must love with a lofty and serious intimate sympathy, with strength, with intelligence: and one must try to know deeper and better and more. That leads to God . . .'[1]

Painters have long been suspect in traditional Islam for fear their delight in natural form should tend towards idolatry. Vincent Van Gogh, the Dutch artist, might well on that score be a doubtful kinsman of the Qur'ān and there is no evidence that he knew it. His words, nevertheless, come close to the basic Quranic sense of the external world as a realm of 'signs', disclosing a divine glory and requiring an attention at once deep and intimate. He was writing, in July 1880, to his brother Theodorus, in a long and searching letter of self-scrutiny, justifying his seemingly idle and disreputable ways as a condition of spirit wistful for reality beyond convention and for beauty in the ordinary, a spirit that refused to be regimented by formality or hardened by vulgarity.

His temper, in another idiom and against a different landscape, is well captured in the words of Marcel Proust.

> 'Suddenly a roof, a glint of sun on a plain, the smell of a road, made me stop because of a special pleasure they gave me, and also because they seemed to be hiding beyond what I saw something which they were inviting me to come and grasp.'[2]

This feeling of being arrested by phenomena, this reading of experience as an invitation to grasp and comprehend, is exactly what underlies

[1] *Van Gogh: A Self Portrait, Letters Revealing his Life as a Painter*, selected by W. H. Auden, London, 1961, p. 55.

[2] Quoted from André Maurois, *From Proust to Camus*, translated by C. Morse and R. Bruce, London, 1967, p. 11.

the Qur'ān's insistence on the quality of the natural order as the intimation of mercy, power and goodness. The identity between the two may be greeted with a certain initial scepticism by strangers to the Qur'ān, and the occasions of recognition must vary, of course, endlessly between the landscapes of Europe and Arabia, between gentle pastures and volcanic hills, between meandering streams and oases in a sandy vastness. The Muslim will not sing with Kipling, in his *A Tree Song:*

> 'Sing oak and ash and thorn, good Sirs,
> All on a midsummer's morn:
> For England shall bide,
> Till judgement tide,
> By oak and ash and thorn.'

He is more likely to exult in the date palm, the cedar and the olive. But the impulse to possessive gratitude and assurance is the same. It is this awareness of the presence of nature in the Qur'ān which warrants and inspires the theme of 'the sacramental earth'.

It turns on 'the grand perhaps' we have already taken as crucial to the Islamic Scripture, noting how the particle *la'alla* occurs with impressive reiteration throughout the book, followed almost always by verbs having to do with intelligence, recognition, understanding, thankfulness and reverence. 'Perhaps you may come to your senses', 'peradventure you may realize . . .', 'it may be that you will be grateful . . .', 'if perchance you may know that mercy is being done to you. . . .' The phrases occur some seventy-two times with verbs and pronouns in the second person, fifty times in the third, in either case in conjunction with the *āyāt* or 'signs' of God. Always there is the double association of idea—a significance attaches to the natural event and it needs the attentive recognition of the perceptive soul. The meaning, though always there, is lost upon the casual or the callous. It fails to register in the absence of that reaching out to grasp in response to gratitude and wonder.

The word *āyah* (sing.), *āyāt* (pl.) means precisely a 'sign', a locus of significance. It is sometimes translated as 'miracles', but the element of extraordinariness makes that an improper reading. It is rather in the very ordinariness of natural phenomena that the sign quality resides. The word occurs also frequently as a synonym for the

Qur'ān itself and has come to be applied as a name for each 'verse' of the Scripture. The whole then constitutes a 'sign', a token of divine communication. It must be read and received in its proper import and status. This confluence of terms is interesting and suggestive, allowing as it does the conviction that the external world is a kind of 'scripture', intimating in its own realm and within its own order that divine knowledge which, in history and prophecy, in word and action, speaks Quranically to mankind, so that the one is not unworthy to be denominated in the same term with the other. But this observation aside, our concern here is only with the sphere of nature as a realm of human experience which points towards the divine. The 'signs' say, in the words of the poet:

> 'Come forth, and bring with you a heart
> That watches and receives.'

They invite men to a religious response to the world of everyday phenomena.

This invitation, of course, is very close to what, in perverted form, is the impulse to idolatry. The perversion arises only because the 'signs' are taken, not as a call to go beyond them, but as an end in themselves. The idolater falsifies what, taken in its due significance, is the occasion of a true worship. So nature is the first ground and the constant test of the authentically religious temper—the temper which does not sacralize things in themselves nor desecrate them in soul-less using and consuming. Between the pagan and the secular, with their contrasted bondage and arrogance, lies the reverent ground of a right hallowing where things are well seen as being for men under God, seen for their poetry, mystery, order and serviceability in the cognizance of man, and for their quality in the glory of God. That this glory is actual in the natural order and potential in the human trust is the meaning of the *āyāt*. Since the point of the revelation is to summon men to that sense of the divine glory, there is deep point and eloquence in having the same name for the verses of the Scripture and the phenomena of the world. These two realms of the *āyāt* illuminate each other.

Here, too, are the springs of all cult and culture. It is always nature which yields the material out of which symbols are drawn and sanctuaries are built. The visible, audible, tangible world is the ever fertile renewer of the will to wonder and the urge to adoration. By the standards and instincts of some religions, Islam has been severely Spartan and rigorous in its cultic engagement with the natural order. Yet within all its reservations about the arts both of image and of sound—reservations for which there were powerful historical reasons inseparable from its own vocation—there lies a sure sense and use of the sacramental which no perceptive visitor to the mosque can fail to register. There is a characteristic 'baptism' of space, colour, pattern, line and light, a geometrical expression one might almost say of 'the signs of God'.

It is, then, to the mosque, not the laboratory, that in their Quranic meaning the *āyāt* are meant to lead the thoughts of men, to the practice of adoration, not the measures of analysis. The attentiveness they evoke means an exploration with the heart, not an exploitation with a technique. We have already noted, and rejected, in Chapter 5, the pseudo-scientific claims that read scientific attitudes into religious meanings. In the Qur'ān's own day this religious sense of the 'signs' was quite capable of co-existing with a pre-scientific world of *jinn* and spirits. To the problem latent here we will return. But it was a religious sense, nevertheless, capable of exemplifying for every age and context of men the benediction of 'the heart that watches and receives', and so joins together the divine honour and the human gladness.

Though religious in its character, this Quranic sense of the natural order can well be the very nurse of science. For it liberates the worshipper from the tyranny of a chaotic naturalism. It unifies the order of experience under a single sovereignty, freeing the mind from plural fears, and so making possible the empire of science. In knowing his heaven unified man discovers his earth possessable: in the rule of the One God is the clue and the means to his own mastery.

> 'By emptying nature of divinities you may fill her with Deity, for she is now the bearer of messages. There is a sense in which nature-worship silences her—as if a child or a savage were so impressed with the postman's uniform that he omitted to take in the letters.'[1]

In this sense, the religious apprehension of 'the sacramental earth'

[1] C. S. Lewis, *Reflections on the Psalms*, London, 1958, p. 83.

is profoundly scientific in its potential. For the same reason, it is the surest antidote to the idolizing impulse. The theme of the *āyāt*, therefore, lies very close to the Quranic iconoclasm. The mere negation of idols, even if propositionally successful, leads only to an iconoclasm of the mind. The effective dethronement of the false deities can occur only in the realm of the emotions, in the instincts and habits, the fears and hopes, of ordinary folk. Such dethronement is only attained when the endlessly plural phenomena in life, of birth and death, harvest and family, food and pasture, wind and tide, are radically dissociated from diverse powers, understood as peopling nature and infecting it with their own disorder and their chronic fickleness. Only when natural events are, as it were, enfranchized, freed to be seen as phenomena within a universe, can they be comprehended, earlier or later, immediately or eventually, in a scientific sense. The probable time-lag here is not itself relevant. The possibility of science lies essentially in the realization of worship, in the negation of the tyrannical multiplicity and the acknowledgement of the single Lordship. That this Lordship is first recognized in the religious terms of wonder, dependence and authority, is the only and the sure matrix of its recognition in the scientific terms of intelligibility and the invitation to explore, investigate and employ resources that are no longer 'divine' because only God is God. Is not this the operative meaning of the Muslim *Shahādah*, or 'confession of faith', that 'there is no god save God', to which we may apply the dictum that 'the affirmative can only issue out of the super-imposed negation'. It is the meek who possess the earth, only because it is they alone who deny its possession of them. The idolater, by definition, is he who has refused to let events be 'signs'.

Yet, equally, the scientific enables and deepens the religious, if the *āyah* quality is not confined to intelligibility. A fully scientific possession of nature can remain a lively, poetic, ardent relationship that does not forfeit the splendour in formulating the science. Laurens Van Der Post has vividly noted this situation from the opposite end in pondering the impact of African travel on sophisticated thinking.

> 'One of the remarkable features of life spent in these circumstances is that nature becomes an affair of personalities. Any scientific notions one might have held about it vanish quickly until there is nothing of the abstract left in one's mind. Sun, moon, stars, wind, lightning and rain

all become great magnetic beings and one's relationship with them intensely personal.'[1]

Intensity of experience, which ignorance pluralizes into superstition, abides and sharpens, as the spur to art and humility, when it is securely rooted in the singular submission.

The *āyāt* take in the whole panorama of the Arabian scene and the vicissitudes of Arab life. 'Know that God brings the ground to life out of death', runs Surah 57: 17, 'for truly We make clear to you Our signs: it may be that you will apprehend'. When rainfall turns the barren soil into fertility the minds of men will surely sense a grateful wonder. There are the dependable sequences of night and day, with their kindly alternation of toil and rest (for example Surahs 28: 75, 30: 46 and 35: 12), and the mysteries of clouds and storms (24: 43), the birds wheeling on the wing (24: 41), and everything in the heavens extolling God after its own order.

Recurrent with the theme of gratitude is the fact of the subjection of nature to the purpose of man. God, says the Qur'ān, has set the world under the dominion or caliphate of mankind, harnessing or, in the old military sense of the word, 'impressing' them into human service. The beasts in their strength (22: 36, 43: 10) and the winds in their courses bend to the ploughs of the peasant and the sails of the seamen. The ships on the Red Sea had a strong fascination for Muḥammad who returns frequently to the strange facility whereby men turn the very gales to their traffic and their merchandise (35: 12, 45: 12, etc.). The skins of animals house and clothe the people, fur and wool and hair affording warmth and shelter and comfort (16: 80 f.). And there is the salt of the sea and the sweet of the well—'the two waters' which diversely care for the necessities of man, cleansing and refreshing, purging and gladdening his habitat (35: 12). Crops, vines, dates, 'the fig and the olive', and all the fruits of the seasons join with the dependable hills in the sustenance of humanity and in the celebration of God (16: 11 f.).

It may be argued that the examples, as in the Book of Job, bespeak a simple husbandry and a primitive economy, and that they tell little with the sophistication of modern man who dispenses with the crude candle, clothes himself in the garments of chemistry rather

[1] In *The Heart of the Hunter*, London, 1961, p. 20. See also *The Event*, op. cit., Chapter 5.

than of the flock, travels without the stars for beacons and does not alternate with day and night. But, as in the Biblical case, so here, the awareness of reverence and of responsiveness—the responsiveness of nature to man's will and of man's will to nature—these are unchanging and unchanged, and in their enlarging dimension belong no less with the complexities of technology. In either case there is no essential distinction in the inner relationship of mystery and mastery. The Qur'ān is not, in these themes, invoking some rough argument from design that might be discredited by the arts of human interference. Though pre-scientific in its simplicity, it is hailing that inherent quality of answerability to man in natural phenomena from which all technology proceeds and it is insisting that this amenability ought properly to be recognized as requiring not only the exploitative, but the thankful, instinct. When man is really awakened, mere efficiency no longer satisfies. There is no more urgent truth of the human condition, nor one so timely.

It emerges most clearly and critically of all in the fact of sexuality as the most elemental of the realms of human dominion. The miracle of procreation, as we noted in Chapter 6, repeatedly awes and fascinates the Qur'ān reader. The power of self-perpetuation entrusted to the human species is an ever-renewed evidence of the stature of the human and the mercy of the divine.

> 'And among his signs is that He has created you counterparts in sex, so that you might dwell together, and He ordained love and compassion as your mutual bond. Truly, *there* are signs for those who think and ponder' (Surah 30: 21).

The same Surah goes on to set that generative 'sign' in a sequence of mortal experience within the created world, diverse in race and colour, frail, acquisitive, sustained, renewed and awed, returning to dust and from the dust to God. These all are, it is sure, 'signs' of the power and purpose of God.

But always and only signs for the perceptive. The import is lost upon those who see without insight and take without noting. Hence the perpetual 'perhaps', the critical capacity for the critical awareness. And always, again, at the core of this faculty of recognition the capacity for gratitude. It is the grateful who are perceptive and the perceptive who are grateful. *La'allakum tashkurūn* is one of the most frequent of the participle phrases: 'haply you will give thanks', and sometimes there is the eloquent deploring comment about a graceless humanity: *aktharuhum la yashkurūn*, 'most of them are thankless' (10: 60, 27: 73, cf. 2: 243 and 12: 38). Surah 40: 61 protests: 'Surely God is bountiful to mankind, but the most of them give no thanks. . . . How then are you misguided, as those who give the lie to the signs of God?' (v. 63).

In this theme the Qur'ān is close to the springs of all art and poetry as well as the impulses of faith. For it interprets the natural order as only safe in the human custody when humans are themselves in awe. Gratitude is neither tyrannical nor tyrannized. It makes for a hallowed *imperium* disciplined by consecration, undismayed either by terror or despair. Nature offers both delight and duty but only in unison. Economy and ecology, wealth and habitation, are as it were a constant interrogation of the soul of man. It answers to the steady interrogation of his environment by the mind of man. The questioner is himself questioned. The answers to man have to be matched and sanctified by the answer from man. It is these together which are the essence of the sacramental. The good earth is the earthly good: they require each other. Together they turn on the human crisis. Or, as Ezra Pound has it, in *The Altar:*

> 'The flame, the autumn and the green rose of love
> Fought out their strife here, 'tis a place of wonder.
> Where these have been, meet 'tis, the ground is holy.'[1]

'Perhaps they may understand . . .'.

It is illuminating to find this Quranic injunction to gratitude linked in a few passages with the repeated theme of *kufr* or 'atheism'. This term is the most basic of all Islamic concepts as the antithesis to *islām*. The *kāfirūn*, those who commit *kufr*, are the negators of the divine, the unbelievers, the deniers of truth. *Kufr* is the total rejection of what has to do with God. The *āyāt*, then, become a ready touchstone of whether or not *kufr* is intended. For it is in them that the divine claim and reality are intimated to men. That is their whole point and character. When they are ignored or despised God is belied: He is disregarded in his tokens. Such active denial is not so much a metaphysical scepticism as a practising neglect. The signs of God become the occasion of the larger repudiation. We then have to speak,

[1] *Selected Poems of Ezra Pound*, edited by T. S. Eliot, London, 1928, p. 69.

not so much of the God men decry credally, but of the God they merely ignore. The *āyāt* are then the point where our implicitly selfish character becomes an explicitly atheistic attitude and an active disregard of the divine. The really tragic atheism is not to disown God in a formula, but to exclude Him in a habit, of rejection. It is to behave as if He were unreal.

Such gracelessness is the ultimate unbelief. The nature of theism is the perspective of gratitude. Reverently responding to experience is, for the Qur'ān, the temper of belief. Thus the Surah of Luqmān (31) reviews the power and splendour of creation and continues: 'Give thanks to God: the man who gives thanks finds his own being in thankfulness [lit. 'gives thanks for his own self']: and when men disbelieve (*man kafara*) God is still there, altogether rich and praiseable'. There is thus a plain contrast between gratitude and unbelief. A similar passage occurs in 27: 40 in the narrative of Solomon and the Queen of Sheba: 'this', said Solomon, 'is a bounty from my Lord, whereby to test me whether I am grateful or graceless. For the grateful man becomes thereby a real self (the identical phrase as in 31: 12) and as for the unbeliever, my Lord withal is altogether rich and gracious'. Moses, in 14: 17, warns the people: 'Your Lord declared: If you are thankful, I will surely increase you, but if you disbelieve [i.e. are thankless] truly my retribution is severe', while in Surah 2: 152 there comes the summons: 'Remember Me and I will remember you: give thanks to Me and be not ungrateful'. Surah 76: 2 affirms that man from the womb is guided on his way, 'whether he is thankful or unbelieving'.

Few as these passages are, there is no need to discount or minimize their implication, coinciding as it does so closely with the frequent denial of the *āyāt* by the attitudes of *kufr*. The association of ideas admits the very exciting possibility of relegating old, barren, contentious concepts of 'atheism' where dogmas anathematized each other in neglect of the religious emotions to which they related—emotions often warped or atrophied by the competitive vehemence of the dogmas themselves. If thankfulness and wonder are indeed the primary element in doctrine about God, then community may be found even where tenets quarrel and perhaps, in measure, even idolatry may be redeemed instead of broken.

The Qur'ān's, of course, is a thoroughgoing iconoclasm, as the times and occasions required. But beyond its negative task of disavowal and dethronement there abides this ultimate and perpetual battle for the sacramental sense of the world as the steady form of the cognizance of God. Here the instincts even of idolaters have relevance. For their superstitions, howsoever ignorant, are at least alert to the awesomeness of phenomena and the precariousness of man. Is it in this context that we must see the sturdy survival in the Quranic world of the *jinn* that peopled with unpredictable surprises the psychic universe of pre-Islam?

At first sight their persisting in the Qur'ān would seem to be inconsistent with any effective monotheism. We have already argued that the doctrine of the signs of nature liberates man from the arbitrariness of plural and unruly forces, of powers and demons, fortuitous in their devices and fickle in their ways. For that doctrine relates and refers all events in the natural order to a single Lordship and sees them as merciful and intelligible. It is true that Quranic discourse does not employ any terminology about 'order', 'symmetry', 'design', or 'system'. Such vocabulary is remarkably absent from the Quranic lexicon. The scientific implication of the signs is latent and derivative, rather than explicit: the words throughout are religious only.

Nevertheless the unity is there, enthroning God alone and thereby expelling the chaos of fear. The Muslim, by the finest of definitions, is he 'who fears nought but God' (Surah 9: 18), God whose worship is neither shared nor diverted, as by gross idolaters, nor debased into a superstitition, as by compromising confessors of the unity. His prayer coincides with that of John Donne:

> 'The God of heaven sanctify to us our natural religion that it be never quenched nor damped in us, never blown out by atheism, nor blown up by an idolatrous multiplying of false gods, or a superstitious worship of our true God.'[1]

For such 'natural religion' is precisely this awareness of the impulse to reverence which the external world exerts, which idolatry falsifies and a discerning worship truly obeys.

Seen in this double sense of the divine glory and the human dignity and of idolatry as distorting both together, what has to be said then of the *jinn* of the Qur'ān, seeming, as they do, to flout the one and dispute the other? There can be no neglecting this question, for it

[1] *Collected Works*, London, 1912, vol. 2, p. 356.

recurs in almost every context of the book. We cannot have the Islamic Scripture without the demons, nor Quranic man without the *jinn*. 'Surely We created man from clay, from moulded loam, and *jinn* We created before him of burning flame' (15: 27). There are, in all, some thirty references to the *jinn* as denizens of the world and as forces among men.

It would be possible to treat the problem by dismissing it as a simple consequence of time and place, as a surviving element of superstition characterizing the locale of the Qur'ān and dating its psychology. But such a merely antiquarian stance, apart from any other factors, offends against the principles laid down in the Introduction of taking the Qur'ān in terms consistent with its authority and veneration by centuries of Muslims. This, as we argued, does not mean any exemption from critical respect, but it certainly precludes both the impatient and the superficial judgement. The *jinn* of the Qur'ān are not to be so crudely scouted if we are to reckon with its real quality.

What becomes clear from a careful study is that the idea of the *jinn* does not jeopardize the doctrine of the unity nor detract from the significance of natural phenomena as we have been reviewing it. The *jinn* are thought of in relation to the moral and spiritual actions of mankind and not the events or vicissitudes of external nature. They do not disrupt the 'sign' character of the latter nor revert to chaos the order by which the cosmos gives God praise and man dominion. Rather, they represent and denote the genii, mostly evil, which underlie the vagaries and perversities of human action. It is 'men and *jinn*', '*jinn* and men', of which we read (for example, 6: 130, 7: 38, 41: 25, 46: 18, etc.) in the inter-acting shape of wrong, of calumny and of discord. They are the lurking enemy of the prophets (6: 112), distorting their true word or conspiring to discredit and to rival the revelation. Surah 17: 88 refers to them as partners in the (vain) attempt to match the eloquent Qur'ān and they figure repeatedly in the allegation that he was merely a poet so often levelled against Muḥammad (cf. 26: 28 and 37: 36, etc.). In a world accustomed to the idea of spirit-possession, as explaining unusual or astounding states of mind or verbal powers, it would be surprising if the Qur'ān did not reflect these assumptions and find them present in the stories of the patriarchs, as David and Solomon (cf. 27: 39 and 34: 12).

But it does so within its overriding thesis of the divine authority.

The ultimate unity is not merely unimpaired by their presence: it is vindicated and counter asserted (51: 56). *Jinn* are seen as acknowledging and revering the revelation (46: 29 and 72: 2 f.) which their wiles cannot gainsay. Some modern writers have taken this as relating Muḥammad's mission to the whole universe in a cosmic sense. The obedience of the Quranic *jinn* is then sometimes contrasted with the obduracy of Jewish and Christian 'satans'.[1] Created beings (6: 100), who come into judgement (6: 128), they are not denied but demoted by the Qur'ān, where demonic forces are real enough but not absolute.

Surah 72, which has 'The *Jinn*' for its title and is largely given to this theme, projects the issues of human existence—faith and unbelief, good and evil, *islām* and unruliness—into a sort of twilight world, or companion realm, of mortal existence. So doing, it heightens the human meaning and invests its affairs with an aura beyond the mundane. Just as eschatology solemnizes the content of time, so this daimonism of the book accentuates the events of mortality. The existential world is haunted, in its crises, by this circumambient world of the sinister and the dire. History is thus more than man's devising and cannot be read aright without the shadows in the wings and the spectres at the gates. Yet, encompassing and subduing them all, is the One Knower of the unknown, the Sovereign Seer of the unseen. In Quranic perspective the *jinn* are in no sense competitors with God. They do not even usurp the natural order. The signs of God are inviolate against them, conspire as they may with men's disowning them.

It needs to be remembered in all this that Muḥammad's mission in the Qur'ān had to do with a monotheism of the imagination as well as of the mind, of the emotions as well as of the creed. Conversely, his iconoclasm did not aim merely to disavow the divinities but to dispossess them. The second of these purposes is always the more difficult, since men's idolatries are more tenacious in their yearnings than their theories. The world, too, remains indisputably plural and disconcertingly manifold, whatever the dogmas of unity. The endless manifold of experiences defies reduction to uniformity. 'There is no *god* but God' truly: but one must also add: 'God is greater'. 'Greater', however, than what? seeing there is nothing exempt from the negation and, therefore, nothing to enter the comparison. How can a gram-

[1] Cf., for example, Muḥammad 'Aziz Lahbābī, *Le Personalisme Musulmane*, Paris, 1964, p. 112, remarking on the defiant quality of the Biblical Satan.

matical comparative, even with an unstated and unstatable and non-existent 'comparable', nevertheless remain an urgent necessity of reiterated witness? Can the non-entity have 'inferiority' *vis-à-vis* the singular? But events, in their multiplicity, all persist—peoples, tribes, rocks, winds, rains, valleys, beasts, trees, markets, the young, the old, the high, the low, the living and the dead. In their presence in experience they have been the occasions of endless fears and hopes and worships. They have been divinized in passionate devotion.

What the Qur'ān demands is not their (impossible) elimination, but their proper subjection, not the atrophy of the emotions that greet them and cling to them, but their direction into the obedience and confession of a single sovereignty through and beyond them. Then, and only then, and necessarily then, the manifold elements of experience, of participation, aspiration, dread and delight, have their authentic fulness, precisely because they are no longer pretentious, disorderly, discordant or tyrannical. Where there is no doubt of the Lordship that rules over all, there need be no inhibitions against the imagination or the heart. These can worthily love the proximate because they are armed against it as the usurper—usurper that is, not only of the divine authority but of the human benediction.

There is no intention to claim this conclusion, so articulated, for the immediate world of Quranic struggle. But it is certainly the final relevance of 'the signs of God'. Without these, the awareness of God's sovereignty is starved of the springs of wonder. For then the majesty has never come near. Without Him the sense of their mystery and meaning dissolves into enigma, into strife and futility, into degradation. Only a sacramental earth can be the divine footstool and the human domain. To see it unhallowed would be to find ourselves denied and God dethroned. To know it consecrate is to confess his kingdom and our creaturehood. 'Thus do We manifest our signs to a people who have minds to understand' (30: 28).

There are several fascinating conjectures which belong with this theme. How does the frequent emphasis on the discerning few square with the assumption of a religion identical with the whole community? Politically and legally constituted, Islam has always confidently comprised an entire solidarity and seen itself a faith without exemption, solidly coterminous, minorities aside, with the total population. This conception was embodied and enforced in the idea of *Dār al-Islām*, 'the house of the faith'. Nevertheless, here is this necessary selectivity of religious truth. 'Most of them do not apprehend' runs the loyal realism of the Qur'ān. 'In their stories [patriarchs' and people's] there is indeed a point—for those who have perceptive minds' says the conclusion of the Surah of Joseph (12: 111). There is, somehow, mysteriously, a minority status about the vitally religious, a quality of apprehension of meaning lacking in the superficial majority, in those who bring no attentiveness to the significance of their experience in the human world.[1]

This sobering reflection, with its warning against an optimistic institutionalism in the things of faith, has, nevertheless, a deeply cheering potential. For it hints at a possible kinship of spirit across the frontiers of formal definition and communal identity. Where creeds and dogmas, for all their service to truth, must necessarily scrutinize and exclude in the tests of belief, gratefulness and wonder may well embrace and include, in the gist of belief. Community in *shukr* may override excommunication in *kufr*. If gratitude be the criterion, the outsider, by credal norms, may qualify for welcome within. 'The signs of God' in nature do not especially present themselves to dogmatists: perhaps the contrary. They have a clear impartiality *vis-à-vis* the *dārs*, or households, of conformity. Nor are they concealed or obscured to the strangers in the gates and the sceptical of mind. The only criterion for their recognition is the will to apperceive. Like the rain that falls on the just and the unjust they do not discriminate against the dubious or for the devout. Their relevance for either is on the same ground of factuality for both, of mystery and grace for each.

> 'Yet doubt not but in vallie and in plaine
> God is as here, and will be found alike
> Present, and of His presence many a signe
> Still following thee, still compassing thee around
> With goodness and paternal love, His Face
> Express and of His steps the track Divine.'[2]

Milton's imagery of footsteps is perhaps bolder than the Quranic sense would warrant and 'paternal' is, as yet, *verboten*. But need these discrepancies impede the discovery of a unity of conviction across the distinctions of religions?

[1] This point should not be confused with the philosophical aristocraticism or the Ṣūfī *gnosis* discussed in Chapter 3.

[2] John Milton, *Paradise Lost*, Book II, ll. 349–54.

This is not to say that all awareness of a sign-quality about events in the natural world is ready to see them as 'signs of God'. Richard Jefferies, in *The Story of My Heart*, left one of the most passionate and lyrical confessions of the sense of nature where objects 'seemed like exterior nerves and veins for the conveyance of feeling to me'. Yet he strenuously refused to allow this ardour any theological significance, though he loved to lie 'prone on the greensward in token of deep reverence', watching the scudding clouds and crumbling the chalky soil between his fingers, as he let the immensities of sky and earth enthral him. In all such interrogation of nature, however, there is a kindred temper in no way alien to the affirmations of faith. It is part of the very shape of the signs that they await, and do not compel, a recognition.

All this, then, tends to open, without blurring, the frontiers between theism and unbelief which have too long and too often been rigorous and belligerent. But there are considerations here, also, between faiths. Islam has always been urgently unitarian. Its very determination to be uncompromising has been liable to compromise the full relevance of this faith in unity, by giving it a severity born of fear when magnanimity would have been a fitter quality. This, no doubt, goes back to its first time and place. Idolatry, in the original century of the Qur'ān, was so chronic and pervasive that only a thoroughgoing surgery could suffice to eradicate it. The iconoclasm then had to be total and absolute. Only so might the instincts of the *Jāhiliyyah* be overcome. In this radical destruction of the idols, however, there was an unintended sacrifice or rejection of the whole realm of symbol, the force of which has been slow to reckon with its own success and to admit a time when its own victories had finally made symbolism safe from idolatry.[1] It would be odd to imply, by a perpetuated anathema

[1] A sense that there might be a positive point in the instinct behind idolatry is present, if rarely, in some Islamic thinking. Thus, for example, the great Al-Bīrūnī, in the fourth Muslim century, in his treatise on India, argued that human need underlay representation. Simple minds could not think in the abstract. Forms and images aided their comprehension. But, inevitably, as he believed, these aids degenerated into actual objects of worship and became usurpers of the reality they signified. Thus they require to be utterly vetoed. See *Alberuni's India*, chapter 11, in vol. 1, of Eduard C. Sachau's translation, London, 1910.

It is intriguing to find that Al-Bīrūnī uses exactly the same argument as other Muslim intellectuals employed in apology for the sensuous passages of the Qur'ān which he both justified and deplored as the necessary form of spiritual ideas for vulgar minds.

The whole rationale in both cases is unfair to symbol, and liable to intellectual arrogance.

on the world of imagery, that fourteen centuries of Islam had achieved no success against idolatry.

Aside from this historical aspect of the matter, it must surely be clear that the Quranic doctrine of the signs in nature, as expressive of the divine power and mercy, admits of the belief that the events surrounding them may be celebrated in festivals, enacted in liturgies, and depicted in art. It seems further to allow such response as authentically part of that very alertness it enjoins. If spring is truly a token of the divine grace and, in its recurrence, of the divine fidelity, the painter, the musician, the dramatist, must capture its sign-quality with brush, or song or word, and thus release its joy and meaning into the popular soul and into corporate cognizance. The artist, in icon, or statue, or image, may surely reproduce the beauty, or recall the wonder, of every sign-event and thus imprint it the more eagerly upon the human recollection. There need be nothing artificial, or superstitious, about such a proceeding. The idolatry, if it be present, lies not in the art but in the will and there alone can be expelled. No veto can preclude it without quarrelling with the very signs of God. For of these the artist is the ally and the friend.

It belongs, then, with the concept of the signs in nature that the worship of God must engage the imagination. External experience is no neutral ground, where the worshipper stands in atrophy of sense and sterilization of thought. The iconoclast is frustrating the very will to unity if he thinks to make it so and his enterprise is futile. The *true* end of idols is the beginning of worship. And it is also a recovery of symbol, a recovery now safe, sane and sure. Without the discipline of image and of symbol, man would be attempting to respond to the divine by the denial of the evident and the experiential, and in defiance of the signs. Like a flagrant asceticism, such a philosophy denies God in despising his creation.

The Quranic signs are thus a deeply potential, reconc iling, mediating, truth, calculated to give pause to the asperities of insensitive conviction and to the militancy of those who do not stay to discriminate where they denounce. It encourages us to seek, as it were, a reverence for reverence, and to correct the idolatries of men without violating their shrines. For these, even if perversely, may represent what they have done with the signs. The task of the faithful is to retrieve the perversity without dispelling the significance. This apart, what does monotheism itself avail? Why does unity 'matter'? If it is merely a passion about something arithmetical, it is barren and frustrating. It matters because, as a tradition of Muḥammad has it, 'whosoever makes all his cares a single care, God will suffice him as to all his other cares'. As Jalāl al-Dīn Rūmī observed:' Whoso preserves his tongue from ascribing partners to God, God undertakes to cleanse his spirit of the weeds of polytheism.'[1]

Here, then, in Leo Baeck's words, is 'a monotheism of the senses'.[2] We must resolve never to close our faculties to their benediction in God. Rather let

> '. . . the open sky sit upon our senses like a sapphire crown, the air (be) our robe of state, the earth our throne and the sea a mighty minstrel playing before it.'[3]

It was just a failure to live in these terms which Thomas Traherne in the seventeenth century described, in an oddly Islamic phrase, as 'my apostacie', by which he meant, exactly, this lapse (so characteristic of the adult world) into the negligent, casual and graceless attitudes the Qur'ān steadily reproaches. 'All his care', therefore, in the enjoyment of the senses and the mystery of their felicity, was 'to be sensible of God's mercies and to behave himself as the friend of God in the universe'.[4]

[1] *Discourses*, translated by A. J. Arberry, London, 1961, p. 90.

[2] *This People Israel: The Meaning of Jewish Existence*, translated A. H. Friedlander, New York, 1965, p. 174.

[3] *Letters of John Keats*, selected by F. Page, London, 1954. Letter of 14 September 1817, pp. 25–6.

[4] See *Centuries of Meditations*, new issue, London, 1960. Century Iv, 41. See also Century v. 9. This work lay in MS. undiscovered until this century. It is a great treasure of simple and reverent delight.

Chapter 10
DESIRING THE FACE OF GOD

Among the greatest of twentieth-century western minds in the study and awareness of Islam was Louis Massignon. Through half a century of patient research and personal relationships, and with a rare quality of spirit, he made the mysticism of Islam an inward experience of his own being as a scholar and a Christian. He was convinced that Muslim theology was essentially a mystical structure deriving from the Qur'ān itself as the primary source of its development. Those immediate features of the book and of the Prophet's career, which seem to place them both squarely in the sphere of dogmatism, autocracy, power, and sharp contrasts—aspects broadly incompatible with the true mystical temper—Massignon was bold to claim, in their proper perspective, as the very proof of his case. Quranic vocabulary as the vocabulary of mysticism was the central clue of his scholarship. The prophetic figure behind it and within it he saw as the intense focal point of a sense of religious destiny—'a contraction of truth within historic time'.[1]

Massignon's career, which it is not meant here to explore, serves as a lively reminder and symbol of a dimension of the Qur'ān that needs a careful appreciation. We have been led to it through all the foregoing chapters. *Ḥifẓ* plainly lends itself to a feeling for the 'mystique' of the whole as more than a document. The idea of 'surface' and 'depth' within the text, of the 'subtlety' behind the 'obvious' and of a selectivity of readership, easily made for an élite status of understanding and discernment. The deep, dramatic 'personalism' we have seen in

[1] Louis Massignon (1883–1962) made his first contact with Islam in 1901 in Algeria. He travelled in Morocco, corresponded with Charles de Foucauld and studied in Cairo. From 1907 until 1922 his main energies were devoted to the study of the Persian mystic Al-Ḥallāj, a task which contributed to a deep Christian conversion, and transformed the whole temper of Massignon's work. His significance as a pioneer of Muslim-Christian exchange still awaits definitive treatment.

Quranic portrayal of the human calling and crisis—though it can well underwrite a sharp orthodoxy at odds with mystical intuition—has within it the urgency about the self which so often characterizes the mystic's concern. The concept of *Tauḥīd*, even in its most dogma-conscious form, readily serves to yearnings after absorption in the One where credal confession of the unity becomes superfluous. The seeking of forgiveness may pass into the experience of one-ness in which both guilt and pardon are transcended in the embrace of non-duality. Most evident of all, the 'signs' that call men, through the gate of the senses, into the divine friendship are capable of the readiest mystical translation into the language of ecstacy and unitary love.

The purpose of this chapter is to summarize this area of the Quranic mind, the book, that is, as it might be taken and as it has been received. The literature is immense. For Sufism—the familiar Islamic term for mysticism—has often been the major element in the religious history and the popular experience of Islam. It served over long centuries to interiorize the terms of Islamic dogma. Even those who dispute the claim of Massignon, and of many other scholars, that Sufism derived from wholly inward and Muslim sources and was not evoked by external factors, must, in so disputing, concede the remarkable fact that a system so instinctively authoritarian and absolutist as Islam, and so essentially confident about political sanctions in religion, should nevertheless have generated so sustained an achievement of mysticism. For the mystic will gladly defy the dogmatists, keep his inner freedoms against rulers, dream away the holy *Ka'bah* and insist that no mere journey makes a pilgrimage. He will find his exegesis as he pleases, be his own *Imām* and set the inner light against all caliphs and pundits. It says much for the resilience of Muslims that an original religious history so sharply assertive in its creed, and an establishment so confident in its statehood, could nevertheless through the centuries have produced so rich and spontaneous a quality of spiritual adventure.

The Qur'ān is clearly at the centre of this paradox—if such it be. For the book has been at once the guardian and fount of the orthodoxy and the origin of the mystical vitality. The very *waḥy*, or 'revelatory' inspiration, which, through the Prophet, is the ground of its sacrosanct status serves in some measure as a paradigm and an aspiration.[1]

[1] Aspiration in the sense that Muḥammad could be taken as a practising mystic whose example could be followed. See *The Event*, op. cit., Chapter 1, for a study of the *charisma*

Prophecy, albeit irrepeatable, is a phenomenon which may kindle a discipleship of the experience as well as a submission of belief. The vocabulary in which the final revelation speaks may be borrowed to carry the inner apprehensions of truth, as the mystic learns them for himself. The same book which authorizes the shaikh energizes the saint. Where the Schools interpret with a call to submission, the mystic appropriates in a personal quest.

Ṣūfī awareness of the Qur'ān can best be measured for our purposes by reference to notable passages and salient vocabulary terms, the first of them supplying the chapter title, namely 'the desire for the face of God'. *Waj Allāh* and man's *ibtighā'*, or active yearning towards it, express the essential mutuality between the divine and the human which, through all its rich and complex forms, is the central experience of Islamic mysticism and, by the same token, the point of its deepest divergence. It formulates in the sublimest terms the devotion which speaks its heart in crying: 'I am Thine.' But it may also be claimed for the ecstatic word: 'I am Thou' in which the mystic utters his entire absorption into the single reality where the finite creature sheds the illusion of individuality and is lost in the eternal One. The dualism with which devout awareness always begins—and which traditional exegesis finds inseparable from the very nature of *Ibtighā' Waj-Allāh*—the monistic forms of Sufism find fulfilled in its transcendence. The large issue implicit here belongs with almost every other realm of Quranic/Ṣūfī terminology, and takes its place in the inherent tensions of dogma and devotion which belong with all religions.

It is important, however, to note that consistently in the Qur'ān the phrase 'desiring the face of God' belongs in the context of human compassion. Surah 2: 272 has to do with expenditure on behalf of the needy and joins the moral worth of such acts strictly to a 'desiring of the face of God'. Al-Baiḍāwī has a very direct comment on this verse. 'Wealth is the full brother of the spirit.'[1] He goes on to observe that to spend both our goods and our selves is to authenticate Islam and cleanses the giver from love of things. He clearly sees the meaning within the ordered regimen of *Zakāt* as one of the pillars of Islam.

It is just this context of religious dutifulness and practical alms-

of Muḥammad and the clues to its ascertainable psychic aspects and what they might mean for Muslim devotion.

[1] *Fa inna-l-māl shaqīqu-l-rūḥ*. For the phrase *Waj Allah*, see J. M. S. Baljon, 'To Seek the Face of God', in *Acta Orientalia*, vol. 21, 1951, pp. 254–66.

giving which figures in 13: 22 and 92: 20, where the identical phrase occurs, except that 'his Lord' is read instead of 'God'. The latter reads:

> 'He who gives his substance to cleanse himself, and not with a view to the compensating favours of anyone around, but only responsive to the face of his Lord the Most High—he will be requited' (92: 18–21).

In other verses the verb *arāda* replaces *ibtaghā* with almost identical meaning. The association throughout is that the sense of human need, taken up into an active charity and a communal solidarity, belongs with a perception of the divine glory. The heavenly countenance is realized in actively responding to the human neighbour.

There is, here, one of the deepest themes of Quranic religion, which it would be wrong to reserve for esoteric Ṣūfī interpretation. For it has to do squarely and firmly with the ordinary, legal, institutional patterns of established Islam. 'The face of God', in these verses, is emphatically un-ecstatic in its down to-earth implications for day-to-day piety in the duties of allegiance. The Qur'ān, to that extent, would seem to have little sympathy with the the more pretentious forms of Ṣūfī spirituality, or at least with their claim to some *élitist* experience of divine relationships. It is tempting, of course, though it would be academically precarious, to derive Muslim mysticism itself from what might be called philanthropic sources—in the desire for personal asceticism in revolt against Ummayyad luxury and for quietism and compassion in contrast to the robust politicizing of the Khawārij and other militant groups within the struggles of early Islam. Certainly the practical emphases of the 'face of God' passages are clearly discernible in the detachment from worldly wealth which characterized the Ṣūfī Orders of later centuries and in their disciplined brotherhoods of human solidarity.

But our only concern here is with the Quranic factors and with the mystic's 'case' from the book. With the point of the preceding paragraph rightly made, we are ready for the more obvious Ṣūfī 'potential' of other verses about 'the face of God', notably those which contrast the abidingness of the divine with the fleetingness of all else. 'Everything is perishing', says 28: 88, 'except His countenance'. The previous clause is a pronounal form of the *Shahādah: Lā ilāha illā Huwa*, 'there is no god but He'. Surah 55: 26 and 27 runs: 'Everyone upon the earth is transient (*fānin*): the face of your Lord abides, majestic, glorified'. The two verbs here belong with the oft-quoted pairs of the divine Names: *Al-Awwal wa-l-Ākhir* and *Al-Ẓāhir wa-l-Bāṭin*, 'the first and the last, the outward and the inward', if read in the sense that empirical reality known to man in time is no more than the manifestation of the absolute and the eternal. They also correspond to the two pivotal terms of mystical thinking, namely *al-baqā'* and *al-fanā'*, the ever-enduring and the ever-fading.

That distinction, of course, could simply attach to mortal existence as temporally conditioned, in contrast with the unconditioned 'world without end'. Ṣūfī exegesis, however, understands it to describe the passing away (*fanā'*) of the empirical self into the unitive state of entire non-duality, akin, in its most assured forms to the Hindu *advaita*, where God has ceased to be an 'object' of worship and the worshipper, likewise, has ceased to be, as a separate 'bringer' of worship, but all is bound in a single 'We'. There remains, no doubt, a paradox in that pronoun, or, rather, in the fact that it has to be plural—wherein lies the central dilemma of 'the not to be and yet to be' of mystical 'personality'. Inconsistently, perhaps, in theory, yet gloriously in fact, mystical absorption into the One has, nevertheless, given back the self to itself in heightened and, indeed, distinctive identity, and thus produced the most creative and dynamic religious *personae*, like Jalāl al-Dīn Rūmī, Al-Junaid, 'Abd al-Qādir al-Jīlānī, and the *aqṭāb* or *foci* of Ṣūfī discipleship.

It is, again paradoxically, the very force and fervour of such figures which sends us back to the 'way' (or *ṭarīqah*) by which they became what they became. The 'theory'—if such it may be called—is not disproved by its illogicality. For it is the mystical reading of the meaning of *Tauḥīd* itself. That term, so dear to the Islamic dogmatists as the great antiseptic, banishing all pluralism and affirming the central creed of the divine Unity against all idolatrous 'competition' and all plural trustings and prayers, becomes for the mystic the sure descriptive of a unitary experience, where individuality has been transcended, where phenomenal existence has been left behind and the soul is lifted out of all self-desires. This is the true *fanā'*—not the mere physical transience of the mortal world and the universal destiny to die, but the willed death to the self in its acquisitive character, so that its clinging pre-occupations of appetite and pride are shed, and it ceases to be aware as an *ego* and consequently all separateness dissolves and only God remains. Yet even He, hitherto misconceived from within our selfish 'reverence', is no longer the great 'Other' to Whom we ascribe our remote praises, but the One in Whom we cease to be—and are.

It is, truly, one of the most remarkable evidences of the spiritual resilience of the Islamic Scripture that it could undergird in one and the same religio-cultural history two so contrasted patterns of divine-human relationship, that *Tauḥīd* could be understood from it in so sharp a diversity. For is there not a clear polarity between the sovereign transcendence of orthodox theology, with its *Rabb-'abd* relationship of absolute submission enjoined and paid, and the unitive aspiration of Ṣūfī discipline where *that* God and *that* worship come within an illusoriness which must be superseded? Is there not in the first a transcendence which, for the second, must be itself 'transcended'? Is there not for the former a quality of sovereignty before which the latter must seem intolerable, at odds with the real human as well as with the true divine? That theological tension has to be appreciated, quite apart from the unmistakable practical tensions that emerge over the requirements of ritual and the demands of law. The mystic was well able to repudiate pilgrimage as an unnecessary rite, when he was to himself a better *Ka'bah*. Or he could readily identify the meticulous worshipper in his *Ṣalāt* as no better than an idolater clinging to the visible and imprisoned in the tangible, a patron to himself even while he patronized a distant *Allāh*.

In view of this the temptation to surmise that mystical reading of the Qur'ān derives from alien impulses and factors external to a native Islam, is strong. But it would seem well, nevertheless, to resist it, and simply to register instead the evident flexibility of Quranic usage in Muslim hands. For it is this which holds many practical implications for the present time. No religion, of course, is exempt from adjacent influences and Sufism, no doubt, registers them within Muslim history with more obvious hospitality than any other segment of thought. But it is itself so influential within Islamic continuity, and vital to it, that its way with the Qur'ān cannot well be seen as other than congenial to the Scripture. One cannot deny that there are verses and concepts of the book susceptible of such patterns of interpretation. This is not to say that they are necessary.[1] It is the 'liability' of the

[1] The situation has many counterparts elsewhere among the religions. There are, for example, several vital matters in Christian faith and practice which Scripture *can* be honestly understood to sustain without it being right to claim that it *must* be taken as doing so.

Qur'ān to this 'style' of understanding which in the end is the significant thing, rather than any mandate of the text that this must be its meaning.

Examples are numerous, elaborating the fundamental idea of *Tauḥīd*, and of *fanā'* into it. 'God well-pleased with them and they well-pleased with Him', says 5: 115, adding, in the re-iterated Quranic phrase: 'that is the great victory', or 'the supreme achieving' (*al-fauz al-'aẓīm*). The context of this divine pleasing, in both senses, God's and man's, is consistently the bliss of the believers in paradise (cf. 9: 72, 89 and 100, 45: 30, 57: 12 and 64: 9, etc.). In view of this there is some arbitrariness in building a doctrine of spiritual self-transcendence upon it, apart, that is, from the mystical import of bliss and the *summum bonum*.

The same double sense resides in the much-loved: 'So remember Me and I will remember you' of 2: 152, which the Ṣūfī masters have taken in the sense of the unitive mutuality of the soul in God and of God in the soul. It centres on the concept of *dhikr* which becomes in Islamic mysticism the very core of the discipline. It *can* mean simply and uncomplicatedly, the recognition of the Qur'ān as the divine reminder to men (*dhikr* being one of the titles by which the book is described), and the devout remembrance of God in the fidelity of the daily prayers. But its technical sense in Sufism develops into the elaborate and cumulative disciplines of the Ṣūfī Orders. There the call to awareness of the divine 'signs', reviewed in the previous chapter, becomes a studied technique of attention and desire, whereby the egocentric situation is turned towards its escape into the all absorbing recollection of God. These complex and exacting paths to the Ṣūfī attainment of *al-fauz al-kabīr* are best considered within the inclusive notion of the *ṭarīqah*, or mystic's way.

Perhaps significantly, this term in its fully developed connotation is not Quranic. The word does occur in 20: 105 in a somewhat enigmatic passage about the surmising of the resurrected as to the space of time since their mortal term. *Amthalum ṭarīqatan* will say that it was no more than a day. The phrase is variously translated 'the justest of them in the way', 'the well-informed of them', 'the best of them in conduct', 'the fairest of them in course', and 'the most exemplary of them in his way'. The noun in the accusative is most readily taken in a quite general sense, the more so as the context has to do with unbelievers. The usage can hardly bear the whole weight of the technical *ṭarīqah*. The other occasion is 72: 16, where the hint of the previous verb *istaqāmū* suggests simply the sense of 'the straight path' of the *Fātiḥah*. In one context where *ṭarīqah* occurs with the possessive 'your' (pl.) it belongs with the history of Moses and the wiles of Pharaoh.

Here again, however, the lack of Quranic definition of the technical *ṭarīqah* does not curb the assurance, nor check the intuitive resources, of Ṣūfī commentary. There are several terms which fit into the pattern of the stages of the soul's progress towards the unitive state. It begins in the sense of need and 'poverty' of heart, out of which the seeker comes in the beginning of his course. Here may be borrowed a comment of Moses in the story of his watering the flocks of the daughters of the man of Midian, one of whom he subsequently took to wife in his exile from Egypt. Surah 28: 24 runs: 'O my Lord I am needy for (*faqīr*) whatever You will cause to come upon me.' Seyyid Hossein Nasr writes:

> 'He who participates in *Taṣawwuf* is called a *faqīr*, or poor, according to the Quranic verse: "And God is rich and ye are poor" (47: 38). . . . The *faqīr* seeks to realize . . . that he has nothing, all comes from God . . . metaphysically he is nothing. God is the one and only Being.'[1]

The plural word *fuqarā'* is used in several places in a purely literal sense, describing the appropriate recipients of alms (for example, 2: 273 and 9: 60) though even here a certain metaphorical meaning may be arguable and 'being in want of' stands as a physical parable of a spiritual hunger conditioning the divine satisfaction. In 35: 15, however, 'O people, you are the poor ones unto God [lit.], and God is rich and praiseworthy', is liable to a deeper implication than a material dependence, though many translators take it only in that way.[2]

The *murīd*, or would-be finder,[3] is only constituted by a willingness to count the external world loss and accept a voluntary 'poverty' of spirit, or disciplined *zuhd*. This basic Ṣūfī term does not occur in the

[1] In *Ideals and Realities of Islam*, London, 1966, p. 131. The author's usage *Allāh* has been changed to 'God'.

[2] For example, Arberry, Syed 'Abdul Laṭīf, Pickthall, Dawood. In 2: 268 we have the only use in the Qur'ān of the noun, *faqr*, or 'poverty' there identified as what Satan bestows in contrast to the plenty which is the gift of God.

[3] *Murīd* is the active participle from *arāda*, used above in 'the face of God' passages. It means 'the one who seeks'.

Qur'ān. Nor is asceticism approved, though there are friendly references to monasticisms outside Islam.[1] But the Ṣūfī, in foregoing the distracting and diverting appetites of the natural man, can claim to be carrying to a further point and a more conscious technique the fundamental notion of *imsāk*, or self-restraining which is the familiar, universal posture of the Ramaḍān fast. In *zuhd*, or abstinence, he is paying the necessary cost of the divine *Riḍwān*, or pleasing.

Some mystical thinking understands a progression from *īmān* (faith) and *islām* (surrender) to *iḥsān* (true weal). The first two are related in either direction, that is, the submission (*islām*) which does not yet exercise authentic belief, as in the case of the acceding tribes of *badū* in Surah 49: 14–16. Or *īmān* is seen as a firmer, fuller stage of the *muslim* as *mu'min*. Either way, *iḥsān* is, then, a further stage again, where the individual believer—whose individuality is necessary to, and confirmed by, the credal piety—passes into the unitive experience. 'Shall the return of *iḥsān* be other than *iḥsān*?' asks Surah 55: 60. The immediate meaning seems to be that the bounties of God expect and deserve a proper hallowing, a due and a just and a compassionate receiving, in the meaning, we may assume, of what we have already pondered in 'The Sacramental Earth'.[2] But mystical reading of the sense of *iḥsān*, in passages where it is not obviously material in meaning, claims it for this status of attained 'will-into-God' seen as the true well-being, well-doing, beyond all formal religion or obligation of piety. Where *iḥsān* is closely linked with *dīn*, or 'religion', and would, thus, seem to belong squarely with orthodox devotion, Ṣūfī thinking enlarges the range of *dīn* to embrace all its own esoteric meanings. Such passages are numerous with the plural participle *muḥsinūn* or *muḥsinīn*. Surah 7: 56, for example, bids men 'call upon Him with awe and ardour', and concludes: 'The mercy of God is near to the *muḥsinīn*'. Surah 29: 69 assures those who struggle in God's way of His guidance and His presence. 'Truly God is with the *muḥsinīn*'. With this term, as with others, the general reader is aware far more of a Ṣūfī liberty, than of any exegetical necessity, about the *iḥsān* of the *ṭarīqah*.

[1] Notably in Surah 24. See below. There occurs in 12: 20, in the narrative of Joseph, the active participle (pl.) *zāhidin*, 'setting little store by him', i.e. Joseph.

[2] Though Al-Baiḍāwī takes it simply in the sense that the (human) *iḥsān* of good works deserves the (divine) reward of paradise. It might be claimed that the context sustains him. *Muḥsinūn* might be awkwardly rendered 'the well-being ones'.

The verb 'to struggle' (*jāhadu*) in the passage just quoted is another conspicuous term in the Ṣūfī vocabulary, with perhaps a more persuasively potential ambiguity than *iḥsān*. The general sense of *jihād*, or 'effort in the way of God', has to do, incontrovertibly, with the active propagation of Islam in the emphatic patterns familiar from Islamic history, involving and sanctifying the political order, and the military arm, in the cause of the faith. But that very phrase *fī sabīl Illāh*, 'in the way of God', allows, if it does not suggest, a different temper—and arena—of 'struggle' on behalf of God, within the soul. So it is that the mystics developed the notion of the 'inner' or the 'greater' *jihād* in contrast to the 'outer' and 'lesser' *jihād* of rulers and armies and legists. Soul-*jihād* became the test and proof of the will to discipline which alone sustained and accomplished the stages of the Ṣūfī progress through repentance, abnegation, resignation, obedience and patience, to the ultimate awareness of unity in God.

While the major Quranic passages in this field have to do categorically with the outward and the communal sphere and with the sanctions of power, there are latent potentialities for Ṣūfī interpretations in others. Even the most adamant irreconciliability can be spiritualized into the soul's implacable opposition to its own enemies. Thus, for example, Surah 60: 1, shortly after the *Hijrah*, warns the *Muhājirūn*, or emigrants from Mecca, not to compromise their exodus by harbouring a secret love for their former fellow citizens in the abandoned city. For these are now indicted as 'God's enemies', as well as being foes of the Muslims. Having gone forth to exile and to struggle 'in My way and for My good pleasing' (*fī sabīlī wa ibtighā'a marḍātī*), says the Lord, it would be playing false to stay emotionally bound to those one has forsaken and not to effectuate one's own decisions totally. The situation is immediately parabolic of the absolute claims of the *ṭarīqah* and the committedness required of the *murīd*, if he would become the *wāṣil*—the one who has attained. That 'there is no discharge in that war' is a truth the outer struggle readily affords to the inner. Enmities against God, to be uncompromisingly resisted, then become the passions and temptations of the flesh, the self-delusions of the ego-centred life, the foes of 'the real' as, for example, Al-Ghazālī expounded them in the third section of his monumental *Iḥyā' 'Ulūm al-Dīn*.[1] He called them *al-muhlikāt*, 'the things that

[1] Abū Ḥāmid ibn Muḥammad al-Ghazālī (AD 1058–1111), perhaps the greatest of all Muslim theologians. His 'Reviving of the Science(s) of Religion' is pre-eminent among

destroy'—gluttony and sensuality, the pitfalls of speech, anger, malice, envy, avarice, hypocrisy, arrogance and conceit, and the worldly goods which nourished these deceptions of the heart. All these had to be countered by *al-munjiyāt*, 'the saving things'. The struggle within man has its seat in *al-nafs al-lawwāmah*, the reprehending self, the inner censor of the spirit, often associated in moral psychology in Islam with *al-nafs al-ammārah* of Surah 12: 53, the soul constrained towards evil and needing, therefore, the incessant watchfulness and curb of an inner *jihād*.[1]

The external *jihād* is often understood as having its own sanctions within itself, as an overriding obligation, not unlike the Marxist sense of destiny. This same inner authorization can, likewise, be borrowed for the urge to disciplined concentration of will, all deterrents apart. The point emerges in the context of the intriguing phrase in 22: 78: 'Struggle in God His due struggle' (*jāhidū fī-llāhi ḥaqqa jihādihi*) which is followed by the observation: 'He has chosen you and has not laid upon you any *ḥarajin* in religion.' *Ḥaraj* usually means an impediment, burden or constriction. But it contains the idea of that which is inhibiting.[2] The *jihād* that is truly God's can then be seen as that which relates all means to the one end and has within itself the justifying principle. This could certainly be said by the Ṣūfī of his *ṭarīqah*. For he is therein bound over—if one may venture a legal phrase—to his sole cause. This 'concentrating' of the self is the perpetual condition of *Tauḥīd*. It is precisely that injunction to whole-heartedness which finds eloquent expression in the words of Surah 9: 24:

'If your fathers, your sons, your brothers, your wives, your families,

the major works of Islamic moral thought and a crowning achievement of religious awareness.

[1] Cf. above, Chapter 6, pp. 86–97.

[2] Some translators take it materially as 'hardships'. The comment of Al-Baiḍāwī is interesting. '*Jāhidū* etc. means for God and on His behalf against the open foes of His religion, the deviationists, and against inner enemies of passion and the soul. It is said that the Prophet remarked on returning from the expedition to Tabūk: "We have come back from the lesser *jihād* to the greater *jihād*." . . ."He has not laid, etc." means any anguish by reason of what it may cost you to carry it through. The reference is to the fact that there is no prohibiting it to you nor excusing you from it, or else to your being authorized to disregard in exceptional circumstances what is otherwise incumbent on you. The Prophet said: "If I have commanded you to do something, do it to your utmost", inasmuch as there was for them a way out of every trespass and a door open for repentance, in permitted circumstances. . . .'

or the substance you have acquired, or trade you may fear will be put at risk, or homes you are very happy in, are more precious to you than God and His Apostle and venture (*jihād*) in His way, then hold off until God brings about His will . . .'

The clauses here about a loyalty that counts the cost have to do directly with immediate history and crisis. But they have an evident relation to the decisions of a disciplined *taṣawwuf* and its critical demands. As with every other sphere of Quranic vocabulary that lends itself to latent as well as patent meanings, *jihād* avails for sainthood as well as for policy.

The Ṣūfī path, mapped thus in terms of the book and trodden with a scriptural devotion, leads to the attainment of gnosis, or *'irfān* and *ma'rifah*, to the inward knowledge which rewards the patient seeker but is hidden from the rational wisdom and the formal pietist. These two pivotal terms are, in fact, non-Quranic, but they are readily comprehended within the concept of 'illumination' and the metaphor of *Nūr*, or light, which is one of the Names of God. The most notable passage of all, in respect of Ṣūfī exegesis, is the Surah with the title of 'Light' (Surah 24). It takes its name from the most celebrated of all verses in this regard (vv. 35–37).

> 'God is the light of the heavens and the earth.
> The likeness of His light is as a niche wherein is a lamp.
> The lamp is in a glass, and the glass, as it were, a star for brilliance.
> The lamp is kindled from a blessed tree, an olive neither of the east nor of the west, the oil of which is almost incandescent of itself without the touch of fire.
> Light upon light.
> God guides to His light whom He wills.
> God affords these striking similitudes on men's behalf and He has knowledge of every thing.
> This—in houses God has willed should be established in which His Name should be remembered, and wherein, glorifying Him by morning and by evening, are men whom neither trading nor merchandising divert from the remembrance of God, the performance of the prayer rite and the bringing of alms—all in awe of a day when hearts and eyes alike will be in consternation.'

The concluding phrases keep very close to the familiar features of the *Sharī'ah*, *tasbīḥ*, *Ṣalāt* and *Zakāt*, and to the concepts of *hudā*, or guidance, and *yaum al-Dīn*, the day of judgement. What so pointedly sustains and almost invites the Ṣūfī exegesis is the warm commendation of the 'monastic' principles of withdrawal from the working, bartering, acquisitive world, and, even more, the wide potential or implicit meanings of the cluster of terms at the opening of the passage, with their inter-depending significance—light, likeness, lamp, niche, glass, star, oil and kindling fire.[1] For these perfectly fit the mystical notion of the soul's illumination, its being absorbed into a light beyond and yet within it. As the lamp is to the light so is the soul to the One. As the glass is to the lamp so is the empirical self to the unitive self. As the fire is to the oil so is the truth to the fuel of the heart. There are almost endless theosophical and esoteric themes and principles capable of being read in these rich metaphors and all with the authority of God Himself having 'struck' such 'similitudes' for the sake of humanity.

'I gazed upon God', wrote Abū Yazīd al-Bisṭāmī, in the third Muslim century (d. 875)

> '. . . with the eye of certainty, after He had advanced me to the degree of independence of all creatures and illumined me with His light, revealing to me the wonders of His secrets and manifesting to me the grandeur of His He-ness . . . Through God I gazed on God and I beheld God in reality. . . . He created me an eye out of His light. With the tongues of His goodness I communed with God and by His light I gazed on Him. I knew that through Him I lived. He opened to me the door of the palace of unity. . . . He bestowed on me a name of His own essence and addressed me with His own selfhood. Singleness became manifest; duality vanished. No trace of me was visible. . . .'[2]

In like vein, the renowned Shihāb al-Dīn al-Suhrawardī (1153–1191), known as 'the master of illumination', who was put to death at Aleppo, on ground of 'heresy', when only thirty-six years of age.[3] He drew his *Ḥikmat al- Ishrāq*, or 'Wisdom of illumination', from the analogy of the sun, irradiating (we might even say, 'orientalizing') the world. The primal light (*al-Nūr al-Qāhir*), descending through degrees of light, drew the soul in yearning (*al-dhauq*) to itself. That yearning

[1] On the fascinating questions of detail here and, in particular, 'an olive neither of the east nor of the west', see *The Event*, pp. 93–7.

[2] *Muslims Saints and Mystics: Episodes from Tadhkirat al Auliya'*, translated by A. J. Arberry, London, 1966, pp. 105–108.

[3] Not to be confused with his namesake of Baghdad, Shihāb al-Dīn 'Umar al-Suhrawardī (1144–1234), a nonagenarian.

was itself the perception by which the irradiated being of man transcended his contingency.

Deeply congenial to the 'light' metaphor and all that gathers round it in Ṣūfī exegesis is the bewilderingly rich term, *Al-Ḥaqq*, among the divine Names—'the true', 'the real', 'the authentic'. 'God, He is the true' (22:6). 'Exalted be God, the King, the true, there is no god but He, the Lord of the gracious throne' (23:116). It lends itself to all the versatility of Ṣūfī esoteric reading and sustains, indeed, the counter-conclusion that it is the exoterics, the literalists, the 'concretizers', who have missed the inner sense of the book. 'The reality of realities' (*Ḥaqīqat al-Ḥaqā'iq*—not itself a Quranic phrase) is the all-embracing One, beyond and through all individuation and cosmic particularity, the essence to be identified in the symbols of the revelation taken, not in collective subjectivity—as is the way of commentators—but in their transcendental meaning. The real, then, invites the spiritually apperceptive back beyond his empirical being into the state of re-integration into divine reality, where he knows himself such as he was before the illusory manifestation into temporal being. The words of Surah 64:3: 'He created the heavens and the earth with the truth', then carry the sense that the creation mirrors 'the principal possibilities' which, according to the Ṣūfī concept of the Creator (*Al-Khāliq*), are effectuated into time and things. In a similar sense, Surah 31:28: 'He created you not, nor brought you forth, save as a single soul', is taken to mean, not an identity of all mankind in the created order, but the undifferentiated reality where individuation—such as the true Ṣūfī transcends—is known for the illusory thing which unenlightened subjectivity stubbornly wills to be.

The resources of Ṣūfī reading of the Qur'ān in the mystical sense of 'the real' may be further illustrated from two intriguing verses. In Surah 11:56, the prophet Hūd, remonstrating with the tribe of 'Ād, declares: 'There is no crawling thing but He takes it by the forelock (*bināṣiyatihi*). My Lord is on a straight path.' That concluding *ṣirāṭ mustaqīm* phrase encourages the reader who is so minded to understand the passage as affirming a principle of reality, pervading all things, and passing through the intelligence (the crown of the head), understood, not as the mere empirical reason that leads to science, but as the spiritual intellection by which man realizes his essential absorption into 'the real'.[1] It may be asked how this relates to the

[1] The phrase has the sense of mastering, or effectively controlling (cf. 'Take time by

insect and animal spheres which the verse plainly includes, or to the inanimate worlds which it must needs involve. But that question only underlines the ready ingenuity—if such it be—or the confident assumptions, of such exegesis. The will to enlist the Qur'ān for an existing structure of thought is the more impressive where its very case is dubious.

Witness the sense of Surah 21: 18: 'Nay! but We cast the truth upon the false and it subdues it. Lo! it vanishes away. Woe to you over your (false) ascriptions.' The context has to do with a vigorous refutation of the idolaters and asserts the deep significance of the creation and of life. However, according to a prayer of 'Abd al-Salām ibn Mashīsh, a sixth (AH)-century Moroccan mystic and teacher of the great Abū-l-Ḥasan al-Shādhilī, founder of the Tunisian Shādhilī Order of Sufism, the 'false' here is the illusion of empirical selfhood, which is exposed and destroyed by the awareness of the unitary self.[1] The 'false notions' (*mimmā taṣifūn*), that is, 'what you describe', are then seen, not as the idols of the *mushrikīn*, but as the egocentric deception of individuation not yet freed from the bonds of its unawareness of the real.

The twin issues here of Quranic exegetical liberty, or pretension—as the case may be—and of the initiatives which could venture them, can both be pondered under one further, final, Quranic term, sometimes recruited by the Ṣūfī mind, namely the *bay'ah*, or 'allegiance' of the believer. This term has clear, historical, political, implications in the Qur'ān. Surah 9: 11 calls upon the believers to take joy in the bargain they have with God, referring to the bond between God and themselves, in which they exchanged the pledge of allegiance for the pledge of paradise. Using the same verb, to vow allegiance, Surah 48: 10 speaks of a fealty sworn to Muḥammad as a fealty sworn to

the forelock'). Dawood translates: 'There is not a living creature on the earth whose destiny He does not control.' If we are to apply this to mankind perhaps we must associate with it the implications of Hamlet's: 'What should such fellows as I do, crawling between earth and heaven?'

[1] The verb means 'to hurl, or throw or fling', and in a derivative sense, 'to invalidate or refute'. The term *zāhiqin*, here ('vanishes away') is not the *fanā'* root. It may well refer simply to the progress of Muḥammad's mission in the struggle for an effective monotheism. Ibn Mashīsh's prayer ran: 'Strike with me on vanity that I may bring it to naught.' Quoted from Titus Burckhardt, *An Introduction to Sufi Doctrine*, translated by D. M. Matheson, Lahore, 1959, p. 15. Burckhardt adds: 'To the extent he is effectively emancipated the contemplative ceases to be such and such a person and "becomes" the Truth on which he has meditated and the divine Name he invokes.'

God. That 'God's hand is upon their hands' seems to mean a sacrally solemnized oath. Surah 48: 18 adds. 'He knew what was in their hearts and He sent down the *Sakīnah* upon them, and gave them the reward of a prompt victory.' Surah 60: 12 uses the same *bāya'a* verb of women coming to accede to Islam. There seems no doubt that specific historical occasions, verifiable in the *Sīrah*, or biography, of Muḥammad, are identifiable in these allusions.

It has, however, been possible for this 'allegiance' or 'homage' or 'selling of oneself' to be given a mystical significance. The Prophet, in this role as the focus of loyalty, may be seen to command the soul-magnetism by which private souls cluster around the real so as to pass over into its identity. The light metaphor suggests this parallel meaning. To belong is to be suffused into unity. As light indwells, so allegiance identifies. The soul is yielded into the irradiation which both achieves and annihilates it, as the mere lamp in the glow of the light.

There is also a further discernible, if elusive, sense here. Mystical 'allegiance' to Muḥammad may be held to take the disciple beyond the literal text of the Qur'ān. For, antecedent to the Prophet's oral communication (though not to its celestial counterpart) and, therefore, to the text of the Qur'ān in earthly currency, was the direct awareness of the Prophet's consciousness of its content. May not the disciple participate in that prior reality, through his discipleship, and so enter an immediacy of apprehension only possible within such 'allegiance', and in an *à priori* relation to the textual Scripture and its normal study? In this way the Qur'ān as a document could become secondary to its mediation through a 'master' in sequence to the Prophet himself, in so far as such a 'master' enjoyed a spiritual unity with him and could communicate it to his disciples. Hence the pattern of Ṣūfī devotion within 'orders' of allegiance received as foci of Quranic light.

All esotericism tends, of course, in this direction, since, by its cult of immediacy, it pre-supposes continuing inspiration and continual manifestation. So it was that the traditional Ṣūfī loyalties gathered around eminent founders or *aqṭāb*, each the axis of the soul's devotion. The vicissitudes and technicalities of this development do not belong with our present concern for the Qur'ān. It suffices to note that the personal relationship of the believer to the Prophet, through the *barakah*, or 'virtue' of the *quṭb*, or with the order-founder as the mediation of the Prophet's claim on the soul, could be seen in the pledges of the *bay'ah*. They were solemnized in rites of initiation and perpetually expressed in the techniques of *dhikr*. The note in 48: 18 about the *Sakīnah* (or Shechinah-presence), coming upon the pledgers, served greatly to sustain this Ṣūfī exegesis. For it was a favourite term, denoting the soul possessed of, and by, its Lord. It was close to the *iṭmi'nān*, or 'tranquillity', that figured prominently in Islamic vocabulary as a reward of the remembrance of God (cf. Surah 13: 28, and 89: 27).

So strong were the emotions associated with Ṣūfī allegiance that they could well replace, without embarrassment or compromise, even the ritual, legal, obligations of 'ordinary' Islam. The bond of discipleship provided also the necessary continuity through which the stages of Ṣūfī disciplines could be ensured and guided. On every count the Ṣūfī understanding of the soul and God, of love and faith, required the framework or fabric which *bay'ah* connoted. But there can be no doubt that the development was the inner logic of Ṣūfī assumptions, rather than the necessary logic of the texts they used.

Reflection on the great prototypes and foci of Ṣūfī devotion, their spiritual kin and their lesser kindred in every order, serves to underline the paradox we have encountered throughout, namely, the supreme personal achievements of stature and spirit which were the crowning fruit of a system that proclaimed the illusion of the personal self. It would appear that the central principle of *Fanā'* and *Tauḥīd* contradicts itself in fulfilling itself, and that the personality which strives to lose itself as illusory stays to find itself in a deeeper fulness of reality. For all the arguable vagaries which can be detected in Ṣūfī exegesis, that paradox abides as a steady measure of the range of the Qur'ān, experienced and possessed.

There remains one final consideration of this 'desiring of the face of God' in Ṣūfī readership—a consideration which points forward to the themes of the next chapter. Such mystical exegetes represent what we may rightly characterize as the outstanding example of the assimilative capacity of Islam. Even the most ardent champions of the view that the genesis and growth of Sufism are authentically Islamic are bound also to concede this assimilative quality. There is no sphere where the parallels with other faiths and attitudes, Hindu, Buddhist, Christian, Jewish, are more evident, and the textual liberties more self-justified and confident.

Moreover, the theory itself of Sufism turns on the notion of the exoteric, the orthodox and the literalist, as being only the veil, or 'surface', of meanings these attitudes do not exhaust or even understand. Claiming spiritual sovereignty over the logical and ritual forms of religion, it sees itself as *qalb al-islām*, 'the heart of Islam', possessing the normal ideals and symbols in its own way, in independence of their traditional significance. That independence is fundamental to the esoteric and to a characterization of the exoteric as merely preliminary or obtuse—a collective dullness. There could hardly be a more devastating posture of superiority to received authority than this.

It compels on the modern observer the question whether the same kind of assimilative freedom may not well be claimed in quite other directions. If authority, dogma and rite, can be an exoteric realm a true insight knows how to decipher and, so except in terms of its own, to discard, why should not a like liberty suggest itself to the non-Ṣūfī, modern, intellectualist mind, re-conceiving authority, dogma and rite in *its* own image? Mysticism seems to be one of the major casualties of the secular world.[1] Its greatest days are probably past. But its example survives. Others, too, can claim to leave behind the witless 'exoteric'.

Why, for example, should the psychologists and the social scientists not do likewise with the explicitness of Islam, seeing its meanings other than its seeming, and reading them in their own idiom? An instance is readily to hand in the recent writing of Dr Muḥammad Kāmil Ḥusain. Some brief note of it may serve here as a useful foil, and as a contrasted 'revising' of what might be understood by 'desire for the face of God'. His understanding of Islam turns on its psychological and social role in achieving peace of heart (*iṭmi'nān*) and conducing to the realization of human well-being. Religion has even a physiological basis, being the restraining brake on human animality and excess, the nourisher of conscience against the modern idolatries and false absolutes of wealth, or nation, or pride or greed. *Tauḥīd* and *Tanzīh* and *Raḥmah* in Islam need to be understood and interpreted in terms of soul-quality, soul-reverence and soul-peace. In a sense, all religions exist for these ends and their doctrinal structures and liturgical forms are a matter of indifference, provided their function

[1] See the concluding chapter in J. Spencer Trimingham, *Sufism and the Sufi Orders*, Oxford, 1971, for a careful survey and estimate of the contemporary standing of Islamic Sufism.

in the soul of man is achieved and sustained. The real miracle of the Qur'ān is its effective transformation of a pagan society, and this remains the text of its meaning. God is merciful to men through men's mutual mercy. 'Desiring His face', therefore, means seeking and doing what He has willed for the human situation, where all tests return.[1]

We are almost akin, with these thoughts from within Islam, to Matthew Arnold's familiar dictum about religion as 'morality tinged with emotion'. There is much, at least in western, secular writing today, which would reject it out of hand, as simply further proof of the will to illusion underlying all religion, the will to a comfort and an equanimity which the real world cannot yield, an attempt to unburden ourselves of the weight and futility of our existence, where the honest man, by contrast, shoulders the sombre truth of the void. Dr Ḥusain doubtless has his answer for those secular minds who equate the courageous with the comfortless and believe there is 'nothing so real as nothing'. It is a fascinating discussion. But, whether facile or perceptive, sanguine or authentic, as an account of religious meaning centred in a human function, his view represents an assimilation of Islam, no less worthy of recognition, no more questionably 'esoteric' in respect of authoritarian Islam, than the different ventures of the Ṣūfī mind. To attempt to relate their relative acceptability would be too pretentious a proposal. The only concern in this context is to note that one assimilative capacity may suggest another. 'My soul is ever in my hand', wrote the psalmist (Psalm 119: 109). The faith is what the faithful take it to be. Ṣūfī exegesis of the Qur'ān is both a telling, and a pointed, exemplification of that principle.

The great Leonardo da Vinci used to describe himself as 'a disciple of experience'. So, in their own sense, might the Ṣūfīs. The essential question is which determines the other—experience the discipleship, or the discipleship experience? Men in Islam have long been subsuming the world to their religious text. There are many now who are disposed rather to see the text through the priority of the world. What, then, in that more likely mood of the future, is a Quranic discipleship likely to mean in experience?

[1] See his article 'O God, Make Strong Islam', in *Al-Zahrā'*, Cairo, 1971, pp. 9–14 and, more fully his *Al-Wādī al-Muqaddas*, Cairo, 1968. The theme of false absolutes occurs notably in his *Qaryah Ẓālimah*, Cairo, 1952 (English translation *City of Wrong*, Amsterdam, 1959).

Chapter 11
DIRECTIVE AND DIRECTION

'Sometimes a lantern moves along the night
That interests our eyes. And who goes there,
I think, where from, and bound, I wonder, where?
With, all down darkness wide, his wading light.'[1]

Almost certainly the Quranic lantern of Surah 24:35 was fixed in a sanctuary with steady reserves of oil and tended by contemplatives.[2] Yet to think it moving in the hand along the ways of life is to do justly by its themes of guidance and the present self of its people. The purpose of this final chapter, with the initial help of G. M. Hopkins's imagery, is to see the faith-community of the Qur'ān, as it were, carrying their illumination. In religious existence there is this seeing and this following in reciprocal relation. We see by what we take: we take what we see by. 'Wading . . . down darkness wide' is no strange poetry for our current flux of perplexity.

Hence the concluding title. The Qur'ān in its authority is directive—emphatic, revered, fundamental. But what direction do its possessors take with it and from it? Every religious authority, in the end, turns on the terms of the obedience of those who receive it as authority. Even where the authority is unquestioned, it is because acceptance is unquestioning. The guidance is always a receiving by the guided and the quality of the one will hinge on the temper of the other. However men understand the light in their hands and how it came there, it is they who relate it to the darkness into which it shines. Islam is what the Qur'ān defines and enjoins: it is what Muslims read and acknowledge.

[1] *The Poems of Gerard Manley Hopkins*, 4th edition, edited by W. H. Gardner and N. H. Mackenzie, London, 1967, p. 71.

[2] See the sequence about houses of prayer in which men live, all merchandise apart, to praise the divine Name.

In previous chapters we have noted what it is to have the Islamic Scripture by heart, and have taken some stock of traditional exegesis and its cast of mind. We have isolated certain dominant features of the Quranic understanding of man and his experience of personal significance, his vocation to divine relationship, his involvement in evil, his pardon and God's mercy, his invitation both to dominion and submission, his liberty to be idolatrous and his true liberation in a hallowed world from the menace of his pride. All these are at once idelibly Quranic and universally human. They are the Muslim's inward and religious world, yet also the one, common context of mankind.

If text and meaning are properly seen in the foregoing, they admit of certain closing reflections relating them to the present practice of Islam. We have in mind three decisive aspects which might be broadly formulated as (1) being Muslim with the Qur'ān, (2) being Islamic in the world, and (3) being religious by Islam. These are, in effect, the faith-question, the secular question and the ecumenical question. If the distinctions seem somewhat cryptic and puzzling at the outset, it is the business of the sequel to give them clarity and point. The hope, in what follows, is to explore the Muslim receiving of the Qur'ān, the Islamic way with the secular/religious problem, and the role of Islam in a plurally religious and irreligious humanity. How do we understand the Quranic allegiance? Is the secular/religious issue Islamically solved or soluble? If there is a wider ecumene of religions what has Islam to bring to it and receive from it? All these, surely, in the poem's phrase 'interest our eyes'. But more, they interest our humanity.

Being Muslim with the Qur'ān is perhaps put usefully into focus by beginning with a western-style query frequently encountered in several forms. Is there any serious textual criticism of the Islamic Scripture? How far have Muslims gone in taking the Qur'ān in proper terms of historical analysis? Are they not impossibly fundamentalist in their attitudes? When will the break come? Will it not be the more devastating for having been so long delayed? Behind these and kindred questions there lies, of course, the claim, familiar to the intellectualist and the critical historian, by which all religious sources must be open to radical scrutiny and dogmatic pretensions suitably disciplined by cold, objective fact. No areas can be held in sacrosanct immunity from rational interrogation. No text can rightly enjoy an authority that is absolute or be exempt from sceptical investigation. Can the Qur'ān then abide, in the strong traditional, even sheer, authoritarianism by which it is taken as 'the book of God'?

It needs a certain courage—and owes a careful statement—to feel that these in the end are the wrong questions. Of course, history and historians have obligations to truth and truth to critical questions and critical questions to free rein. These obligations, however, must be pursued within the fact that what finally matters, and signifies, about the Muslim reception of the Qur'ān is a religious finality. This has been our emphasis throughout the foregoing chapters. The sense of man under God and the living issues of his rightfulness in that relationship are not demoted or disallowed, and they are certainly not answered, by views or debates about the theory of Quranic origins and sources. They persist in their cosmic and religious urgency and no contributory questions can assume priority over them.

This is not to say that scholars should not interrogate the text of the Qur'ān and speculate about its antecedents. It is not to say that some sort of Islamic doctrinal positivism, taking the Qur'ān in miraculous terms, has the right to veto all question of its autocracy. It is not to say that, by intelligent criteria, faith in the Qur'ān would not be sounder to perceive the human element authentically within the act of God and to conceive of the latter as moving with and by the former. For prophetic revelation is not the less divine for being also, instrumentally, human. And the instrumentality of Muḥammad in the Qur'ān deserves, and will no doubt eventually receive from Muslims, far more adequate exploration and recognition than it has yet enjoyed.

It is, none the less, to say, and say decisively, that in the end the Islamic authority of the Qur'ān is religiously beyond these questions. It is also to say that, practically speaking, 'criticism' of the Qur'ān is not likely to develop, or to prove, in any essential sense, a test of religious existence. Even Muslim writers keenly aware of the secular doubt of religion and the menace of religious obscurantism, who are anxious for a sound rehabilitation of the role of religion in society, do not see their duty in terms of textual criticism. On the contrary, as Dr Muḥammad al-Nuwaiḥī observes, it is impossible to foresee such a sense of liability in Islam, either today or tomorrow. The same writer, with a concern for western susceptibilities, declares that belief in the divine origin of the Qur'ān is bound up with the conviction of what he calls 'the actual, verbal utterance of God'. To admit human elements in the structure of the Qur'ān is impossible to Islamic religion.[1]

The argument is not simply that it would be impolitic to expect it and so there must be a tactical patience while a proper question is shelved. It is that the religious authority of the Qur'ān, as the charter of human meaning before God, is sacramentalized in *this* account of its origins. Its being 'the divine word' *is* literary, in strictly scriptural standing and its *I'jāz*, or divine credential, belongs in that sphere of inspiration understood as altogether 'bestowed', 'given', 'made to intervene' into the vacant place of the human agency. That character, religiously received, is its status.

The outsider is certainly free to speculate on prophetic receptivity, on contemporary factors, on psychic elements, on the human in full relevance to a phenomenon which could not exist without it. He will indeed be wise to do so. He may even excite or inspire the Muslim to follow suit. But, with or without this phenomenological study, the Islamic sense of what here we can only call 'Quranicity' will remain a matter of divine gift and divine sanction and divine activity and such conviction will remain the religion of Islam. It will not be altered in essence should there ever come about a pattern of thought which understood such divine initiative as having vital room for human participation and human travail. Muḥammad would then emerge in different terms effectively, while remaining what for Muslims he has always been essentially, namely the prophet of God.

The debate then about the How? of the Qur'ān is proper and fascinating. It is a significant, objective, historical and scholarly pursuit. But whether allowed or disallowed, alien or congenial, it will leave intact the Quranic allegiance in Islam, the conviction, that is, of a revelatory directive as to the meaning of man. The orthodox theory of the Qur'ān, as heavenly dictation, is no more, no less, than the form of its definitive authority to faith.

It is fair to note, in this whole connection, how different any way are the textual issues in the Qur'ān from those of the Biblical literature. It is confined to twenty-three years and one locale and one solitary spokesman and personality. The period between its utterance and its canon is relatively brief. There are of course endless duties of scholarship here about textual matters, destroyed versions, vowels and diacritical points, variant readings and cases and the rest. There

[1] Quoted earlier in Chapter 4.

are also tangled questions of content, sequence, context and occasion, and all the accumulating unimaginative-ness of much tradition and commentary. But at this juncture, and in full retrospect, the surest, most appropriate, posture of religious study is to take the Qur'ān with the Islamic *imprimatur* we have noted and reach, as we have tried to do, into its deep and abiding themes of God and man. What we, or Muslims, say of it is rightly subdued to what it says of us and of the humanity that is ours.[1] It seems clear that the supernatural idea of the Qur'ān is the dimension *within* which, not *against* which, the main development of modern resilience and change comes and will come in Islam. The dogmatic status of the book is not reduced but its contents re-interpreted, on practical grounds, by understandings that do not take upon themselves the fundamental criticism—a task which, to that frame of mind, is both ill-considered and unnecessary.

In these terms there is a very wide practical reformulation of Quranic loyalties which bespeak a remarkable flexibility of Quranic meanings. It is not, in the main, that reformers find new ideas desirable and take them from outside in neglect of the Scripture. It is rather that they find them Quranic and claim them as its meaning. There is a strong tendency to insist that basically the problems of Islam are not intellectual but social and legal, that the writ, as it were, of the religion does not face any challenge for its authority, but only for its specifics. The Qur'ān, as the constitution for mankind, remains inviolate. But the by-laws under it may be renewed and reviewed. The former ensures the will to *maṣlaḥah*, or public weal. The latter enforce its detailed demands. This distinction, often made by Muslim writers, has obvious bearing on the explicit and the implicit studies in Chapter 3. It is frequently corroborated by a distinction between *uṣūl* and *furū*ʿ, the elemental and the derived, the roots and the branches.

In these ways a remarkable flexibility can be achieved within the classic shape of Quranic authority. The text is given an elasticity

[1] Such Muslim studies of the Qur'ān as have been made in the last half-century focusing on the human authorship of Muḥammad in effect sustain this conclusion. For they leave a religious allegiance to the Qur'ān intact, however they may venture to re-formulate the Prophet's role in it. There have, for example, been efforts to explain the shape of the patriarchal narratives and their divergence from earlier parallels as due to conscious literary adaptation much as Shakespeare, for example, refurbished, to great advantage, the material he received. But whether these are convincing, or not, and whether conscious authorship rather than otherwise is provable, are discussions which do not alter the Islamic role of the Qur'ān.

which orthodoxy might be expected to deny but which remains viable in its non-provocation of dogmatic belief in what relates to Quranic status. Thus, for example, 'Alī 'Abd al-Rāziq, in a now historic *tour de force*, was able to argue from the Qur'ān the non-necessity of the caliphate to Islam despite assumption of its indispensability through all the Muslim centuries.[1] The Qur'ān certainly survived the crisis of the end of the caliphate with surprising ease. Yet in retrospect it is not surprising at all, since the Qur'ān in fact could not be proved to sustain it.

It has proved similarly resilient over the question of its translatability—a matter very close to its sense of itself as a linguistic miracle and long, if not originally, an object of sharp anathema, in many orthodox circles. For almost all the several passages which speak of its Arabic form link that fact with intelligibility to the hearing community which was, of course, Arab. Thus, for example, Surah 42: 7: 'Thus We have inspired you with an Arabic Qur'ān, in order that you may warn the mother of the villages'.[2] Taken dogmatically this Arabic form could preclude and veto translation. For translation un-forms in one language to re-form in another, which might be taken as implying a divine miscalculation, or rejecting a divine disposition and presuming to alter it. But taken intelligently, the Arabic serves the substance, as a form which the paramount purpose requires should bow to intelligibility, that is, to translation. In ways like this it is possible for the exegesis of passages almost completely to reverse itself, the status of the text being all the time intact.

This happens, of course, most readily in the sphere of law.[3] While it is true that the radical changes in Turkey under Ataturk in the 1930s militantly repudiated Quranic sources, legal adaptations else-

[1] In *Al-Islām wa Uṣūl al-Ḥukm* (Islam and the Principles of Rule), Cairo, 1925. French translation by L. Bercher, in *Revue des Études Islamiques*, vol. 7, 1933, pp. 353–91 and vol. 8, 1934, pp. 163–222. See also this author's *Counsels in Contemporary Islam*, Edinburgh, 1965, pp. 69–72.

[2] Thus 12: 2 adds to 'an Arabic Qur'ān' the phrase: 'Perhaps you will understand.' 43: 3 uses the familiar verb, be alerted or intelligent. 20: 113 has the phrase 'perhaps they may fear', and 39: 28 'for a people who know'. 41: 44 makes the precise point that a foreign tongue with an Arab people would be ludicrous. Frequently there is the emphasis that the Qur'ān is clear, forthright, without dubiety, a book, as 39: 28 has it, 'without crookedness'. Opacity, where translation is needed and withheld, would certainly mean dubiety.

[3] Cf. J. N. D. Anderson, *Islamic Law in the Modern World*, London, 1959, and N. J. Coulson, *History of Islamic Law*, Edinburgh, 1964.

where have generally argued their case within the *Sharī'ah.* They have been presented, not as an abandonment of the sacred law, but rather as its re-presentation in progressive terms. Examples are numerous from almost all segments of Islam. The most conspicuous might well be the development of the well-known passage in Surah 4: 3 f. about plurality of wives. Traditionally understood as a specific authority for plural marriage within the limit of four, the verse in question is now widely claimed as a virtual prohibition of plurality of wives and an implicit intention of monogamy. The point turns, mainly, on the sense of the condition *in khiftum an lā ta'dilū*, 'if you fear you cannot behave with equality', or, 'be just . . .'. If material matters are in question here, justice is feasible and the proviso attainable and the plurality therefore allowable. If, so the argument runs, moral, emotional and deeply marital matters are meant, then, clearly, the proviso is virtually un-attainable and the permission is withheld. The debate here runs deep. There is confident espousal of wifely rights here requiring the monogamous state. There is equally insistent rear-guard action rejecting it. Social changes on a wide scale certainly underlie and necessitate the debate. The point here is simply that the debate does not take the form of pro- or anti-Qur'ān. It is a controversy for the authority of the Qur'ān as that which both the old and new invoke and revere.[1]

Similar flexibility in the practical directives of the Qur'ān and the direction they afford to its community derives from the argument from time and the very effectiveness of Islam. It can hardly be supposed that emphases and injunctions urgent in the original pagan setting of the first Muslims would need to be perpetual throughout the centuries of Islamic existence. For this would be to imply that Islam itself had somehow failed in the effective making of Muslims. A quite absolute veto on representation was right and defensible in a chronically superstitious society. But Muslims do not remain such. For they have achieved a true monotheism where idolatry is no longer a disease or a temptation. Need they then be subject to the

[1] The notion, here, of what is virtual as a prohibition, if so it be, confirms the continuing dependence on the Qur'ān. For the monogamy it sustains does not go further and ground itself on the conviction that the prohibition has to be absolute or that the mere idea of plurality is itself injustice to an existing wife. For these positions, with their sacramental sense of the marriage bond, as inherently inalienable, are not and could not be, drawn from the Qur'ān. Virtual prohibition still leaves the option open to put things to the test and the failures, if they occur, are *post facto* and the marriages exist.

first vetoes in perpetuity? Clearly there must be social and legal recognition of the achievement of Islam itself.[1]

When direction by the Qur'ān is responsibly sought with that consideration in mind—the on-going lantern as it were—it is notable how many supposed indispensables of Islam do not enjoy specific or categorical support in the text itself. The caliphate is a salient example, predestination another, nationalism another. Even the bodily postures at prayer and the explicit authority for the numbers of sequences in prayer and the five-fold occurrence daily are not found in any Quranic verses.[2] They are, of course, deeply with its spirit and have an authority that could hardly conceivably fail of Islam. Yet they are also striking examples of the need to see the Qur'ān as a court of reference for Islam rather than as the always categorical dictation of what Islam was, or is, or shall be. Like every other Scripture, whatever the scriptural status is taken to be, it presupposes its community-in-trust and cannot be Qur'ān to them without them.

So change happens pragmatically and though it revolutionizes centuries of Quranic reception it still makes bold and makes good the claim to be Quranic.

The foregoing is in no way intended as justice to a vast theme. 'Being Muslim with the Qur'ān' must needs go back over all the preceding chapters and much more besides. But in broad terms it has brought us to our second inquiry about 'being Islamic in the world'. For all these responses to time and circumstance involve the fundamental issue of the viability of Muslim religious existence in the modern context. Like every other God-oriented allegiance, it is hard pressed by secularity, and it has features that make it, in serious ways, the most hard pressed of them all. Is the secular/religious issue within Islam soluble?

The question is not made easier by the fact that, from one angle, it should not be formulated. For Islam has always stood for a rejection of the secular understood as a category of something exempted from the divine rule. It has boldly claimed to include all things under God. It does not separate the religious and the political. It concedes, at

[1] There is an interesting example of this in 'Muslims and *Taṣwīr*', by Aḥmad 'Īsā, in *The Muslim World*, vol. 45, no. 3, 1955, pp. 250–68, being a translation from *Majallat al-Azhar*, 1951. The main subject is representational art.

[2] There are references to morning and evening and 'the midmost' prayers and to multiple times of prayers. The absence of an explicit 5 figure has no operative significance.

least in theory, no sphere to the specifically religious. All is under the divine sovereignty. In the restrictive sense there is nothing religious and nothing secular. All are *muslim*, tributary to God. The only distinction that applies is between *islām* and non-*islām* with *jihād* enjoined to subdue the one to the other. But *islām* is not religious and non-*islām* secular. On the contrary the latter is idolatry and under anathema, while the former is *Tauḥīd* and under *jihād*.

In old or static times the great divide could be drawn in geographic terms. *Dār al-Islām*, the house of Islam, was an expression on the map, with frontiers separating it from *Dār al-Ḥarb*, the house of strife not yet subdued to the law and order of Islam. But this physical or military distinction is plainly out of date. Its age-long institutional expression, namely the caliphate, is defunct. There is no feasible prospect of the forceful expansion of Muslim rule ending in universal dominion. Modern forms of the specific creation of such rule, for example, in Pakistan, concede in their very circumstances the non-Islamic set-up outside them.[1] There has to be co-existence within a world community, not reducible, indeed not divisible, by these concepts.

More significant than this fact of life, as it denies for ever the old theory, is the issue of Islamic existence inside the sphere of *Dār al-Islām* itself. Does not the latter really have to be now understood as a domain of yieldedness to the divine, as a realm of human obedience to God, taught by the Qur'ān and the *Sharī'ah*, but sustained in personal existence,[2] and dynamic not static, a struggle not an assumption? It still has, of course, its institutions, Ramaḍān, pilgrimage, *Ṣalāt*, and the rest, by which to be identified. These abide as its marks of identity. But they are not religiously neutral in the sense that Islam is achieved in them irrespective of their quality and their incidence. Around them, as well as within, are the ultimate questions of intention, authority and relevance. They have all the time to be effectively related to problems of society and culture and the wider

[1] For the large Muslim minority in India, and elsewhere, must continue to be Islamic without benefit of that Islamic statehood which the Pakistani thinking declared to be indispensable to such full existence. In a modern secular state Muslims have to be Islamic simply in religious terms which is to use the word 'religious' in a restrictive sense Islam has never approved.

[2] The use of 'personal' here is not meant to imply that religion, as argued by Wilfred Cantwell Smith in *The Meaning and End of Religion*, London, 1963, only really belongs in personal terms—a concept which is liable to atomize shared, and indeed corporate, realities.

world. Islam has always insisted that what we may call the intensively religious acts, the ritual obligations, are within a larger submissiveness to God extensively realized everywhere.

It is just this inclusive character of being Muslim which is at stake in the contemporary circumstances of secularity. If we think of the religious sphere from the angle of its anchor in ritual, in sacred law, in *tafsīr* and tradition, in the authoritative sanctions of life, then it has to be conceded that these are in recession, in the popular mind, in technical education, in social practice. Religion, for all its will to be inclusive, becomes at least *de facto* a preserve, *qua* authority an expertise, *qua* public loyalty a diluted thing. To this extent the secular/religious distinction does and must exist. Muslims are actually, partially, sometimes deliberately, secularized. Or, conversely, they are religious in tacit erosion or, by contrast, in conscious and insistent conservatism. Either way, the observer and the participant have to reckon with at least an actual distinction between the secular and the religious. There has to be strenuous effort if secularity is not to fall altogether away from being Muslim under God and if religion is to make good its vital rejection of the diminished sphere and relevance which such a falling away would leave to it. For, ideally understood from its genius in history, Islam cannot tolerate that indifferent secular nor acquiesce in that partial religion. Its very genius consists in believing the distinction unnecessary and derogatory to both. For God is one and His rule indivisible.

The question persists, however, whether in point of fact the modern secular mind does not make effective disengagement from religion. Prominent in Muslim political and legal thinking, in the last half century of new states and constitution-making and defining, has been the concept of 'repugnancy to the Qur'ān and the Sunnah'. Muslim laws and societies should not consciously legislate or envisage in practice what could be said to be uncongenial to the sacred sources. There has been wide disparity of view as to how this non-repugnancy should be judged, whether by *ad hoc* committees of referees learned in the minutiae of these sources and entrusted with the task outside electoral processes, or whether it could be assumed that legislatures elected by universal Muslim suffrage and having only Muslim membership could be relied on to ensure Quranic fidelities.

Aside from the procedural aspects, the concept itself is interesting. Its negative form, focusing on what might be contrary, suggests that there are wide areas of neutrality, or non-specificity, which are matters of silence and so of indifference, to the text of the Qur'ān. Though there is, of course, no neutrality in the liability of the Godward relation, the effective distinction leaves large room for the idea and the pursuit of secular things. The religious becomes, in this sense and from one angle, that which the Scripture specifies. To go one's own way elsewhere clearly gives the secular broad rein, and this view of the divine documents, as not being exhaustive and onerous and inquisitorial, has long been a deep and firm conviction of the Islamic mind. To that degree it is an ally of the instinct to secularize, to deny to religious authority the sort of dominance which its custodians often assume and to which its instincts always tend.

Even so, the obligation to acknowledge God in unlimited liability is the heart of Quranic faith. The secular cannot be allowed to be irreligious. There may be areas of neutral silence in the divine documents. There are no areas of neutrality in the divine claim. The principle of what is repugnant exists, surely, on behalf of what is consistent. When one turns the criterion round to that of consistency or loyalty to the Qur'ān, one is back with the problem of having all things rightly religious. One cannot, in Islam, let the secular go unrestrained, as in the west. For this would be to forego the very meaning of Islam as a religious interpretation of life. Yet one cannot retain it on accommodating terms without risking the integrity and meaning of that religious interpretation and its achievement. If we disallow the distinction between the secular and the religious, we fly in the face of contemporary realities. We are then liable either to make the religious task too easy and to under estimate its real *jihād* and struggle, or to disserve the secular in its deepest problems, by a naïve assessment of how it might be sacred.

Could it be, then, that in this whole context we are close to a new and contemporary meaning of the call of *jihād*? The mystics, as we saw, often spoke of the lesser and the greater *jihād*, by which they meant that the struggle against the evil self was sterner than that against an unbelieving enemy. Are not the two struggles in fact one? Should we not see the battle-points of the God-relationship running through the whole of human society and standing within the Muslim soul itself? If there is indeed a struggle, a necessary dynamism, a real fibre, in faith, must it not also mean that there are areas of human existence and of human choice that want to exempt themselves from the recognitions of God which we call religion? Does not the secular world have this potential intractability, this implicit independence of such religion, this will to secularity? How else, without such, could *jihād* be needed? Is not this dissent from the sacred the final meaning of *Dār al-Ḥarb*, in any present sense?

To concede the right to secularity in these terms is not, of course, to compromise what ought to be. It is merely to admit what is. And such admission is the beginning of wisdom about its due correction. It may also be in the end the necessary condition of even the sacred itself. Men do, and will, secularize very extensively in Islam, both as to law and thought. That secularity is measured greatest by those whose criteria of religion are the most conservative and static. In that fact is the danger of a polarity by which each is anathema to the other. The sacred then forfeits fulfilment in the secular and sinks into a ghetto mind, while the secular is no longer opportunity for the sacred. Neither can well abandon its proper tension with the other.[1] *Jihād* could well be understood, therefore, as this situation by which the world, being secular, is an arena of struggle for its proper meaning in religion, and religious faith, being alive by that struggle, must needs achieve its meaning in the secular. Even for Islam the distinction between the secular and the the religious is a primary constituent as well as a prevailing circumstance of faith. It can never again be seen as a frontier on a map or a border between states. It runs as a tension, a mutuality, within the individual heart and through all the fabric of the *Ummah* and the world. Being Islamic in present history means just this encounter with the un-Islamic, understood as the secular as it would be if no rule of God claimed it, as it is until the rule is known and served.[2]

So we reach our third concern. From the faith question and the

[1] There is of course a widespread tendency to do so. There is a firm conviction in many quarters that Islam can never be 'secular'. The whole secular/religious vocabulary is a western way of thought. There is a parallel to the Islamic *mutatis mutandis* in the Jewish view. For example, Ignaz Maybaum, *Creation and Guilt*, London, 1969, pp. 147–50. 'One cannot speak of a secularized Judaism.' But this is a kind of positivism, either of identity or faith, which does not concede an operative negation.

[2] The essential problem of secularity in Asia and Africa today is psychologically complicated by the fact that its historical origins are from the west and considerations of cultural defensiveness are deeply involved. A sound post-imperial independence of mind can confuse the issues and miss the common human essence of the modern destiny.

What is at stake for the future of religion has to be seen as an inclusive test of the contemporary mind from which there is no immunity in dissociation or distance. It is not wisely taken as a geographical invasion to be held off by local resistance. A privacy of religions, whether culturally defended by politics or artificially preserved by dogma, secular question, we come to the ecumenical question. All the foregoing, though phrased here in terms of Islamic *jihād*, the struggle to be right in religion, clearly belongs to every system of faith. The fact that it does so means that each is involved with every other. Though disparate in claim, in dogma and in soul, they have in their plurality a common interrogative and a unity of obligation about man. Modern development has brought them into one arena of urgency within which their separate and crucial convictions about finality, authority and destiny must necessarily 'come clean' and take scrutiny, the old seclusions and isolations being ended. If their very inward loyalties are to be rightly maintained they must be alert to their common denominator in the human crisis.

If, in this sense, there is a wider ecumene,[1] it becomes possible to ask in broad terms what being-religious-by-Islam has to bring to, and receive from, such active relation of religions. The question obviously includes the relevance of the Qur'ān to those outside Islam, which we have throughout been studying. But it asks, further, how that relevance might avail for others from the lively custody of Muslims and how others might speak, for its sake, to its custodians and heirs. In its appeal to thoughtfulness and its claim to inclusiveness, the Qur'ān certainly allows such dialogue. The time impels it.

We end with the open question, with the question open. For we are only at the beginning of this kind of reading the Qur'ān outside its own community. It is a temper new and perhaps still suspect to its own proper readers. There are still taxing questions of attitude and doctrine to surmount and resolve. But to reckon first with the right intention is a true Islamic approach. The rights of God rightly known and served, as the condition of a rightful humanity, might fairly claim to be a definition of Islam for purposes of religious ecumene. For that is the meaning of *Allāhu akbar*. 'Let God be God', and none other. To identify and disown every pseudo-absolute as a menace to man as servant and a blasphemy against God as Lord; to see that issue as the crux of personal destiny and as the vital theme of history,

would seem to be the worst posture for a present spiritual concern about the secular. Even the causation factors only seem uniquely western if we have short historical memories. The implicit demands are universal.

[1] The phrase is used, for example, in Ignaz Maybaum, op. cit., p. 143 f. Cf. also Eugene Hillman, *The Wider Ecumenism*, London, 1968. Are the instincts and goals of the ecumenical movement in any sense extendable beyond the borders of Christianity itself? For Maybaum the ecumene is 'monotheistic'.

being so defined in revelation and re-iterated in prophethood; to believe it embodied in the claims of ritual and the patterns of symbol—this is to be Muslim in the power of community and the bonds of *Ummah*, as these are shaped by habituation in the practice of *Dīn*, and established and defended in the political order and the meaning of the state. To see it culminating in the grand assize and in the great divide of eternity; to know it interrogating your own existence within that destiny; to feel it brooding significantly over all the attainments and pretensions of technocratic man—such is Islam.

Such will always be its witness to the community of religions, to the diversity of mankind. And in that trust of the rights of God, as the clue to man, Islam has boldly grappled with the problem of power, has firmly invoked the political on behalf of the religious, accepting—as the Qur'ān itself indicates—the liabilities which go with external success and with the sanctions of force, counting hypocrisy a necessary risk in a larger aim, and power a lesser evil than sedition and survival a surer thing than innocence. From the time after the *Hijrah* when Muḥammad justified truce-breaking as proper in the interests of peace-enforcing, and such palliatives of evil less worthy than its eradication, Islam, more than any other creed, has been uninhibited in the acceptance of power. It is futile for good causes to wait till history favours them. They must take and discipline and employ the sinews they need. Only in the militancy is the sincerity. For there is no greater evil than non-*islām*. The lesser ones that serve to its defeat are answered in that fact, but only under the right sovereignty.

Summary is always a precarious venture. But are not these two, the divine Lordship and the prophetic service robust for that Lordship, the core of the Muslim witness in any ecumene of faiths? God and the apostle is the single formula. Apostolate, in the event, is both *balāgh* and *ḥisāb*, both a message to deliver and a cause to make victorious.[1] Each vindicates the other. The cause is right only because it belongs to the faith. The faith would fail, in fact and in duty, if it did not achieve the cause. All is *fī sabīl-Illāh*, 'on behalf of God'. In the plural perspective of religions Islam has the great strength and the great burden of this involvement with power—with power, not as an aberration from its ideals or an episode in its moods, but as the

[1] The distinction is a frequent one in the pre-*Hijrah* period. Cf. 42: 47: 'Your only duty is the preached-message (*al-balāgh*)', and 16: 37, 84; 29: 17 and 36: 16. It even continues after the *Hijrah*, cf. 24: 52 and 13: 40. The latter reads: 'Yours is *al-balāgh*, Ours the reckoning', i.e. the requiting, the issue.

central and integral quality of its conviction. It, therefore, represents in elemental terms a crucial decision in religion.

If we ask, conversely, what it might take from the conversation with other faiths, the answer must clearly lie in the sphere of its strength. It may well be formulated as the question of transcendence, not any question *about* transcendence—for that would be to ask Islam to deny itself—but a question *for* and *within* transcendence, the sort of question which would invite Islam to be itself more radically. The reason is already clear from Chapter 8. The outsider, thinking with the Qur'ān, moves with an overwhelming sense there of the divine Lordship. But he is likely to register, for that very reason, a steady disquiet about the immunity of that transcendent rule from the human realm which creation proclaims to be its responsibility. Creation surely matters to the Creator. Given that sublime sovereignty and Islam's splendid commitment to it, how can we forebear relating the recognition of it to the whole range of its meaning in history, in the history of the humanity which is its definitive sphere? How can we exclude the criteria by which we know how great it is from the dimensions of the human situation to which its rule relates? How shall we separate the mystery and the suffering of our humanity, in its most authentic self-awareness, from the superlatives of power and majesty which we ascribe to God?

All ecumenical religious converse must, then, confront Islam with the question of its adequacy to the theme of man in his tragic quality, in pain and despair. It was for this reason that we gave special attention in Chapter 6 to the Quranic measure of man in mortality and reckoning and judgement. It is not that Islam lacks the *gravitas* which is inseparable from religion *per se*. On the contrary, it gives it a profound expression and, geographically, an almost universal pattern of participation. In its own household it sacramentalizes and gives ritual shape to the experience of human finitude. Yet religions around it, respecting that existence under God, are the more bound to ask it, in the very loyalty of respect, whether it fully measures what man must mean to God and God to men, consistently with the reality of either. At least in its majority Sunnī form, Islam has need of the invitation to ponder this mystery more radically.[1]

That invitation must not be pressed as something drawing its relevance from outside Islam. What to do with it may need external

[1] One needs to say Sunnī Islam here, since the Shī'ah segment of the house of Islam

witness. But the heart of its urgency lies in that which is also the heart of Islam, namely, man in creaturely significance and God in undoubted sovereignty. It is not to be escaped by pleading a refusal to be over preoccupied with evil. For there can be no over preoccupation where there is an assurance of divine reality. To be un- or under-occupied with the mystery would be the questionable theism. It is because God reigns that sin is significant, and significant most of all for belief in an eternal power. A concern that is not insistent enough, whether in thought or in deed, about the human tragedy is, by the same token, a dubious confession of the Lordship of God. If there is to be a dialogue of religions which takes Islam in its own seriousness, this will be its first necessity.

Nor is the theme to be evaded by taking refuge in irresponsible or inadequate theses about omnipotence. Even that very term can be a trap for the sanguine or the doctrinaire. We may recall the old theologian who thought of the omnipotent as able, by dint of being so, to create a rock so heavy that even he could not lift it (he, that is, who was omnipotent). 'I believe in God', added the theologian, 'and I believe in the rock.' But this kind of omnipotence that has overreached itself is not the Quranic doctrine of creation. Nor is it the Islamic understanding of God. To say *Allāhu akbar* is to repudiate notions of omnipotently frustrated omnipotence, of omnipotence precluded from coming true in history, or captive to arbitrary assertion.

Our purpose here is not to pursue what the wider ecumene must venture. It is only to begin to identify its great exchanges of giving and receiving. There is a deep sense in which the times as well as the dogmas converge to point them out. By this criterion also tragedy is well taken. For it belongs with the world in which religion must be re-discovered—the world of refugees, of peoples tangled in hostility, of national economies showing ever greater disparities of wealth and poverty between the hemispheres, and this grim inequality threatening to become coterminous with the anger of races. There can be no ecumenical or true converse of religions which does not bring its issues of faith and worship into the living sympathies of a common humanity moving darkly in the earth.

has faced the mystery of suffering within its own history and been shaped, both dogmatically and emotionally, thereby. This very development in itself, and its long standing continuity from the earliest days of Islam, might be taken in itself as evidence of the point we are suggesting.

Index

The Glossary of technical terms in *The Event of the Qur'ān*—companion volume to this study—is not repeated here. It is hoped that to an adequate extent the meaning of these terms will be clear from the contexts the Index notes.

Quranic passages quoted in the text. Those noted by reference only are not listed.